Show Me the Way to Santiago

by Peter Kay

This is the author's account of a 600-mile journey of discovery along the way of the Via de la Plata from Sevilla to Santiago de Compostela in Spain.

ISBN: 978-0-9574905-2-9

Edited by E. Rachael Hardcastle
Formatted by E. Rachael Hardcastle
Written by Peter Kay
Photographs taken by the author and/or others on the pilgrimage are used with permission.

Special thanks to Maureen Wakelin for her knowledge of the Spanish language.

Most names have been changed to protect the identities of those involved. Permission has been granted from others to use their names and stories for the purpose of this account.

Published by Curious Cat Books, United Kingdom
For further information contact www.curiouscatbooks.co.uk

Also available as an e-book.

First Edition

Show Me the Way to Santiago

Also by the Author:

A Pennine Way Odyssey: Self-Published in 2013

For and in memory of Christine Straker

Christine was a great friend to Sandra and I. She was my 'unofficial' book marketing salesperson in the north-east.

All the royalties received from the sales of this book will be donated to the Motor-Neurone Disease Society.

Also in memory of Terence (Tel) Wakelin

Tel was married to Maureen and sadly passed away just prior to the publication of Show Me the Way to Santiago. He is referred to in the book and was a great partner, father and grandfather. A good friend, who had a wonderfully dry wit and an avaricious capacity to read.

Like Christine, he will be sorely missed, but not forgotten.

About the Via de la Plata

The Via de da Plata, or Way of St James, is a long-distance walk, like many others. However, it is surprising, given its beauty and connection to an ancient Roman route and its significance as a pilgrimage route, it is not better travelled and documented. It stretches from Seville in the south of Spain and travels virtually due north for most of its route, to finally arrive in Santiago de Compostela, some 1,000km (606 miles) later.

It passes through some of the most beautiful parts of Spain, crosses rivers, fords, streams, traverses high plains, cuts through valleys, divides walled fields, passes and dissects woodland and takes the traveller on a journey of discovery. It provides opportunities to explore some splendid cities and a number of interesting towns and small villages, many with their own secrets to reveal about the history, culture and fabric of the many communities that have and continue to make Spain such a fascinating country. It runs for the most part south to north, up the eastern side of Spain, running parallel to the border with Portugal.

The flora and fauna also provide the walker with much to enjoy and admire and occasionally be entertained by. The 'Way' is negotiated by following a

i

series of yellow arrows. These can be painted on walls, roads, specially constructed signposts, rocks, and can be depicted in many ways. There is no pattern or regularity to their appearance, albeit they tend to be in greater evidence when a change to walking in anything but a straight line is required.

The route itself is an extension of the Roman road that linked modern day Merida (Augusta Emerita) with modern day Astorga (Asturica Augusta). It was developed in the early Christian era by using, adapting and extending older roads, typical of Roman route development of the time. The route was kept alive during the Visigothic and Islamic eras between 750 and 1492. The name Via de la Plata comes from the Arabic term 'Bal Latta', which means 'paved way'. From Zamora, there are two options to choose, either to Santiago via Astorga, linking up with the 'French Camino', or by turning north-eastwards towards Ourense and on to Santiago de Compostela.

I chose to follow this latter route.

Author's Note

Following in the footsteps of the thousands of people who made this journey before me, often with far greater self-sacrifice, served more than any other event in my life to convince me of our interdependence as a human family.

The book is a personal, humorous and impressionistic account of my journey of discovery and the people I met along the way. It chronicles how I came to undertake the journey, including my reflections about family and life. It also charts the stories of some of my fellow travellers who were happy to share with me what lay behind their journeys, these became intrinsically intertwined with my own. Finally, the book is about humanity and friendship; the first week being shared with a good friend, Maureen and the remainder with my close friend and soul mate, John.

It is not intended to be a guidebook. It may, however, be of interest to those contemplating a similar journey or those armchair long-distance travellers, who simply enjoy reading about the experiences of others who bravely or foolhardily undertake such journeys of self-discovery and the kinds of people one is likely to meet.

If you are contemplating undertaking the journey yourself, I would strongly advise checking on an appropriate website beforehand to glean knowledge about which refugios and albergues are currently known to be operating. This is particularly important in places/destinations where there may be no other accommodation options and/or where there may be a good distance before the next potential stop over place.

Prologue

Two angry red blisters on my right heel have been inflamed for a while, their throbbing is a constant reminder of the miles I've walked and of my endurance during the past two days in the searing heat along the Camino. My feet aren't just complaining but shouting at me and my brain questions my sanity. On my own, I might have found a way to ignore their protests and carry on—I have a room booked in a hostal in Salamanca in two days; only a further 92km separated me from that haven. However, I'm not alone. John, my soul mate, kindred spirit and walking companion's feet are in a far worse state than mine and it would be madness to carry on and inflict escalating pain and suffering on him. He bares his increasing discomfort with a determined stoicism—a testament to our strong friendship.

16 days ago, I set off from Sevilla on my quest to walk the route of the Via de la Plata to Santiago de Compostela. It has been my slow-burning ambition for the past six years. A friend, Maureen had shared memories and photographs of her journey of self-discovery along its 1,000km path, which so many had trodden, and along which many more would hike in the future. Is my faith strong enough or do I need my lapsed religion, too? That was the question that had

nagged Maureen into exploring the Camino. She'd been rewarded with a new-found determination in life and many stirring memories of her fellow pilgrims.

Ever since Maureen had shared her stories of the Camino, my desire to become one of the peregrinos, had grown until it became an ambition. To follow in the footsteps of those—who for centuries have travelled it before—is my way of connecting with my fellow humans. Maureen readily agreed to share the start of my pilgrimage and we'd walked together for seven days, before I linked up with John in Zafra. Her knowledge of the Spanish language and of the Camino's idiosyncrasies had boosted my confidence.

I started the walk with a life dilemma to resolve, and I know Sandra (my life partner for the past 43 years), is back home grappling with the same one. What troubles me as much as the dilemma itself is whether she and I will reach the same conclusion. Faith, for me, is three-fold. How much can I look inwards and manage my confidence, humility, strengths, weaknesses, passions and failings? How reliable am I? Am I resilient enough to succeed in self-imposed challenges like walking the length of the Via de la Plata?

I also have great faith in my fellow human beings—not just those close to me; the ones I love and choose to spend time with—but in wider humanity. I've been struck by Maureen's description of those she met along the Camino.

For the past 16 days I've shared my journey with Martin and Marion, who hail from Denmark. Their warmth and compassion for each other and for fellow pilgrims is evident. With Inieste—a Dutch-Basque woman in her 30's—her search for redemption is due to her never seeking out her long-lost Spanish father whilst he was alive, and it haunts her. This drives her to walk the Camino. Then, there is the German duo of Karl and Hermann, with their pre-dawn whisperings and their jovial evening reminiscing. Andreas, at 22, is the youngest pilgrim we've met, he has linked up with a fellow German peregrino, Marie, who is around 15 years his senior and their 'Gruppenführer', Jesus, who is Spanish and is now their self-appointed guide. There is also Millie and her golf trolley, plus many others.

Giving up so soon will not only mean I won't complete the Camino, but will mean losing contact with my new Camino family.

Chapter One

Sevilla to Zafra

Monday 21st March

Arrangements have been made, flights booked and enough of my family and friends informed I can no longer back out. I'm going to walk 1,000km across Spain! I've visited Sevilla (our starting point) before and remembered the heat, the orange trees, and a wonderful park. I've tried to recall the many public statues, the buildings and the cathedral with its cool, cavernous inner spaces and tower, which is one of the tallest in the world.

For the past six weeks, Spain in general, (including the route I'm walking) has experienced heavier-than-usual levels of rainfall and there has been widespread flooding. Packing as light as possible (given I will be my own beast of burden) was something of a challenge. I also had to pack a sleeping bag, as many of our overnight stays will be in 'refugios' equipped with bunks, but no bedding. My rucksack and its contents were packed in a fold-up canvas bag for the flight, so I can stow it in the hold. The bag also contains my walking pole and a knife for cutting bread, cheese and fruit.

I am sitting in the train with Maureen, who will be walking the first leg of the Camino with me, reflecting on these matters. We will be at the airport in less than an hour's time.

I've known Maureen and her partner, Tel, for around 25 years over which time we've become good friends. Maureen is a calm, caring person who looks out for those less fortunate than herself. Along with Sandra, my partner, we have been involved as trustees of a local charity for several years. Sandra and I have been on holiday with them and had a common narrative in terms of our children. Maureen's eldest son was in the same class at upper school as our eldest daughter. When our children were young we were part of the same babysitting circle. Maureen was a keen walker and amongst other walks she and I shared was part of my Pennine Way Odyssey in 2012. Maureen has a strong moral compass and Tel delights in making outlandish statements—in mixed company—enjoying watching her squirm with embarrassment. It's done in a tongue-in-cheek, provocative way, but still makes her blush. Their idiosyncratic but strong relationship is a delight to behold. Tel's had some health challenges and the care and support Maureen gave has been buoyed by the self-confidence and determination she gained from her Camino experience.

I've been planning the trip for over a year, so as the plane takes off from Stansted, I experience a sense of intense anticipation, interspersed with waves of trepidation. Sections of the route are described in some journals as having bulls and wild dogs to be wary of. Having a walking companion (Maureen initially and for the remainder of the route, John) will, I hope, help to ward off such wild beasts! Maureen will walk as far as Zafra with me and then return to Sevilla for her return flight home. John and I would link up in Zafra and walk the rest of the way together. Maureen is also a friend of both John and his partner, Caroline.

John and I are close friends who have much in common and have walked together in the UK on many occasions. Coincidently, we both originate from the same Lancastrian town, support the same football team and have similar tastes in music. We've followed similar career paths and it was work initially that brought us together nearly 30 years ago. Like Maureen and Tel, John and Caroline have children of a similar age to ours and we've shared holidays together. John and I both have a love of the outdoors, especially long-distance running and fell-walking. Over the years our shared passions have taken us on a journey from friendship to soul-mates.

***

The flight from Stansted to Sevilla takes two and a half hours and on the way Maureen and I hear about a golf trip to Portugal being embarked on by a large group of men, who originally worked together as prison officers in London, but who are now scattered far and wide. In conversation with two of them, we are told they maintain contact through their "annual pilgrimage to golf courses in Spain or Portugal."

My pilgrimage is of a different kind, instead following the alleged route of Saint James from Seville to Santiago along the Via de la Plata. Maureen had undertaken the whole journey in 2010 over a period of 46 days. I'm not sure how long it will take me, or if indeed I can make it the entire way, but I have allowed up to 45 days to try and complete the walk, with a return flight booked from Santiago on the 46th.

I was inspired to undertake my pilgrimage walk, partly by Maureen's tales and partly by my self-imposed challenge to get fit following a health scare. The idea of walking it grew over time until I was obsessed with a compelling desire to become its 'companion'.

As our taxi takes us from the airport down into the heart of Sevilla, I have no idea that during my time on the Camino I will manage to lose a pair of trousers, unwittingly re-enact a Laurel and Hardy sketch, visit a ghost town, discover the birthplace of one of my father's favourite poets, and several times make a fool of myself.

Nor do I know that those I meet along the way will have their own captivating stories to tell and that for some of these fellow travellers, their lives will become entangled with my own. Millie and her golf trolley. Sergio and his big dilemma. Karl and Hermann and their morning whispering routine. Bernhard and his search for a Viennese señorita. Erico and his journey to declare his undying love to his intended. Keith and Susan and their relationship dramas. Marie, Andreas and their self-appointed Spanish 'Gruppenführer'. Inieste and her homage to her Basque father and last but, not least, Martin and his devoted maid Marian. Others will share my journey more fleetingly, but nevertheless will still leave their mark.

***

In the lead up to today I've become increasingly interested in the history of the country and the impact it's had on both the landscape and its people. The route has origins in Roman times and along its length are reported to be some examples of this impact during different periods of Roman, Christian and Moorish domination. There is also said to be stark reminders of more recent events that characterise the terror and impact of the Spanish Civil War, some of which still create divisions.

As we leave the taxi at the 'bullring', it's a warm, pleasant first evening in Spain, while we walk to our hotel. The solid walls of houses, apartments, shops, hotels and bars, are all around us and the sweet and savoury smells of food seem to be at every turning. Our hotel The Zaida, is small, comfortable, clean and hidden away. We have to weave our way through the narrow and twisting cobbled streets until it reveals itself. It is designed in a Morroccan style with coloured tiles and ornate carvings. Leaving our rucksacks at the hotel (mine will be a constant companion for the rest of my journey), we find a bar and eat tapas and a small beer.

I visited and stayed in Sevilla in 1998 as part of a two-week Andalucian 'White City' tour which Sandra and I enjoyed enormously. Sevilla is the capital and the largest city of the Andalusian region and has had a chequered history dating back over 2,000 years. In the 12th Century the Almohads arrived and Sevilla took over from Cordoba as the seat of Arab-Andalusian power. The impressive Giralda, the Plaza de Toros de la Maestranza and the Alcazar all date from this era. I can remember being fascinated by both the age and the condition of these magnificent buildings on my previous visit.

Arriving on the day of the spring equinox seems apt, signifying the transition between one season and another. For me, the transitions between the day-to-day responsibilities of life at home and a six-week journey into the unknown are stark. My priority each day will be about travelling from A to B, but not always knowing which B I will end up at and not being sure I will have somewhere to lay my head when I get there. My journey will, according to Maureen. also bear witness to how spring impacts the flora and fauna for almost the whole southern to northern length of Spain.

Being back in this city, which holds so many positive memories of my time here with Sandra, reminds me of my own mortality and our current dilemma. A few years ago, I was rushed to hospital with a suspected heart attack, which thankfully turned out to be something less serious. It did lead me to spend the best part of two days in hospital and to decide I needed to take steps to improve my health and fitness levels. To that aim, I lost weight, took up running and in many ways changed my lifestyle. I considered myself lucky to have been able to do that. It also led me to refocus on the importance of family and friends and the things I still wanted to achieve. Walking the Camino is both a personal ambition and a way of expressing my gratitude for being fit and able to consider completing it.

Sandra has been hugely supportive of my efforts and had selflessly acknowledged I will be absent from home for at least six weeks.

I also wonder whether, during my time on the Camino, I will reach a conclusion about our current dilemma. Our lives are moving on and we are both facing the challenges that come in later life. How do we maximise our independence and where do we spend our later years? We are up for the challenge change will bring and have already fully explored options around extending and altering our current home, where we have lived for 27 years, happily raised our family and have so many positive memories. However, we both know people who left it too late in life to move to another and more suitable property. For this reason, moving to a new house is very much an option. Should we stay, or should we go?

As I am about to set off on my walk, this is still an undecided matter.

Sightseeing in Sevilla

Tuesday 22nd March

The day dawns and continues to be beautiful with temperatures reaching 27 degrees at times. We get up and have breakfast at a little café across from the hotel. Our plan is to spend the day in Sevilla and for our pilgrimage walk to start on Wednesday morning.

Maureen delights in showing me the first steps of the route we will take as we walk to and across the Puerta de Triana Bridge spanning the Guadalquivir River. We follow the way-marked yellow arrows that would be our guiding lights along our journey for about one kilometre and then left at 'tomorrow's route' to visit the Santa Maria de las Cuevas Monastery, now the Modern Art Museum, which unfortunately is closed.

Our walk continues alongside a huge music venue and Spain's equivalent of Cape Canaveral to the main Expo 92 site, which brings back memories of my previous visit to this wonderful city. At Isla Mágica we are afforded and take the opportunity to board an open topped bus for an enjoyable 90-minute tour of the city. I am told during the tour that following Christopher Columbus's discovering the Americas in 1492, Sevilla experienced its apogee. The Chamber of Commerce was created to deal with the trade between Spain and the overseas territories. This meant Sevilla became the wealthiest and most cosmopolitan city in Spain and in the 16th Century led to Spain becoming the most powerful nation in Europe.

Leaving the bus, a pleasant stroll back along the river follows, as we take in the sights and sounds of tourists, children, cyclists, joggers, dog walkers and locals on their way to and from work. We stop once to purchase some water and more frequently to shade our eyes from the sun.

Leaving the river, we head deeper into the city on a thoroughly enjoyable and leisurely walk through a myriad of narrow streets, so characteristic of the older part of this and many of Spain's towns and cities, stopping for lunch at two o'clock in a little café in the Calle San Vincenti, before returning to our hotel for a siesta.

I recall my previous visit to Sevilla and my memories of it. Sevilla's cathedral is reputed to be the largest in the world and it was designated as a World Heritage Site by UNESCO in 1987. It took over a hundred years to build and was completed in 1506. I well remember being blown away by its capacious interior and by the myriad of side chapels and the various alters and separate little places of worship that lay within. The gold, jewels, paintings, carvings and wealth on display is formidable too, a reminder of the power and control the church held over the lives of so many people for so many years. I admire the architecture, the craftsmanship and the artistry but feel a sense of anger at how these were used to subjugate the masses. The adjacent bell tower, the Giralda, may predate the cathedral and is the most recognisable landmark of the city. It is 105m high and climbing it in 1998 was certainly a highlight for me. The views from the top give a sense of being able to watch over the whole city. Sevillanos are particularly proud of their cathedral and of the Giralda.

Two events in the 20th Century added to the city's cosmopolitan history. These were the Latin American exposition in 1929, which led to the building of several pavilions to represent the various countries from across the Americas. These magnificent buildings are splendidly contained within a large park, which also has lakes, waterfalls and plants from all the various countries involved. I have happy memories of walking through it 18 years ago. In 1992, the Universal EXPO was created, representing the scientific achievements of mankind; many of the features of which I also witnessed during my earlier visit. The city today boasts a population of around 700,000 and is generally dry all year round with long summers stretching from May to October. It sits on the plain of the Guadalquivir river, which flows southwards from Sevilla to the coast at Cádiz.

As well as thinking about the history of Sevilla, my siesta allows me to recollect 1998 and the special time Sandra and I spent here and in other parts of Andalusia. Our relationship endured a challenging time earlier in the 90's, but our 'White City' tour in Spain marked a new closeness and gave us a strength we have both drawn from ever since. Few relationships run smoothly all the time, but it's comforting to have confidence you will share the rest of your lives together.

Feeling both reconnected to the city and rejuvenated from my siesta, I link up with Maureen and we re-emerge into the warm afternoon sun at five o'clock and walk to the cathedral at my request, only to find that the last entry for tourists has been and gone. Instead, we follow the 'Camino' route from the start at the cathedral to re-join our earlier steps of the morning to find the registration point and obtain our 'pilgrim passports'; including one for John. These will serve as our credentials as pilgrims.

My 'Credencial del Peregrino' now contains my name, address, passport number and unfurled has 40 separate rectangles, each designed to be stamped at each of my stop-over places to confirm the details of my journey as it unfolds. On the flip side, it shows the route from southern Spain to Santiago and all the major towns and cities along the way. It will no-doubt become my most prized and tangible reminder of my journey, providing evidence of my progress along the Via de la Plata.

Friends of the Camino run and co-ordinate assistance for 'new' pilgrims from their small office in a 'corral' in Triana. We are given information about the route, but in simple terms it is explained that following the yellow arrows will show us the way to Santiago. Our visit to Triana is followed by a stroll back across the bridge for a cooling milkshake and a sit down on a terrace, where two dark-haired, giggly and kilted girls play with their dog. Joggers, cyclists and rollerbladers pass us by, while down on the river below three canoeists glide silently by on the water. Another pleasant walk along the river follows before we head back into the city.

Finding ourselves, not entirely intentionally, back at the cathedral, Maureen expertly negotiates our entrance as pilgrims and we sit through and experience an hour of a service in the magnificent, cavernous cathedral. The coolness of the cathedral provides perfect sanctuary from the heat outside. Some beautiful singing from an older priest is followed by a performance from a much taller and thinner young man, whose vocals give rise to goosebumps on the back of my neck. Making our way back to the hotel, with the warmth from the sun now diminishing, I am filled with a sense of anticipation and excitement for what lies ahead. Now for a drink and shared 'tapas' in the bar opposite, and so to bed for tomorrow when the 'real journey' starts.

Sevilla to Guillena

(23 km or 14 m) flat, gentle rises
Gradient ascended 20 metres

Wednesday 23rd March

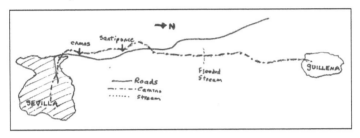

We leave the hotel at ten past eight. Having packed and unpacked my rucksack I discover the micro towel I brought with me for the journey is nowhere to be seen, so I am compelled to borrow a towel from the hotel for the rest of my journey. We cross the river via the Puerta de Triana for the third time and retrace the steps of yesterday until for me, 'new' ground is broken. A welcome breakfast stop is made after an hour walking in Camas (a little town in the suburbs of Sevilla), where a small roadside bar draws us in with its aroma of freshly ground coffee and the smell of toast. I don't realise how hungry I am until we sit down to eat the warm tostadas and enjoy an orange juice and a slug of coffee. The bar, like Camas itself, is rather basic, but on the first morning on the Camino it has everything I want. Maureen stayed in a small hostel here on her first day of walking six years ago and points out the small, squat building down a side street as we pass by. Today, we are walking as far as Guillena.

After half an hour's further walking along a straight path, through fields of green wheat, we meet our first 'fellow pilgrim', Millie, a Polish lady from the UK. She has a large rucksack fastened to a converted golf trolley and an assortment of other attachments too, including what she describes as a magic wand for heating water in a cup. She is amazed at how little we are carrying and says she has been advised that from Santiponce, the usual cross-country route is flooded after the recent heavy rains.

We leave her behind and decide to continue, on the 'official path' anyway given all assurances promised this route was okay when we registered yesterday.

"I think we should stick to the official route, Pete. As I remember it, you'll really start to get a sense of the Camino over the next few hours of walking."

Maureen is absolutely right, as a splendid vista now opens up as we leave the city and suburbia behind. Between us we spot a buzzard, a heron, a small flock of martins, another bird of prey, a lizard and lots of wild flowers. We do, however, have to negotiate our way across and round a flooded ford by leaving the path and weaving our way through a thicket of spindly saplings, and up and over a bank, before sliding down a grassy slope to 'dryish' land on the other side.

"It wasn't like this six years ago," Maureen assures me.

Having successfully negotiated this flooded fording area without mishap, we later take another short detour, rather than wade barefoot across a second ford. At the first of these fords, a white van is virtually submerged by the waters. Was he following his SatNav or was it just a severe miscalculation of the depth of the water?

Two German peregrinos are encountered drying their feet after a stream crossing, just before we arrive in Guillena. After wandering up and down the main street of the village the refugio, our accommodation for the night, is found eventually and quite by accident. It's located within a sports area containing an all-weather football pitch and a small restaurant and bar. We both savour a wonderful meal of Gazpacho soup and homemade bread, venison and the sweetest orange I have ever tasted, and plenty of water to wash it down. The soup here is so good I ask for and make note of all the ingredients so I can recreate it when we get home.

Our accommodation for the night has five bunks (ten beds), a shower and two toilets. We both shower and sleep for a while, and then take it in turns to go for a walk, as at this stage we are the only occupants and there are lots of young men playing football or just hanging around, so it doesn't feel safe to leave possessions unattended in the refugio, which can't be locked.

During the afternoon and evening, eight other pilgrims arrive, Millie, with her converted golf trolley, a couple from Denmark, a couple from France and the two German men who are walking together, Karl and Hermann, who we saw earlier. The final member of our party is an athletic younger woman who speaks in, but is not, English. She appears very self-contained and keeps herself to herself, so we don't know at this stage from where she originates.

For some reason Millie decides I must be an expert hiker and now seeks me out to get reassurance about her trip and her adapted golf buggy. She is so proud of it I feel too embarrassed to tell her she is never going to make it all the way to Santiago across some of the terrain we are likely to encounter, dragging her 'pride and joy' behind her. I certainly don't want to be a prophet of doom two days into her pilgrimage. As she presses further, I resort to distraction and ask her to demonstrate her magic wand, which she is delighted to do

This encounter reminds me of a story my dad told me about his friend, Harry. He lent a drill to the bloke across the street and when he went over one day to get it back, the wife of this chap came to the door. He asked if her husband was in.

"Didn't you know?" she said. "He died yesterday."

Harry stood there perplexed for a moment and then blurted out, "Did he say anything about a drill?"

The football continues under floodlights until late but eventually the lights go off and the noise disappears. I manage some sleep through the coughing, snoring and murmurings of my first night on the Camino; but I am awoken—as we all are—by Millie's alarm clock. Eventually, she is the last one up.

Guillena to Castiblanco de los Arroyos

(20 km or 12.5 m) steady climbing
Gradient ascended 310 metres

Thursday 24th March

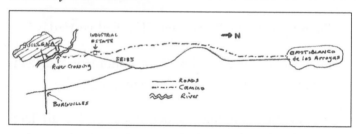

An early rise at seven o'clock and we set off at ten to eight. After ten minutes. we decide against fording a river and take a detour to the road, over a bridge and then down a bank and through a field of cacti to the opposite river-bank to re-join our route—a short but interesting detour. We continue along a track for three kilometres until we stop for breakfast in a very basic café. Our route takes us through a small business park to join the most wonderful of walks up and through olive and orange groves, accompanied all the time by an abundance of perfumed shrubs, bushes and wild flowers: rosemary, poppy, lavender, iris, camomile, rhododendron, azalea and a 'white rose', which Maureen thinks maybe la jara or Spanish Incense plant.

We come across and through our first field of small grazing bulls, who don't seem that interested in us and later see two rather large ones behind a fence… thankfully. There are lots of butterflies in the air; white, blue and tortoiseshell. At a farm, a horse can be seen being 'broken in' and just beyond it I hear something that sounds very much like a woodcock and see a flash of a bird that looks like a golden oriole, only maybe slightly greener. There is stillness and I can almost feel myself relaxing into the peace and tranquillity of our surroundings

A shady spot is used for a rest and we eat pieces of Kendal mint cake and apricots, something that will likely become a feature of our daytime lunch breaks over the next few days. At this point, we exchange words with a couple from Sevilla, who are 'practising' for doing the walk to Santiago in May. In truth, it is Maureen who conducts most of the conversation with them, albeit I do get to elicit how far they are walking today. On arriving at the refugio at Castilblanco de los Arroyos, I am pleasantly surprised (after last night) at the relative luxury afforded us, and the quiet location. There is one room with 16 bunks and another with 12. There are two showers and toilets and somebody on duty during the day, meaning we can leave our rucksacks and belongings whilst in search of somewhere to have a meal. Maureen stayed here before and recommends a small café not far away and we are able to sit outside to eat, although the sun is certainly not as strong as it has been for the last two days.

Castilblanco de los Arroyos has a population of around 5,000 people and is 1,027 feet above sea level. It is the birthplace of Velazquez; not the artist, but a high-ranking civil servant. Francisco Javier Velazquez Lopez is at the time of our visit, the Director General of the Police and the Civil Guard at the Ministry of the Interior. Maybe we should feel very safe here!

Returning to the refugio, I find the water in the shower is cold. Never mind, nothing is going to undermine what has been a very special day! Our late afternoon siesta is disturbed by our first rain and the early evening is altogether fresher with a cooler feel. All our fellow guests of last night are here now, plus a Spanish young man, so 11 of us in all. We wrap up for an evening stroll to get some provisions for tomorrow, as there may be nowhere else to get such things on our route, and it will be between four and five o'clock in the afternoon before we arrive at tomorrow's overnight stop. Bread, cheese, tomato and an orange each are purchased.

Our evening stroll helps us to work out how our route leaves this delightful small town. In a little square there is a statue of an old man standing with his hand gently resting on the shoulder of a seated woman. A wonderfully affirming and positive image of aging, unlike so many images of getting older that seem to both of us to dominate in the media these days. The statue leads to us sharing our thoughts on getting older and our hopes and aspirations for the future. Maureen worked as a volunteer in several albergues in the Pyrenees along the Spanish section of the French Camino. That was how she first met Alison Raju, the author of the guidebook I have with me. Maureen would still like to continue such volunteering for maybe a few more years, but since Tel's heart attack she doesn't want to spend longer periods away from home. She very much enjoys the walking group she is part of back home, too. She and Tel now also have the delights of a grandson to spend time with. For both of us, family time is an important aspect of future plans. I hope to still be running well into my 70's, undertaking other long-distance walks and maybe writing about some of them too.

Our stroll is also helpful preparation for tomorrow. We find the 16th century church complete with nesting storks and swooping swallows and call at a bar for a small beer before returning to the refugio at around quarter-past eight. I don't sleep well as I am cold from my trunk to my knees. I think of getting up to don my jogging bottoms, but in the dark in a room full of snoring pilgrims, this seems like too much trouble. Millie will again be the last one up, despite setting her alarm. Prior to that, I was entertained by the whispered conversation in German between Hermann and Karl as they prepare to depart. My German vocabulary is limited, but even if they had been speaking English, it would have been impossible to discern most of their discussions.

I think this will become a familiar routine for the rest of the Camino.

Castilblanco de los Arroyos to Almaden de la Plata

(29 km or 18 m) flat, gently rising
Gradient ascended 150 metres

Friday 25th March

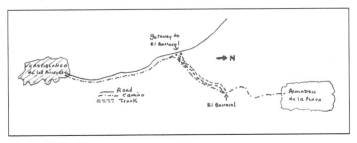

We're up early and set off at 35 minutes past seven, strolling through the village with shops and cafés all closed—no more untill we hit the open road, but no matter, we've got our 'provisions' for the day. The roosting storks are passed, and houses and buildings are left behind as we set out on a 16km stretch of road. At the last building, a solitary stork stands on one leg, like a guard on sentry duty, over a nest perched high above on a pillar. It is quiet though with very little traffic and though it is mainly uphill it is an undulating road. After the rain, the surrounding fields are carpeted with tiny yellow and white flowers, whilst in the distance we can see blue hills and wooded hillsides

25

whilst early morning mists seemed to hover above the valley bottoms. We have the company of fellow pilgrims at various stages. After about two hours walking, a stop is taken for a breakfast of fruit, nuts and chocolate raisins. The weather is overcast, with a cool breeze, ideal for walking.

Whilst we are breakfasting, I share with Maureen my big dilemma. Sandra and I have been debating for some time whether to move to a new house or stay put. We had an architect draw up plans and planning permission has been agreed to extend where we are to try and create more flexible living space. However, we have lived with work going on around us for over two years and further work is planned. Our next-door neighbours on one side had an extension built and the neighbours at the back have recently done the same. This has changed completely the outlook of the property and the private oasis that was our back garden is now overlooked. We now know that the rear garden that we share a boundary with on the other side is going to be built on, too. We have lived where we are for 27 years and raised a family there, but I acknowledge that without major changes to the layout and functions of the existing space, it will very soon no longer be a practical and future-proofed living option for us. Living somewhere that maximises our independence for as long as possible has got to be the major priority. Maureen knows us both well and, like myself can see the pros and cons of both staying put or moving.

"Well," I offer up, "I have got around six weeks to chew the cud on what is for the best and I know back home Sandra will be doing the same."

"She will," Maureen responds, "and I have every confidence that between the two of you, you will make the right decision."

Along the road we see lots of cork trees and hear the first cuckoo of spring and again our eyes and noses are regaled with a plethora of scented wild flowers. We eventually arrive at El Berracol, where the tarmac road can be left behind. El Berracol is a nature reserve dedicated to the planting of trees and after about one and a half kilometres along a wide track we arrive at a complex of buildings. We borrow a key to use some toilets. I think it must have been the first usage of the year—they have certainly seen better days, an interesting little excursion, though.

Back on the track, we carry on until around quarter-past 12, for a welcome lunch stop. Setting off refreshed and rested, we meander along an up-and-down route, which has us fording two small rivers, before branching off to the left along a narrower footpath. The terrain is much more like yesterday's, albeit a bit muddy in places. I hear the pehue pehue of buzzards and looking skywards, see a 'flock' of around 30-40 buzzards, circling and hovering in the thermals. An amazing sight! I have seen maybe six to ten buzzards before but never so many so close together in one place. Heading up our muddy track we hear cow bells to our left. Perhaps it is a warning of impending rain as before long, we finally stop to don waterproofs before becoming engulfed in a heavy shower.

A very steep climb zigzags up to two fine viewpoints, the first 'showcases' our day's journey so far and the second heralds our destination for the evening, nestling as it does some two kilometres below. There is surely no way to easily pull a heavily-laden golf trolley over this stretch, I muse. Almaden de la Plata is famous for its ancient marble quarries, which are believed to have been first created in Roman times. Examples of fine marble quarried here is believed to have been found in both Sevilla and Merida and indeed archaeological research would suggest an overland transport route took the quarried marble south to Sevilla or north to Merida; quite probably along part of the route of the Via de la Plata. Quarrying of marble in the area is thought to have begun in late Augustan times and its wider distribution throughout the Empire expanded in Imperial times.

Almaden is also famous for its Observatorio Astronómico Almadén de la Plata, from which the night skies and the galaxies beyond can be combed. The Observatorio is one of 14 Andalusian institutions devoted to science communication as part of a network established nine years ago (2007) to bring science and technology closer to the public.

An interesting and rocky path leads down to the village and then right to the topmost point of the village to find the albergue, which has one dormitory with 18 beds, packed close together like sardines in a tin. We arrive at the same time as two of our fellow pilgrims, the French couple. After getting out of wet clothes and having a hot shower and changing we have a siesta as the albergue fills up; two cyclists, plus everyone from before except Millie. Will she make it with or without her trolley? The rain is pouring down now as I quickly record the day's events. I think she will be very wet on top of everything else (if and when she arrives).

The albergue has a dining room with tables and chairs and a kitchen, so we have our first hot drink of the day and agree to go out at about quarter-to eight for something to eat. It is nearer to eight o'clock when the rain stops long enough for us to go out and find a café, where we join our two French friends for a three-course meal and a glass of local wine; a veritable feast and all for eight euros.

Outside the rain is lashing down again. I'm not sure how much star-gazing will get done! After the French couple leave to return to the albergue we join the two German pilgrims; Hermann and Karl, who are also in the café for a coffee. Before the rain slackens again, we retrace our steps. We learn that Millie is planning to have a rest day today, to try and fix her trolley, so there is no longer a need to worry about whether she will be joining us tonight.

Maybe somebody else will have the courage to suggest she abandons her pride and joy and just shoulders a rucksack like the rest of us?

There are blankets available at the albergue, so I can ensure I am warm enough to sleep. I do, however, wake at three and then sleep fitfully for the remainder of the night. Despite this, I feel much more rested than the night before!

Almaden de la Plata to El Real de la Jara

(16 km or 10 m) flat
Gradient ascended 10 metres

Saturday 26th March

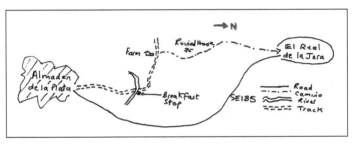

A lovely day starts with a hot drink of tea, before setting off at around quarter-past eight. It is sunny but cool as we leave Almaden de la Plata. A little church at the end of our route out of the village has a stork nesting on the church tower, with two young visible in the nest. The Nuesta Señora de Gracia Church was built in the early 20th century, behind the facade of the former Ermita de Nuesta Señora de los Angeles. I wonder whether there was any marble inside the old hermitage that has been locally quarried or whether marble supplies had been exhausted by the Romans many years before!

Rounding the corner as we leave civilization again, there are fields on either side sprouting solar panels; an enterprising way to make a living no doubt. We hear and then see barking dogs on either side, and then a small flock of sheep appear with a labrador. The dog is herding the sheep on his own, no people around anywhere.

As our route starts to unfold, we embark on a gently undulating path through Spanish oak trees, which keeps us company for most of our walk. We can see, touch and smell wild sage, which we haven't encountered before, but suddenly it is everywhere. Sheep bells are heard and two beautiful Spanish jays dart across our path and through the trees. We arrive at a farm where there are cattle, sheep and many pigs and stay to watch and listen as the pigs run, gather and squeal as the farmer arrives to provide them with breakfast.

On leaving the farm, soon our thoughts turn to our own breakfast and we resolve to stop at the next suitable place. Almost immediately, we reach the summit of a small rise and before us is a small river with a concrete table or seat beside it, just perfect for a picnic. It feels strangely liberating to be breakfasting beside the gurgling waters on cheese, tomato, orange, fruit, nuts and Kendal mint cake. It will certainly keep us going and reluctantly, we tear ourselves away from our splendid surroundings to continue our journey. Undulating tracks follow once the stream is forded with one steeper climb that reveals wonderful vistas towards the higher mountains beyond.

Another farm appears to our left and then leaving the track we join a dirt road. I stop to take pictures of a ruined house that sits within a tightly woven carpet of yellow flowers that seem to be both all around and within the ruins and yet beyond that are nowhere to be seen—nature reclaiming to a magnificent display of colour.

A rather grand house sits on a small hill to our left and beyond that is another farm with goats and pigs. The route at this stage takes us through many gates and the last tells us we should 'beware of loose animals'. I look but see nothing that could be described as 'loose'. Maureen and I both agree that at times today's walk resembles 'the Dales', at others 'the Lakes', particularly the early morning mist below us in the valleys, and yet it is entirely unique and most decidedly Spanish in its own right. We walk amongst or see blackberry bushes, strawberry trees, wild grapevines, oleander, honeysuckle, mock privet, rock rose, cork oaks, gall oaks, willows, mastic trees, ash trees and even one or two poplar trees.

We descend into the small town of Real de la Jara. The town dates to Roman times with some writers even claiming it was founded by King Solomon. It was deserted during the Visigothic period but again resettled by the Moors and obtained emancipation from Cordoba in 1148. It was previously known as Xara, after the bushy vegetation that grows around it. The town was used by King Alfonso XI as his camp before the Battle of Salado in 1340. King Alfonso of Castilia and his namesake King Alfonso IV of Portugal and their Christian armies inflicted a disastrous defeat on the Marinids (Moors) of North Africa; in their attempts to re-conquer the Iberian Peninsula. After the battle the Marinids fled back to Africa. This is one of many examples of Christians and Moors overwriting the landscape of Spanish history in a kind of palimpsest.

In 1498 the Catholic Monarchs granted the town the title of Real (which means Royal) and several other privileges besides. It forms part of the Sierra Norte natural park and is designated as an area of outstanding natural beauty; a privilege that is 'real' and cannot be 'granted'.

The albergue is easily found as we enter the town and see Hermann and Karl marching back up the hill towards us. Apparently to register and get a 'pilgrim stamp' we have to go down to the town hall. The ground floor of the albergue is flooded and not available and a very steep ramp round the side takes us to the door of the floor above. The French couple are already here; the room has ten beds and one bathroom —an en-suite. We leave our back packs and go in search of the town hall. On entering the building, I see a young lady who directs us to go upstairs and along a corridor to the registration point. We come to the area and then find that the young woman has followed to attend to our needs herself.

Whilst we are there a phone call is received (from our German friends), telling her that there is no hot water at the albergue. We are kindly given the option of going to the little guest house at number 70 Casa Molina and only if we do not like this, do we have to go back before two o'clock to pay to stay at the albergue.

The guest house is lovely and only two euros more. We have a room with four beds to ourselves and a bathroom complete with a shower and our own towels. It is strange how you quickly re-evaluate what are the luxuries of life!

The Danish couple are here now too. We decide to stay, leave some things and return to collect our rucksacks. Karl and Hermann have decided to come to the guest house too, which may mean the French couple have what they desire (a private room for themselves). There is hot water now, apparently—one of the German men had simply not turned the right tap on!

We return to the guest house for a shower and to do some washing, which we peg out to dry in a little courtyard in the sun.

At around quarter-to three we go out for something to eat and find a little café just around the corner for a tasty and freshly prepared meal of pasta. Back at the guest house for five o'clock, we both spend time in conversation with our fellow Danish 'pilgrims', Martin and Marian. They are both attentive to the needs and stories of other pilgrims. Marian's English is excellent, and her husband can understand, but is not as fluent at speaking the language. Like myself, he had a health scare recently and takes several pills each day.

"Life is good though," he says, pointing to the sun and indicating all around him.

Marian asks us whether we are planning to walk to Santiago, or whether we will continue to Finisterre, which is what they want to do. I explain that I plan to walk to Santiago, but that Maureen can only walk with me to Zafra. I will link up with another friend, John, there next Wednesday and he'll walk the rest of the way with me.

At the insistence of Martin, Maureen relays to them both the story of her journey along the Camino in 2010. It is a story I've heard before and which kindled my desire to walk the Via de la Plata. I listen with the same keenness as Martin and Marian as the highlights are spoken about. Maureen is typically very modest about her achievement and at times is encouraged by Marian to say more.

I update my diary and keep an eye on the washing as clouds appear and the sun disappears for the day. It did forecast rain later, but on the TV in the café the weather seems set fair for the next two days, with possibly rain on Tuesday and then sunny for the first week in April.

I discover in conversation with Hermann that he lived in Madrid for many years and that the white rose we saw on Wednesday was indeed, as Maureen suggested, the la jara plant, which explains why we could smell incense. It is unusual for it to be flowering so soon, as I guess it is for many of the wild flowers we're seeing. It must be a combination of the six weeks of unseasonable heavy rain, followed by some warmer weather, which triggered this earlier blooming of so many wild flowers. Not that we are complaining!

After a short siesta we go out at seven o'clock to experience the service at the local church, San

Bartolome. A young priest and a large congregation, but it is all over within 20 minutes.

Tomorrow is Easter Sunday and the service will no doubt be considerably longer. As I write, I think the highlight of this evening was the shaking of hands and kissing of neighbours. There are several short walks from the town to viewpoints that look out over the expanse of the Sierra del Pimpollar and the Sierra Padrona, whose high point rises to 911m and is the second highest peak in the Sierra Norte.

We take a walk up to one of these view-points; the little castle, Castillo Real—that is the high point of the village but can't get all the way there because of ongoing renovation work. As we work our way back down to the village, the hubbub of a flock of sparrows draws ever closer. A walk to find the supermarket provides us with the wherewithal to have our usual picnic breakfast on tomorrow's journey. Real de la Jarra has many statues of animals and on our travels, we spot a wild cat, a deer with antlers and an otter.

We meet Inieste again, the rather self-absorbed woman, who on the first night of our journey spoke good English, but who is in fact of Dutch Basque origin. Inieste is not quite so introverted but had been tired and reluctant to engage in conversation with what were, to her, a group of strangers. She tells us whilst her mother was Dutch, her father was from the Basque region in Spain, but that after her parents split up when she was a small child, she returned to Holland with her mother. She has not seen her father since and last year found out he died two years ago. She is walking the Camino in homage to him, a kind of apology for not trying harder to find him whilst he was still alive. A drink and tapas are shared, and we depart feeling a warmth of spirit, borne from a collective commitment to the Camino. I wonder if she will become part of my 'Camino family' in the weeks ahead? She's heard Millie is back on the Camino, albeit now a day behind. I wonder whether she abandoned the golf trolley yet!

Now back at the guest house, I reflect on what has been a most special day in so many ways. Tomorrow we will climb half the height again, in one day, that we have done in the four of our journey so far. In distance, however, we will only cover 20km. I snuggle down in a proper bed with sheets and blankets and drift off into a pleasant sleep, dreaming of things to come.

El Real de la Jara to Monesterio

(22 km or 14 m) gently rising
Gradient ascended 275 metres

Sunday 27th March

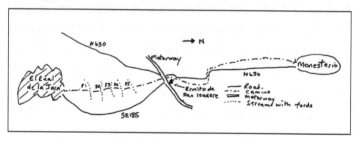

This day takes us up to the high plateau to the town of Monesterio. It will be the largest place we have stayed since leaving Sevilla, with a population of around 4,400 people. After morning ablutions, we leave the guest house at eight o'clock and are soon out of the village and on a wide track, past a field of sheep, with a single dog amongst them on shepherding duty. The sun is out but it will be a little while before it is hot enough to warm us. We walk to the sound of more cuckoos and come across the first broom in bloom. Our track gives views of the mountains, complete with cloud cover at first and there is a Lakeland feel to the landscape, apart from the numbers of holm oak and olive trees.

We eventually catch up to the French couple, who stop to have breakfast and our steps for an hour or so keep us in touch with each other. We have the excitement of negotiating several fords, five in the day, and the first three are in company with our fellow French pilgrims. At the last one of these we spot and take a picture of a tortoise, struggling valiantly along the cloying mud slope at the side of the flowing water; still no deer though!

After a little while, we come to the road over the motorway and see the Danish couple having their first 'pit stop' of the day. I spot a solitary buzzard circling overhead. A perro pastor guides a flock of sheep across our path, with a large loose limbed short-haired labrador assisting him in his manoeuvres. It takes us a while to negotiate the roundabout and road intersections and then to our right on a small hill we see a small building, which is a shrine to Ermita de San Isidro. Here we re-join a path that winds through eucalyptus trees. Some rocks near the shrine provide a perfect place to stop for our breakfast. Whilst we are 'refuelling', Marian and Martin pass us and disappear through the eucalyptus trees.

San Isidro was born in Madrid in 1082 and died in 1172. Legend has it that whilst the saint was praying, two angels ploughed the fields for him. Among the miracles attributed to him, it is said that once when he was building a well, his son fell in, but that through his intervention, his son was miraculously brought back to the parapet when the waters rose, causing the child to float.

The trees continue for around three kilometres, before we re-join a road again for a short while. Just before the junction we come across a flock of sheep. This short stretch of tarmac is significant as it marks us passing the 100km point of my walk, one tenth of the way to Santiago. Our path takes us off and then on the road again until we reach an underpass, where steps have been created for us to finally leave tarmac behind again and join a dirt track. The Danish amigos are enjoying lunch on the last step, as we swing right and reach a rise. We also spot the French couple having their lunch, too. Warm greetings are exchanged all round.

The track rises quite steeply for about seven kilometres and not far from the summit we are joined by a little dog who has decided to accompany us all the way to the outskirts of Monesterio. The town itself is around 755m above sea level. Before we leave the dirt track, we arrive at the Cruz del Puerto, a cross on a hillside and a picnic place. Arriving in Monesterio, we walk up the increasingly familiar N630 into the town and see a hostal on our right but decide to explore a little further.

The tourist information office is closed and in a little bar we are directed back to the hostal (Hostal El Pilar D P), where we are greeted by a very nice gentleman. We are pleased to accept the offer of a twin room with a TV and en-suite facilities for 20 euros each. It seems our evening accommodation is getting better and better each night! Maureen certainly thinks it is a better option than where she stayed in Monasterio six years ago. We take the opportunity to shower and freshen up before going to an adjacent café for something to eat. It has a sign outside advertising 'Pilgrim's Menu'.

A wonderful meal is enjoyed of salad, bread, soup; complete with a whole egg; followed by lamb stew with chips, and more bread (which we keep for tomorrow), coffee and a large glass of wine. This costs us the princely sum of nine and a half euros.

I get a brief phone call from John, back in the UK confirming he's completed the Coniston 14 run yesterday in just under three hours; brilliant news! Had I not been with Maureen in Spain I would have been running with him. I hope he will have recovered sufficiently to be able to join me in three days when we are due to link up in Zafra.

He reassures me he will be fine and that all the arrangements are in place. He will fly into Sevilla the day after tomorrow and stay overnight there before catching an early bus. He should be in Zafra by half-past nine in the morning and we agree to meet at the bus station there. The plan will then be to have a bite to eat before setting off together. Maureen will return to the bus station to get a bus back to Sevilla. Her flight back to England is in the afternoon and she should be back home by half-past ten in the evening.

Leaving the bread in the room, we explore more of Monesterio in the sun, at one café there are 30 or 40 young people enjoying life, a drink and each other's company. Across the square another bar is full of families enjoying a meal and a drink in the sun. This precipitates a conversation between us about our respective partners and families back home which brings back memories of a holiday shared near Carcassonne in France.

A pleasant excursion takes us to the church, where we see the 'floats' that have been prepared for holy week, and in particular for today. In a little square nearby people are clearing away what has obviously been an Easter Sunday event, with party stragglers still enjoying themselves and others tidying away large trestle tables. Our little 'tour' takes us back to our hotel, where we sit for a while in a seat in the sun and meet two 'new' pilgrims, who are from Malaga and started today from our morning starting point. They are taking a week to get as far as Mérida. Sitting in bed to keep warm we find the football channel and watch the last 15 minutes of a Premier League game. It doesn't seem that long ago that Easter Sunday was a football-free zone. Only Christmas Day now retains that privilege.

After a short siesta, I venture on a little walk and spot a gift shop with some very interesting items. Later, I return with Maureen and purchase some silver earrings as a present for Maureen to take back for Sandra, before backtracking to the bar we ate at earlier. Martin and Marian and the French couple both pop in to say hello; such camaraderie. I have a whisky to warm the insides. We then go back to the hostal and to bed. Breakfast, I discover, is included in the price and is available at our little adjacent bar. Until morning then!

Monesterio to Fuenta de Cantos

(22 km or 14 m) gently falling
Gradient descended 205 metres

Monday 28th March

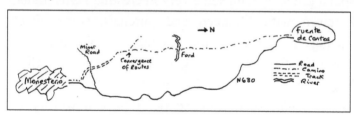

The alarm is set for seven to make sure we are up. We both enjoy a good sleep and it is indeed the alarm that wakes us from our slumber. After morning ablutions and packing we go next door to the café for breakfast. Setting off along the road out of town, it is light but still cool, albeit with the promise of sunshine to come. As we head along the main road through the town, we pass a football stadium and then immediately turn off the road and for the rest of the day, apart from when we arrive at our evening destination, we are away from roads and the noise of traffic.

To start with our route for about three kilometres takes us through and along 'veredas'—lanes with dry-stone walls on either side. Holm oak trees are dotted around, with cows and pigs in the fields and rolling hills, reminiscent of the 'Dales'. The walls give way to more wide-open spaces, with green rolling hills and blue-tinged mountains in the distance. There are fields of brown bushes too and the usual abundance of wild flowers. We pass a solitary gentleman and in conversation we ask him whether there were rabbits, boar and deer around now as we haven't seen any.

"Only on the menu," he says with a smile!

We cross a minor road to continue along a track with only one dry stone wall for company and see irises and a beautiful wild orchid and arrive at a convergence of ways. We are both clear, and are later proved correct, that our route is to the right. The French couple, Bertrand and Cecilia are heading to the left and we have a brief discussion with Bertrand. We point out the arrows to the right, but his wife has gone on to the left and he goes after her, calling 'see you later' to us. At this stage we hope they will find their way to the albergue, which is the destination we are all headed for by the end of the day.

The trees disappear, and we are walking through rolling countryside, much more typical of Spain, with views of distant mountains. Round one bend we catch a glimpse of Fuerte de Cantos, way in the distance some 11km away, which is where we will stay tonight. We encounter a group of cyclists who pass us on the way and later a motorcyclist coming towards us. He stops and shares a word; he is travelling from Merida to Sevilla. He explains there is a ford ahead where he had to help three lady cyclists across safely, a real Spanish knight in shining leathers.

Our track continues for a further two kilometres before we meet our Danish couple, Martin and Marion again and share the conversation with the motorcyclist. They too spotted the orchid we saw earlier and were equally impressed. As we carry on, we see a line of trees in a dip ahead and feel that must be the ford area and resolve to stop there for lunch—we have been walking for about three hours. A stork flies from east to west, sweeping across the green fields ahead. About two minutes later a second one follows. As we near what is indeed the river with the ford crossing, we see another stork nesting in a tree to our right. We cross the ford with a little difficulty (and not without getting feet wet) and on the other side lay out our picnic feast of bread, cheese, apricots and chocolate.

Whilst we are feasting in the sun, drying out and putting on sun cream, Marion and Martin catch us up again and arrive at the other side of the ford. We applaud as they take off boots and socks and don sandals and paddle across to join us. We share some apricots with them and then, having re-booted, they leave us to finish our picnic alone. As we are setting off, a tractor arrives at the ford with a large container, which is then filled from the fast-flowing waters, using just a tube and capillary action. A solitary buzzard is circling to our left, reminding me we haven't had any news of Millie for a couple of days. We are both mesmerised as we watch the silent but graceful fly past of a stork, out looking for food in the wet pastures in front of us.

Refreshed, we continue and discover fields of young pea plants stretching as far as the eye can see. We encounter our first mule, along with a small horse (probably its mother), in a field and then ahead see a cart being pulled by what turns out to be a donkey, with a rider on another mule walking beside it. A shepherd and his dog are watching over a small herd of goats and as we exchange greetings, he complains about the unseasonal heat of the day. Just beyond him and as if to emphasis his point, we find Martin and Marion, both enjoying a rest in the sun.

We continue to the village of Fuerte de Cantos, where they catch us up again as twisting narrow streets are negotiated, arrows spotted in our combined efforts to find the albergue, which is well worth it. It is a former convent with a beautiful view of open countryside to the rear and a small floodlit cloister in the centre, in which a rather magnificent palm tree stands proudly surveying the scene. We are the first to arrive, closely followed by the Danes and 90 minutes later by the tired and weary French couple and then, Karl and Hermann. Our 'party' is coming together again I enjoy a refreshing shower, hang out some washing and then we both go in search of a meal at the Bar Charo, a well-seasoned and warming chick-pea stew with various meats and salad; very nice indeed.

As well as being the birthplace of the painter, Francisco de Zurbarán, Fuerte de Cantos also has a darker side to it through its historical connection to the Spanish Civil War. In 1934 the Mayor of the town was a socialist called Modesto José Lorenzana. He was known for his humanitarian efforts to improve the town and was instrumental in using resources to improve water supplies to all its residents. He also used municipal funds to alleviate the hunger of unemployed families within the district.

The far right moves to destabilise the democratic republican parts of Spain, were reflected in the district by the Civil Governor, Rafael Salazar Alsonso, along with members of the Civil Guard and local right-wing organisations accusing Lorenzana of misusing public funds. On these grounds and with very dubious legal processes he was removed from office. He was later murdered in September 1936, with the far right implicated in his death. Lorenzana's contribution to the development of Fuerte de Cantos is however, now again recognised by the town.

I remember my father telling me of his experiences as a young man in seeking to support the Spanish working people in their struggle to protect democratically won freedoms and to resist the rise of the far right. This was certainly a bleak period in Spanish history and one that saw many people tortured and killed. With hindsight, and in many ways, it was a predictor of the events that unfolded with the rise of Nazism in Germany under Hitler and of atrocities committed during the Second World War.

In Real de la Jara, it was the conflicts between Christians and Moors as each sought to exercise power and control over the area that had historical prominence and here less than 20 miles further along my pilgrimage route, it was the fight between left and right, socialist and fascist, in a bloody struggle that set Spaniard against Spaniard, that had and is today given a greater historical impact.

Our walk has been very pleasant, almost as nice as Friday's; very warm in the sun, though with not a lot of shade. So far, each day has had its special moments. Today it is a solitary buzzard circling on lighter thermals, the silent but graceful flight of the storks, purple blue wild orchids, donkeys and mules and a wonderful albergue at the end of our walk. At the last stream crossing of the day we also hear the 'riveting' of many frogs croaking and are able to spot one or two before they disappear under the water as we approach. Our cuckoo friends keep us company throughout the day, too.

After a short siesta we go outside to enjoy the remaining sun and hear music; brassy bugles and the heavy beat of drums from around the other side of the albergue, as the procession approaches. The figure of Christ on a large plinth is carried by men of the village who are concealed inside to give the impression that the whole structure is floating above the ground. There are many buglers and drummers—men and women, boys and girls—all dressed in their blue uniforms. The albergue we are in was a convent and attached on one side of a square is the chapel, which is still one of the key religious focal points of the village.

As the Easter Monday float approaches it addresses the entrance to the former convent, but is too large to go inside, so instead does a slow 'dance' in front of the doors, to the accompaniment of the music. It then turns and heads back on its slow journey through the narrow streets, back to the main church in the centre of the village. We meet Inieste who also took the route followed by Bertand and Cecille and is feeling very tired. We also meet the Spanish couple again and they too took the 'longer' route. Maureen and I decide to follow the procession on its slow journey. The entire town is out to watch, the girls and boys in their 'Sunday best' and the adults are well attired too. It is certainly the only show in town. After an hour, we go in search of a bar for a hot drink, without success, and return to the albergue, as the sun finally sets on another wonderful day.

Fuenta de Cantos to Zafra

(25 km or 15.5 m) slight fall
Gradient descended 90 metres

Tuesday 29th March

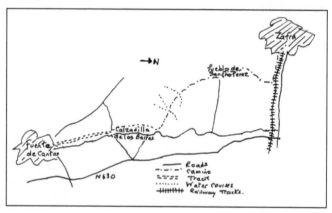

Dawn breaks on my last day of walking with Maureen on the Camino. We have a disturbed night, as Maureen has to dash to the toilets twice to be sick, as I discover on the second occasion having gone out after her, to see if she is alright. I can't get warm during the night and the morning has a much cooler feel to it. We have a later start to the day consequently. The albergue provides breakfast and Maureen is by this time feeling well enough to be able to eat some toast and drink some coffee. We start walking at quarter to nine and agree to take it easy. We head for the church, the final resting place of yesterday's procession, and pick up the yellow arrows of our Camino route and soon see Hermann and Karl, the two German 'pilgrims' a little way ahead. They always seem to set off early.

We cross the road at the end of the village to go down a track and meet two new 'perigrinos', two ladies from the Basque region of Spain. Maureen enjoys the opportunity to converse in Spanish with them, as if she knows that for her, unlike six years before, it will be her last day on the Camino. Apparently, they set off from Sevilla two days after we did, so they are making good progress indeed. Of more interest to me is the fact that they met Millie in Monesterio and she is still pulling her golf trolley, albeit she has reduced its contents somewhat. She has also walked several stretches on the road to better protect her pride and joy.

It is dry with the odd glimpse of sun and a nice breeze to keep us cool. There are certainly more clouds than yesterday. The fields are green and mostly bereft of trees as we take our time to travel the five and a half kilometres to the next village. We see a mule and more pigs and hear the bleating of sheep. There are conical mountains in the far distance and of course, lots of wild flowers.

At the village we stop at a small coffee bar for an infusion of camomile tea and some Spanish cake which we share. As we are leaving the Spanish couple, (whom we first met in Monesterio), arrive and we exchange further pleasantries. After using the facilities, we leave the café and purchase some cheese and a tomato to add to our 'picnic stash' and then carry on, feeling refreshed. We see Inieste ahead, but no sign of the German peregrinos. Marion and Martin are also taking it easy today, as both were unwell yesterday, too. They are not planning to walk as far as Zafra but are going as far as Puebla de Sancho Pérez, which is about five kilometres before it. Indeed, this seems to be where all within 'our family' are headed.

We are now following a sunken grassy lane, between two low walls, which are partly earth and partly stones and see a man tending his vineyard, with his faithful mule grazing nearby. The sun has now completely disappeared, and the sky is getting greyer by the minute. We arrive at and travel alongside a road for a short while and at the next junction an electricity pylon stands guard, atop which a pair of storks have built their nest. We hear the clamouring chatter of the beaks of their young as we approach.

The road is now left behind and our route heads between fields and a solitary figure is spotted ahead. Another stork has built a nest to our left on a smaller pylon. The solitary figure turns out to be a local man who is out bird watching and flower spotting. Our track now reaches a rather tricky crossing point of a river. Our route to the right is thwarted by the instability of a log across the rushing waters. Maureen is encouraged to go to the left, where other peregrinos have found ways across. In the meantime, I reposition the log and using my trusty stick place a stone to wedge it in place. It is a tricky crossing but can be done.

However, within four metres a further obstacle appears in the shape of another water course. It has two parallel logs sloping down and across the rushing torrent for about ten feet. It is a careful balancing act, but I edge across and reach dry land. I re-discover the track and dump my rucksack to go to help Maureen. Despite the gentleman's suggestion, there are no possible crossings to the left and she retraces her steps as I did to help guide her over the two obstacles. We are just about to leave when our Danish friends arrive at the river and we guide them across the obstacles and applaud as they too reach dry land. They decide to have a longer stop and we carry on and say our farewells.

"It's sure going to be a challenge to get a golf trolley across that stretch," I verbalise to Maureen.

"Yes, and if she takes the road route it will add another ten kilometres to her day's walk," adds Maureen.

After about another one and a half kilometres a further river crossing appears, and this time there is no way across and so we are forced to take off our shoes and socks, roll up our trouser legs and carefully paddle across with our shoes and socks in one hand and our trusty poles (both depth testing and steadying us) in the other.

The scenery has been a little boring and uninteresting, but the challenges set by the route have certainly been sterner. However, soon a greater challenge appears in the form of rain and we hurriedly put on our waterproofs and protection covers for the rucksacks and then continue through the now driving rain. After a further two kilometres of relentless rain we cross a road but continue as there is still no shelter to be had.

We march on as the rain increases in intensity. After a further five kilometres I spot a barn to the left which appears to have an opening and would provide shelter, but it is 400m off our track to the left and Maureen is convinced habitation will be over the next rise. We carry on and there is indeed a single farmstead and smallholding over the brow, not quite the habitation we need or are hoping for. The rain is biting cold now and getting heavier still with a few hailstones thrown in for good measure.

We are very wet, but there is still no shelter, so we hurry on, seven kilometres beyond the earlier road crossing. We've now been walking for two hours in the pouring rain and have to cross a railway, too. In the mist we spot a large black bull, at first threatening, but it turns out to be an advertising hording for a Spanish brandy. Exhausted, wet and cold we arrive in Puebla de Sancho Pérez. We debate going to the albergue or heading right to a hostal along the road which should be nearer and serving food and we opt for the latter.

At this point four, bedraggled cyclists pass us having also emerged from the Camino. Arriving at the hostal we take off wet cagoules, shoes and use the toilets to dry and warm wet and numbed hands. We order hot drinks and some food. Maureen is worn out but pleased we have got here and rightly enquires about a room and decides to go no further. After our meal, we go up to Maureen's room, where I shower and change into dry clothes. I then make my farewells as I now head off alone to Zafra, where I am scheduled to link up with John in the morning. Maureen will have enough time to walk to Zafra tomorrow and catch a bus and get back to Sevilla in time for her return flight to the UK.

The rain has now stopped but the wind is stronger and is in my face as I set off along the road on my own. It feels strange to be walking without Maureen and certainly I no longer have the 'comfort blanket' of her Spanish to fall back on. I reflect that I couldn't have done this a week ago, being with Maureen has given me sufficient confidence in my ability to 'negotiate' a way through any linguistic obstacles which may lay ahead.

As I pass the route of the Camino, which crosses the road, I debate which way to go but decide to stick to the road, but after a little while I see a sign for the albergue and decide to change plan and take the Camino route from the albergue to Zafra. I eventually arrive back in the village, my little detour having added two kilometres to my journey, but I am happier following yellow arrows again. My way takes me along a sandy track, which in turn leads to a rail crossing and along the side of the track for a further kilometre until I arrive at Zafra Station, which is on the edge of the city.

The sun is out again as I walk into Zafra in bright sunshine, following the arrows until a big road junction in the centre. I head for the tourist information office and go in the direction indicated by signposts, but as I seem to be on the verge of leaving the city altogether, retrace my steps and concentrate on finding the bus station I will need to be at in the morning to link up with John. With this mission accomplished, I see a bus with Sevilla on it and am tempted to travel back there to meet John at the Hotel Zaida, but then remember that all the hotels are likely to be busy with it being holy week.

Anyway, I discover it was the bus from and not to Sevilla and therefore not an immediate option. The heavens open and I decide to find the nearest hostal rather than search for the albergue in the rain. After a ten-minute walk I find a suitable resting place, check in and go to my room to unpack, sort out my rucksack and put clothes I need on hangers to dry, and wet and dirty clothes in the washing machine. The hotel has a dryer too and so hopefully all will be well for tomorrow.

Zafra is known as a mini Sevilla, because of its Alcazar and other historical buildings. It has a population of around 16,500 and has a history dating back to the Bronze Age. It also has Roman associations and in and around the city, the remains of at least twenty Roman villas have been discovered. In medieval times it was a small border town between the domains of Seville and Badajoz, because of which, in 1030, a defensive fortification was constructed. At that time, it was in Moorish hands and the Arabs named the town Safra or Cafra, from which its current name derives.

During the 13th century it was capture twice by Christian forces; first in 1229 by Alfonso IX and then definitively by Ferdinand III. Its most momentous change occurred when it was granted city status by Henry III of Castile, subsequently it was increasingly fortified and became the dominant city in the area. During the 15th century a lot of this work was completed, with various examples still surviving today —including El Alcazar (Alcazar of Seville) and the Convent of Saint Mary of the Valley. In later years the Alcazar was modernised as a palace.

Zafra remains an important industrial and commercial city serving the surrounding areas, which are largely dedicated to agriculture, as our walk of the last two days testified.

I send a text to Maureen to let her know I have arrived in Zafra and found the bus station where I will link up with John. I wish her a safe journey back. She responds almost immediately and has clearly sorted out arrangements for her travel back to Sevilla in time to catch her flight home.

I then have a rest before going out in search of somewhere to eat. It was sad to leave Maureen, and I am now a day ahead of most of the perigrinos she and I met and have come to know on the way thus far. I wonder whether my path will cross with any of them in the days and weeks ahead. Whilst lost in these thoughts and scanning the menu outside a bar, a friendly voice calls out my name. It is Inieste, who like me, has managed to get to Zafra and is out looking for somewhere to eat, too!

We both agree the menu looks fine and share a table to catch up on the day's walk and the downpour we had to endure. I explain that Maureen is safe and well, but she is staying at Puebla de Sancho Pérez. Inieste is a complex character and still angry with herself for not trying to find her father whilst he was still alive. This leads us to an interesting discussion, as like her, I never sought to find my biological father. He wasn't supportive of my mother and she had a very difficult time having decided to continue with the pregnancy. She was initially disowned by her parents and it was only with the intervention of her brother and one of her aunts, that they relented, and my mother could return home. I was six months old at that time. She was introduced to the man, who later married her and adopted me and who I consider to be my father, by my uncle, and I remember being present at the wedding when I was four years old. Despite being aware of my history and even after being given the name and last known address of my biological father, I never felt the need to try and meet him.

"Why would you not want to do this?" Inieste queries, "Surely you must have been curious?"

"Not really, the man who brought me up and together with my mother gave me a brother and a sister, was in every way the best father I could have had, and I was proud to know him as my father."

I can tell that Inieste is a little taken aback.

"You will never be able to trace back half your blood line," she adds.

"It was different for you though," I suggest, "because your mother and biological father were together for some time when you were a baby. He would have known you."

"I never had a consistent surrogate father like you, either."

"Did he ever try to find you?"

Inieste is silent before she speaks again, "No, he never did. I often wonder whether he ever even thought about me. I would have liked to ask him that question at least."

She immediately asks me about my plans for the next few days, as if to steer the conversation in another direction. She is staying in Zafra for two nights. I explain to her about my linking up with John in the morning and that apart from a hostal booking in Salamanca in 12 days, we will see where each day takes us. We wish each other well and head back to our respective hostels.

I set the alarm for seven to ensure I am up in time to get showered, dressed and packed so I can head to the bus station to meet John. I gather my clothes from the hotel dryer and retire to bed, still ruminating on my conversation with Inieste.

Maureen's Diary Note

Wednesday 30th March

"I don't sleep well but am up in time to pay the hostal bill and walk into Zafra. I catch the bus in plenty of time. It takes the bus just 25 minutes to get to Fuerta de Cantos, where I stayed with Pete two nights ago and a further 18 minutes to get to Monasterio, where we stayed on Saturday. This is like a hurtling succession of déjà vu. Already, the scenery is changing with a welcome return of wooded hillsides, I am sure Pete said this was the most enjoyable part of the walk to date for him. In a further ten minutes, I pass the shrine where we picnicked on our way to Monasterio. I have mixed feelings as in some ways it seems as if the journey is unravelling and I am a little envious of Pete, as I remember back to 2010. It certainly evokes for me happy memories of my wonderful experience on the Camino de Santiago. I hope Pete's journey of self-discovery will be equally memorable. I am awoken from my musings as the bus arrives in Sevilla. I take a taxi to the airport and leave sunny Spain to return to a wet and cold Britain."

John's Diary Note

Wednesday 30th March

"Travel plans worked well, despite several hours of packing and repacking my rucksack to make sure I had everything I needed that both Peter and Maureen had advised. Flight went without hitch and I got a taxi into Seville. Maureen's directions to find the Hotel Zaida were helpful as the taxi driver could only get me to within 400m of it. Most importantly, I was able to pick up my pilgrim passport that Maureen had organised for me and left on reception for my arrival. Found the nearby bus station where I would catch a bus at seven o'clock in the morning. The bus should arrive at Zafra at half-past nine, when I would link up with Peter and Maureen. Later, I got a text message from Peter indicating that Maureen would not be there in the morning but that all was well and a second one from Maureen, wishing me well."

Plate 1
Maureen hiding her eyes from the sun in Sevilla

Plate 2
My pilgrim 'passport'

Plate 3
The Spanish La Jara (incense) plant – Day 2

Plate 4
Tortoise struggling through cloying mud – Day 5

Chapter Two

Zafra to Caceres

***

Zafra to Villafranco de los Barros

(20 km or 12.5 m) slight fall
Gradient descended 90 metres

Wednesday 30th March

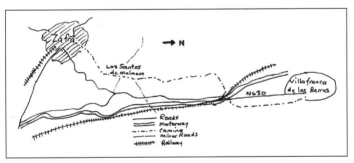

I get up and shower—an interesting experience. The water runs icy cold for about a minute and then turns scalding hot. I finally manage to adjust this to a suitable temperature and am then able to wash, get dry and dressed. I repack the rucksack again including toiletries and a towel, having exchanged the one I borrowed for a fresh one.

I leave my Zafra hotel and head back to the bus station. The bus John is travelling on is operated by the Leda bus company and their ticket office doesn't open for another five minutes at half-past eight in the morning. By the time it does my 'lines' are well rehearsed. I establish which stop it will arrive at and head to Stand 12 to await the express bus from Sevilla. Grey clouds and driving rain will also form the welcoming committee for John. If the long-range forecast is to be believed, it will clear up this afternoon.

The bus (I learn later from John) also stopped at Fuenta de Cantos, where Maureen and I stayed and where we had witnessed and followed the Easter Monday parade. It arrives just before half-past nine and to my relief John is on board, his travel arrangements having gone entirely as planned. After we exchange greetings and hugs, we head down to town along the same route I took yesterday. I had identified several cafés/bars where we might get breakfast. We soon find one and enjoy our first Spanish breakfast together— toast with olive oil and finely chopped tomatoes, plus a coffee.

It's good to be walking with John, we have shared so many memorable walks over the past 25 years. The Lake District was a favourite fell-walking destination for us both. We had spent an enjoyable, but tough, six days undertaking the OXFAM Everest Challenge walk in 1996, ascending and descending most of the major peaks to an equivalent height above sea level of Mount Everest. The weather had been kind too and most of our days were spent in shorts and t-shirts. John also helped me achieve an ambition of climbing all of Lakelands 2,000ft plus summits before the Millennium.

The last of these, which I had deliberately avoided until that time, was appropriately named 'Great End'. It nearly proved to be an almost prophetic choice as I was blown off the summit backwards by a sudden gust of wind. I landed on my back on some rocks in a gulley about 15ft below. Thankfully, I was wearing my rucksack, and this cushioned me from any lasting damage. The look of anguish and concern on John's face as I sailed past him was an image I will never forget. We were staying in a cottage at Grange-over-Sands with Caroline and Sandra for the weekend, and by the time we got back to them later in the day, the story of my fall had been suitably embellished to reflect my near-death experience.

We head back up to the bus station and turn left where we can see a medieval church tower surrounded by blocks of flats. The rain has now stopped but it is still very grey, albeit a lighter shade and a little chilly. We are looking forward to the promised afternoon sun as we follow the road past the church tower and out into the country. I can reconnect with the Camino, and talk to John about the journey so far, the yellow arrows and how we could now 'leave the world behind' for a little while.

To start, we pass lots of dilapidated small holdings; stark indications that generally people in this part of Spain are not wealthy. We walk between huge hedges of prickly pear cacti that seem at home in their environment and yet don't sit right in my head. Maybe it is the cold and the grey sky or the scrubby and unkempt surroundings we're walking through. I spot the first of what turns out to be many blue gentians that we'll pass over the coming days. The further we walk towards Villafranca de los Barros the more abundant they become. A hare suddenly appears ahead, quickly followed by two more, the dark long ears with their small white bandings around two-thirds of the way up give them a haughty appearance. One gracefully speeds off to the left and the other two to the right.

At Los Santos de Maimona, we finally fall lucky in our third shop and get some cheese, bread and bananas for lunch. John carries these in a carrier bag for some distance until we find a suitable spot for a picnic and our first lunch together on the Camino. The sun is now playing hide and seek, but the following southerly wind is our constant companion. We make timely progress for most of the day but during the last eight kilometres slow down—the last three seem to take forever. John's back is playing up and he is in some discomfort and already feeling that he may not be able to continue the walk. I am inwardly distraught at the prospect of having to abort the walk on the one hand; but equally upset at the evident discomfort John's in.

We discuss finding a way to redistribute the weight in his sack and make some adjustments before tomorrow's walk. This strikes as a stark reminder that I have been lucky so far—not everyone who sets out on this journey can see it through. I hope it is just John's body complaining and something we can overcome. This is a symptom of any long walk I have ever undertaken, but usually dissipates on the second or third day. I share with John information about some of the people I have encountered since leaving Sevilla. Maybe this helps to take John's mind off the pain. At least it helps me to take mine off the prospect of him not being able to continue and the ramifications that may have.

About seven kilometres beyond Los Santos we arrive at the Ermita San Isidro (a ruined chapel on the site of where the retinue who transported the body of Saint Isadore to his final resting place paused to rest). Here a huge fig tree promises a bumper harvest in a week or two.

Returning to the Camino we are now travelling between olive groves and lines of vines and can see Villafranca de los Barros ahead in the distance. We detour to negotiate going under the new motorway and to cross the railway track and then go on and over the N630.

We are now on the approaches to Villafranca and I suggest to John, "It would be good to find a little square with some seats for a sit down."

As if by magic one appears ahead, and we take off our rucksacks and do some stretching. I knead the painful area of John's back, hoping this may ease the pain.

We consult guide books and decide on which albergue we should head to and the directions, then set off again, but not before I adjust the straps on John's rucksack to make it sit higher on his back and for more weight to be on his shoulders. At the albergue, we manage to negotiate a bed each for the night. It has a collection of small dormitories and ours has a set of bunk beds and a single bed. It is right next to the bathroom.

The bottom bunk has been taken by a Frenchman, so I take the top bunk and John the bed. We both want showers and a change of clothes. Whilst John is showering, I get into a conversation with an Italian and a Spaniard and later the Frenchman, all undertaken in 'pigeon' Spanish. Tomorrow's planned journey is between 25-35km depending on which of the two books we believe, or 27km if the Frenchman has the most accurate one. Today we walked at an average of four kilometres per hour, so we will use that formula to calculate how far we have walked by the end of tomorrow.

We go to the town and debate eating at one restaurant before going for a beer at a bar. We then find another bar/restaurant that looks good, but the restaurant itself doesn't serve food for another hour, so we purchase two large beers and nurse these until we can go downstairs to eat. I enjoy a tasty pasta dish as a starter and a pork loin steak and chips for a main. The homemade flan is crème caramel. We share a small carafe of house red and finish our feast with a coffee. We then have a dash back to the albergue to get in before the doors are closed at 11 o'clock.

Most pilgrims are already in their bunks. Ablutions completed, I clamber into bed, hoping for a good night's sleep. John hasn't complained about his back this evening, despite me raising the subject. Is he pretending all is well to avoid sabotaging our journey, or is he sufficiently recovered? This is the debate raging in my head as sleep eventually takes hold.

Villafranca de los Barros to Torremejia

(25 km or 15.5 m) slight fall
Gradient descended 105 metres

Thursday 31st March

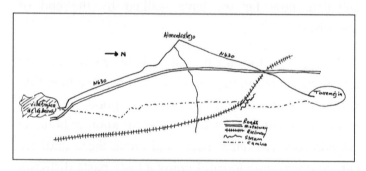

I sleep fitfully as the room is too warm. During the night I unzip the sleeping bag and later discard the blanket covering it, to get some sleep. We get up at around seven o'clock and after using the bathroom and getting dressed and doing most of the pre-packing for the day's walk ahead, wander through to the dining area. This is rather crowded as there are about nine of us in total and the dining table only sits six comfortably. I later discover that Karl and Hermann stayed last night, but as they were in another dormitory and left early as usual, I had missed the opportunity to introduce them to John. There are also some high stools allowing some of us to perch and use shelving along two walls as a dining table. However, people are at various stages of eating breakfast and soon there is room at the dining table for the six of us still eating.

Breakfast consists of toast and jam, juice and coffee. As well as the Frenchman, Italian and Spaniard I spoke to yesterday, there are three other men and one woman in the albergue. One of these gentlemen; who sports a rather large goatee beard, that accentuates even further his rather pointed chin, is later described to me as a French Sports journalist who is seeking to cover the whole distance of the Camino in no time at all by jogging it! I ask him in English if he had considered getting sponsorship from a golfing equipment company and dragging a buggy behind him on his travels? He looks nonplussed and I am not sure whether that's because he doesn't understand or because he considers my question to be bonkers. Then a smile breaks on his face and he responds with, "I see you have encountered Millie too!"

I purchase two half-litre bottles of water for a euro from our hostess at the albergue and by eight o'clock we are ready for our first full day walk. As we set off it is barely daylight and the black clouds filling the sky are looking ominous. It is drizzling too as we negotiate our way out of the town, soon picking up our comforting yellow arrows. They almost, however, cause us to make an unnecessary detour to a school, where lots of energised young people are gathering for another day of lessons. John spots arrows leading us through the school gates, but on closer inspection, it becomes clear that the school can provide a pilgrim stamp for your credentials. As we already have ours, we don't need to go to school today.

The crime rate in Villafranca must be low at this time of the day, as I imagine that every policeman the town employs—at least eight—are on the streets, manning all the crossing points near to the school, ensuring that all the students arrive safely. Soon, after passing the school, we leave the town and are in open country once more.

The problem for the first nine or ten kilometres turns out to be the cloying ruddy brown mud which, after a brief time of walking through it, makes it feel as though we're walking in lead boots. This slows our early progress. We can see several pilgrims ahead of us and at one stage. Despite the handicap of the mud, we are overtaken at speed by the French Sports journalist. He dons rather jazzy shorts and a colourful top, has trainers rather than boots, two walking poles and a French foreign legion style hat upon his head. Soon after passing us, he breaks into a jog and we can see clods of mud being flung in all directions as he ploughs forward to catch up and overtake the next pilgrim. We discover later in the week that he walked and ran from Paris to Rome and is planning to cover the entire length of the Via de la Plata in around three weeks, averaging around 50km per day. I would be happy to complete it in twice that time.

No sooner than the 'mud cloud' created by his feet has dissipated do we have heavier rain to contend with too. This continues to accompany us, before stopping at around 11 o'clock. We are then blessed with occasional sunny intervals, but there is still a cool feel to the air. Finally, we get to a point where we can leave the cloying mud behind and use a post and our sticks to try and remove some of the mud from our boots before carrying on. We are now following a line of pylons and at one point decide to stop and use the base of the nearest pylon as a stretching post. We don't dally long though as whilst we are engaged in exercises the rain starts again and we also realise just how cool it is when we're not walking.

We follow a line of telegraph poles along a broad track that stretches far into the distance. We have fields of vines and olive groves on either side, again as far as the eye can see. The only benefit from this rather monotonous stretch is the absence of the cloying mud, although our boots still give testimony to its adhering qualities! Eventually, we come to a metalled road which crosses our track. We can bear left here and visit

Almendralejo, where we can purchase fresh supplies. However, it is four kilometres away and will also require a similar distance to be walked to re-join the Camino further ahead. We decide to carry on towards Torremejia and the line of hills we can now see running south-east to north-west in the distance.

The rain stops again, and it becomes pleasant. We resolve to stop for lunch around noon, or wherever we can find somewhere suitable to sit around that time. A stone is spotted to the side of the road and it is just big enough to provide a seat for us both and we dine on our meagre rations of yesterday's bread and cheese, pepperoni and yoghurt-coated raisins. We have shared similar resting places in rather more precarious places in the past, not only in the Lakes, but on Arran, in Snowdonia, in Ireland and the French Pyrenees. John and I drove there for a day's walk, during the holiday we shared with Sandra, Caroline, Maureen and Tel near Carcassone. We had followed a route that took us to the Chateau de Peyrepertuse, a ruined fortress with spectacular views. A framed picture of the Chateau has hung on a wall in John and Caroline's home ever since to serve as a reminder.

Whilst we're eating, we are joined by another Spanish pilgrim; he also stayed at the same albergue last night. We share stories about the cloying mud and the challenges of making progress. After a while, he is on his way but not before I think he offers me his cape. Whilst momentarily considering whether he would be offended if I refused his generosity, realisation (thankfully) dawns that he is enquiring as to whether I would help him to get it in place to cover both he and his backpack. We are then also joined for a little while by two Germans—a man and a woman—with whom we exchange greetings before they too are on their way. We later get to know them both and discover he is in his 20's and his name is Andreas and the woman is Marie. Both linked up during their 'pilgrimage journey' because of their common nationality and both are hoping to complete the whole Camino before returning to their respective homes in Germany.

We rouse ourselves from our lunchtime stop and tog up again to continue our journey of discovery. We pass a dead hare on the track and hear skylarks above. They sound out of sorts but later when the sun comes out again their singing appears to be happy and joyous again. Yesterday I remarked about being happy to be following little arrows again and today recalling that, we both try to remember who it was that sang about 'little arrows' way back in the 60's or 70's.

The sun now stays with us for the remainder of our day's walk, apart from a brief shower just before we arrive in Torremejia. This creates an outpouring of singing from me about songs with sunshine in the title;

most notable of which is 'Walking On Sunshine'; which we have no difficulty in remembering was sung by Katrina and the Waves. Apart from recalling song titles, this little stretch of our walk is memorable for our conversations recalling earlier challenge walks we had undertaken together and for me in recalling certain aspects of my Pennine Way walk. John seems to have lost the back pain and the adjustments made to his rucksack have been helpful. It is now and for the rest of the Camino, a feature of our time together, that I ensure the straps on it are in the right place after each of our stops. I am also tasked with ensuring John doesn't forget his walking pole. To aid my task, he lays his stick next to mine whenever we stop.

This time is also memorable for a two kilometre stretch, at the start of which we can spot something in the far distance that could be a pilgrim, probably one of those who passed us earlier… or is it a tree? It seems to move as we continue ahead, so we agree it is a figure, but then it seems to be still again. Has he stopped, waiting for us to catch up? Our debate continues, and our eyes are focussed on the 'object' ahead. For a long time, no matter how far we progress, the figure seems to be the same distance ahead. Finally, we draw close enough to identify our mystery pilgrim is a tree—not long later it is finally behind us.

About six kilometres before we get to the village of Torremejia, we are approached by a vehicle coming along the track. As it nears us it slows and the driver winds down the window and gives us details about a private albergue in the village.

I spot a hoopoe and we watch its flight across the vine fields to our left. Several butterflies also keep us company as they come out to flutter in the warming sun. Finally, vines and olive trees are left behind as we take a left at a junction of tracks and have barren or fledgeling wheat fields for company. We are also suddenly on more tracks of cloying mud and must walk along the field edges as best we can to minimise the amount of mud sticking to our boots and slowing us down. We have our first stop since lunch, under a tree and for the first time, risk taking off cagoules and put on sun cream. About ten minutes later, it starts to rain again. "It'll blow over," I state confidently, but after another five minutes the drizzle thickens to heavy rain and we stop to don waterproofs again.

The path now takes us along and to a railway track, where we branch left underneath it and emerge at the other side to be faced with a wide stream to get across to where our path continues along the edges of more fields. A short stretch takes us along a bank between the stream to our left and the fields to our right. It then follows the edge of the fields until we emerge at the village that will be our home for the night. The last stretch gives us more cloying mud to contend with and the returning motorist passes us and once more encourages the specified albergue!

We stop to consult the guidebook—John had obtained a recently published one just before he left for Spain (Gerald Kelly) and instead set out to find a small hotel—slightly more expensive—but it guarantees the offer of a single or a twin room and a better prospect of a good night's sleep. Before we find it, we pass a café, where for the third time we are propositioned about staying in the private albergue, which is clearly owned by the café owner too. We agree to return should we need to and find the small hotel about 100m further along the street from the café. On arrival, we are informed by a curt response from a rather surly receptionist that it is unfortunately fully booked!

"I don't think they welcome Camino pilgrims, certainly not ones with cloying mud on their boots!" John retorts as we regain the street and our composure. We had stopped before we got there and had another go at reducing the amount of mud covering us both from the waist down. I also zipped off the bottoms of my muddy walking trousers and John readjusted his attire to conceal most of the evidence of dirt.

Like dogs with tails between their legs we return to the café and enquire about the albergue and are given directions. The owner and café proprietor drives, in his shiny red car just in front for the whole route to guide us to the 'jewel in his crown' before giving us the guided tour. A deal is struck on a twin room for 14 euros including breakfast, which we can consume at any time from six o'clock in the morning back at the café.

A lot of the accommodation listed in the guidebook John acquired is new and it appears that local Spaniards have now caught on to the opportunity that there is money to be made from the increasing number of pilgrims. From discussions with Maureen about her walking of the Camino six years ago, it was clear local people always provided encouragement and a wistful smile—now a number were offering much more.

At our 'hidden jewel' we take it in turns to have a shower and both wash some clothes and peg these out to dry in an enclosed courtyard. It starts raining again not long after this, although we leave things out, hoping it may blow over quickly. I also take the opportunity to catch up with my journal. Our four kilometre an hour rule of thumb seems to be working well, with today's walk taking about six and a half hours.

Torremejia is certainly a strange place. Arriving as and when we did, it felt like we were walking into a deserted town from the wild west. I expected a bale of hay to come blowing towards me, spaghetti western music to spring up from nearby tannoys or a sheriff to appear on horseback or even a gunslinger to step out from a side street and challenge us to a shoot-out! Lots of buildings appear to have been recently constructed but are very roughly hewn and put together.

Musing on this, I start to imagine that our persistent 'host' is the 'sheriff' or 'Mafioso'. When we go in search of somewhere to dine in the evening all the other restaurants are either closed or are not serving food. After having a beer at the sheriff's café, we end up back there to get something to eat. At least there is a big screen in the bar area, and we are assured it will be on for the football. Football seems to be the only English or 'universal' word we commonly understand. After we checked in at the albergue the sheriff gave us a map of the town, which only shows the main street and all to the right of it.

During our search for a restaurant, we discover the old town, the church and the municipal albergue are all on the other side of the main street and therefore do not exist on the map he provided. We return to the café at quarter to eight and as soon as we are inside a huge black cloud goes overhead and disgorges its contents on Torremejia. We both agree we won't shed a tear when we leave in the morning. We order another beer and I have a starter of fried eggs and rice, green beans and scrambled eggs for mains, followed by another flan, which probably had eggs in it too! I'm not addicted to eggs, rather that of all the other things on the menu I could decipher, these seemed the only appealing dishes. On the big screen, it's La Liga football but we decide to call it a night and head back in the rain to the 'hidden jewel'.

At our albergue we discover we are indeed the only guests (or suckers) and I retrieve wet washing. We attend to our ablutions before turning in for the night. A text from Maureen confirms that she got back home safely. I respond and agree to periodically keep her in the loop on our progress.

I don't sleep very well. It is very cold and even in the sleeping bag with the one thin coverlet over me, I cannot get warm. At one point during the night, I sit up and fold the coverlet in two. This provides a thicker but narrower covering that helps a little and I do then get some sleep. In the morning, I discover several thicker blankets in the wardrobe. Doh!

Torremejia to Aljucen

(30 km or 18.5 m) relatively flat
Gradient descended 35 metres

Friday 1st April

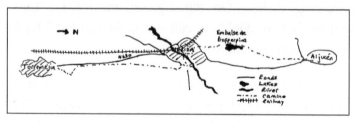

At around six o'clock I am convinced there is someone else in the dormitory next door and see the light go on in the hall, but when I get up at seven the place is deserted and I start to question whether my mind is playing tricks.

Following getting dressed and repacking our rucksacks, we finally leave our twin room and 'private mansion' and head down to the 'meson' for breakfast. Our Mafioso suggests when we are leaving, we head straight down the road out of town. Is that an instruction or a helpful suggestion, I muse? I am still in no mood to trust what he has to say, and we head off at about half eight in clear weather, if a bit chilly, to find the 'official' route out of town. The coolness of the morning means I'm wearing gloves for the first hour or so.

We leave Torremejia with no regrets but are soon back on a track heavily 'iced' with cloying mud and almost lose the path. At a junction, we step aside to let a van go past and continue ahead for a few metres before being redirected by a resident back to take the other track. This leads us after about 400m back onto the road, and we now stay on the N630 for a long stretch. If we had stayed on the road, we would have avoided more mud and almost getting lost. Perhaps our Mafioso was trying to be helpful after all? I curse my stupid inflexibility which led me to view all pushy entrepreneurs with caution and mistrust.

I pause as I spot a greyhound chase a hare across the road ahead and watch as he quickly loses track and stands and stares forlornly into the scrubby field ahead, before he returns to the road and re-crosses more slowly. A stork is spotted too, followed by five more and we watch as they fly gracefully across our skyscape, two or three carefully executed beats before they effortlessly continue by gliding on the thermals. We also hear our first cuckoo of the day and see a hoopoe as it darts away showing to favourable effect its largely black and white plumage. A dead goat carcass is our next offering of fauna, sprawled out beside the road having been largely eaten by insects.

Later in this stretch, I spot a buzzard and wonder whether he dined on goat recently.

We arrive at a newly constructed logging plant and here our Camino leaves the road and we have cloying mud again, before this eventually gives way to rolling farmland and drier sandier paths. We now have the vista of Merida ahead and pass some stables, where some fine examples of Spanish horses have large compounds to wander in and a mule to keep them company. Arriving in Merida, we come alongside and follow the river for a while before crossing it by going over the very impressive Roman bridge.

An hour or so is taken to explore Merida, have a cake and coffee and enjoy the sunshine which has suddenly arrived in a rather splendid square. We see and acknowledge a fellow pilgrim, who like ourselves finds the square a rather pleasant place to take a break. This is yet another encounter with the young man, Andreas, with whom we will come to be better acquainted with as our journey of discovery continues. Merida was established in 25 BC by the Roman Emperor, Octavious Augustus, primarily as a retirement facility for Roman legionaries. It was initially named Augusta Emerita and the location for it was chosen because of the hill overlooking the surrounding plains of the River Guadiana.

As we are retracing our steps back to the Roman bridge to pick up our route again to leave Merida, we pass the municipal albergue and to my great delight, I spot Karl hanging out some washing. I shout a greeting and we go down to him and finally I can introduce both he and Hermann to John. It is during our conversation we discover that they were staying in the same albergue as ourselves in Villafranca two nights ago. Mind you, they never hang about to meet people over the breakfast table! After saying our farewells, we return to the task of navigating our way out of the city, passing the magnificent and significantly intact remains of the Roman aqueduct which dominates the skyline. Storks are nesting on various ruined ramparts as we now start a slow gentle climb up the hill and past the derelict Pan Emirita bread factory.

It is about eight kilometres from Torremejia to Merida and retrospectively if I was to be undertaking this walk again, I would tag those eight kilometres on to yesterday's walk and stay overnight in Merida. That would have the dual benefits of not needing to stay in a place with little to commend it and, instead be able to see more of the sights of Merida itself.

Negotiating a roundabout and going over the motorway, we have a new and rather splendid cycle way to follow and find a good place for lunch on the brow of a hill. It has been especially created with picnic slabs that can be used either for seating or tables. We enjoy cheese, bread and bananas and whilst doing so Andreas catches us up and we again exchange pleasantries and learn a little more about each other. Soon after he departs, our lunch is interrupted by a short shower, which both curtails our rest and means we must tog up in waterproofs again before we make tracks down the other side of the hill and along the road to the Embalse de Proserpina.

The Embalse is a huge reservoir created by the Romans and used ever since, with periodic restorations to maintain its validity to provide water to Merida and the surrounding areas. It now has a range of bars, cafés and houses dotted along it and there are signs that some of the bars and cafés are busy getting ready for the new 'tourist season' that lies ahead. We pass them and follow a rather pleasant stretch of the Camino as it goes along a quite road, rising steadily as it does so, with increasingly rocky outcrops. In an undulating and boulder-strewn field to our right, where the boulders appear to be hunkering down into the landscape, we pass a large cow followed in slow but determined fashion by an even larger bull.

Suddenly there are cows and bulls everywhere we look both sides of us. I watch, fascinated, as white egrets feed off insects on and around the cattle as they nonchalantly continue to graze with maybe a periodic shake of the head. The egrets pick insects from the heads and necks of the cows and then swoop away to go and 'help out' another. In the full heat of the summer, that must be a very welcome relationship to have.

After we pass a single but noticeable white house set back on the left, we leave the tarmac and follow a rather pleasant track past and between Holm oaks, rocks and olives, with an abundance of wild flowers giving us a colourful and aromatic canvas to walk through, until we drop into the village of El Carrascalejo where a dog is waiting under a large olive tree to greet us. He gives us two barks and we carry on up the hill and around a corner where two small terrier type dogs offer their greetings too. In the centre of the village and in front of the small church, our fellow peregrino Andreas is standing and looking a little perplexed. He is heading, like us, for Aljucen today and thinks he has arrived there already but cannot locate an albergue. We explain that we believe this to be El Carrascalejo and that Aljucen is the next village we will come to. The three of us then continue our walk together conversing in 'good English' as far as he is concerned. He is from Dortmund and is intending to complete the Camino and has until the beginning of May to achieve it.

We arrive in Aljucen and find the albergue with a little difficulty and discover there are three rooms each with three beds—a set of bunks and a single bed. By the end of the afternoon, nine of us are there. In addition to the two of us, at least five are German we think, including Andreas and Marie and maybe the other two are Spanish. It is rather cramped but okay. As it transpires and because we didn't 'bag' our beds on arrival we end up in different rooms. We both do some washing and peg things out to dry in the small courtyard at the back. This plan soon gets interrupted by a sudden and very sharp shower, which has us scurrying out to retrieve items. We drape washing over several lines in a small covered outside area that has a waterproof drape as an external wall.

The shower soon passes and Anna our hostess, arrives, and we complete the formalities of booking in, paying our ten euros and getting pilgrim passports stamped. Anna then leads a tour of the little church within the village, before we all go to a little café, The Casa Rural, which is run by Anna and have an excellent meal—three courses and a bottle of wine for seven and a half euros. It is good to be with fellow peregrinos and we spend a pleasant night together but are back at our accommodation and in bed by nine o'clock as we will need to be up at around quarter past six for breakfast at seven at the same café before heading off to Aldea del Cano, where most of us will be staying tomorrow night. We already know the one albergue there only has nine beds too. The sky is red and forms itself into a beautiful sunset over the village as I reflect on the best day so far. One of our German companions tells us it is going to be a sunny day tomorrow. Let's hope he is right. The sunset certainly promises us a warm day.

The bunk beds are tight to the wall on one side and I am in the top bunk again. Andreas is in the single bed, which is under the small window to the room and this sits close to and at right angles to the set of bunks. There is only a small corridor of space between Andreas's bed, the side of the bunks and the door to the room. I don't sleep much, if at all, maybe half an hour at most. I comfort myself with the thought that at least I am resting. I am up as scheduled, trying hard not to disturb one of my fellow roommates—one of the Spanish guys in the bottom bunk below me who told me last night he is not leaving until much later.

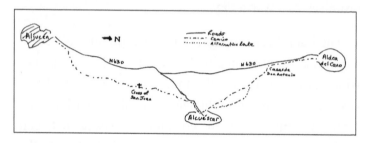

Aljucen to Aldea del Cano

(35 km or 22 m) slightly uphill)
Gradient ascended 130 metres

Saturday 2nd April

The problem with the lack of space and the darkness of the room is there are three rucksacks and assorted items of apparel belonging to three different people in one confined space. I use my torch to locate my clothes but search high and low for my walking trousers to no avail. Meanwhile, Andreas is up and dressed and has vacated the room. I go into the one living/dining room to see if, for some reason, my walking trousers are in there, again with no success. Three of the Germans are up, dressed and about to depart for their breakfast. They haven't seen my trousers, either! I check outside and on the off-chance duck under the waterproof drape that protects the outside drying area. There, thank goodness, are my walking trousers. I have no recollection of putting them there, but finally, I can change back out of my evening pair and into my familiar day wear.

After the consternation of the trousers, I go into the bathroom and discover there is no toilet paper and have to backtrack to rescue a pack of tissues from the rucksack. Finally, and somewhat flustered, I am ready to depart. John and I go down to the café, where our German friends are almost at the end of their breakfast. I remark to Andreas what a contrast it is between the archetypal German efficiency at getting up, dressed and away and the typical 'Brit' who can't even remember where he put his trousers. This causes great merriment all round as he relays my comment to his companions.

Despite my delaying tactics, it is still only around half-past seven when we've finished our breakfast of coffee, jam and toast, paid our dues and are ready for the off. It is still barely light outside and convenient that the first stretch is along the road, otherwise, navigating may have proved a challenge. Heading north out of the village, we continue on the road for around half an hour before bearing right just before a petrol station and for the next 15km are immersed in a wonderful landscape of woodland, meandering and gently undulating paths, flowers and trees; with the singing of many different birds adding musical accompaniment to our progress. There is also dampness in the air after yesterday's showers. The promised sun hasn't quite managed to make an appearance.

At times it reminds me of the Southern lakes, with great boulders providing interest to both left and right. The flowering broom, the fragrant lavender, the aromatic jara and several pretty potentillas being the highlights, but the canvas is completed by a plethora of smaller pink, blue, white and yellow flowers, which seem to dance under our feet. It isn't long before we hear the first cuckoo of the day, too. The skylarks sound happy, blackbirds and song thrushes are in good voice and a woodpecker is busy at work to our right.

We also hear a chainsaw but despite at times it seeming to be closer to hand, we never discover its source. At times sound can be deceptive in the open countryside. At one point the perfume of the jara is so strong that we can both breathe in the incense. We arrive at a place where two cars are parked about 20m apart. We pass close by to one, which is white, looks brand new and there isn't a splash of mud anywhere to be seen. I wonder not only how it got there, but how it remained so pristine in the process!

In places, the paths have seen some recent work to add compacted sand and clay and this combination allows us to make excellent progress. We stop at the summit of a long steady climb to drink some water and eat a banana. We can see three people in and amongst the holm oak trees, obviously gathering something from the woodland floor as we see each stoop at different times, and they appear to be carrying baskets to hold their 'crop'. They are too far away however for us to be able to discern exactly what they are picking up. A jackdaw to our left seems equally curious about the humans with their baskets as he cranes his neck to one side to check them out.

Now the path levels again and the scenery changes, subtly at first, as we wend our way to a large stone cross. This is the Cross of San Juan and Nino Muerta. Legend suggests on a midsummer feast day, to celebrate the anniversary of St John the Baptist, a young shepherd boy was coming to the fiesta from the Valle de la Zarza when at this spot he was attacked and eaten by a wolf.

The path now widens, and we have the pleasure of some sunshine for a while. Out of nowhere, we suddenly hear the approach of (and are then passed by) a van; this is quickly followed by two more vehicles, one in each direction. Yet again we wonder where from and to these vehicles are going. The peace of our walk soon returns, however, although the noise of a helicopter overhead adds to the resumption of birdsong.

We are now on the lookout for a large white house named 'Campo'. Ivan Campo was a great hero of ours when he played for our beloved Bolton Wanderers. We know he has property and a restaurant on Majorca— has he built a retreat in the heart of Spain, too? We need to find the property because we know we need to bear right when we see it and not carry straight on as the arrows may suggest to an albergue. We understand from Anna it is currently closed. We weren't planning to stay there anyway. There are a couple of false possibilities before we finally locate the house and the turning to the right which takes us down a track. We can see Alcuescar in the distance. There are people in the grounds of the house but there is no sign of Ivan!

We promise ourselves a sit down and a spot of lunch in Alcuescar and as we approach the outskirts and leave our wonderful wooded paradise behind, the sun is long gone, and it is starting to feel chillier. We pass a field of horses with one mule amongst them. Eventually, at the main road a right turn is made, a short distance beyond this the Camino bears left along a track, but the town is up to the right and so we leave the route in search of something and somewhere to eat. There is a market going on and we wander through the long line of stalls looking for someone selling bocadillos. All we find are clothes, fruit and vegetables, cheese, ham or tripe.

We head further up into town and finally spot a café. Heading inside, who should we spot but our German trio including Andreas and Marie! Later in the week, we discover that their companion is Spanish, I think he is called Ernesto and having met him during the journey and having discovered his skills, they appointed him as their guide for the rest of their trip. It was in fact Ernesto, who based on his reading of the skies last night, promised us blue sky and unbroken sunshine today. He may be good at reading things on the ground, but obviously weather forecasting is not one of his specialities.

We decide on cheese and tomato bocadillos and I order a tea. Back home, I rarely drink coffee; it may be doing this is not helping in my efforts to sleep. We say goodbye again to Andreas, Ernesto and Marie as they head off once more. We will see them later at Aldea del Cano, as we are all staying there tonight. Two large baguettes arrive and at first bite, we both decide we are hungry, and the cheese is rather tasty. About half-way through the sandwich we decide it was good that we asked for tomato too as it starts to become increasingly overpowering and strong; clearly, it's goat's cheese and cut in large slabs rather than in more dainty slices. I give up before I finish it, but the tea is deliciously refreshing. After visiting the 'aseos', we leave the café and go back past the market to buy two oranges. There is a park between the market and the main road where we will need to find our Camino route as it leaves the road on the opposite side from the town.

We find a bench in the park and take off boots to give our feet some air and to enjoy a rest, both to help digest our lunch and to rekindle our energies before we carry on. I recall that we'd had some rain for a fleeting time just before the cross of San Juan, thus keeping up with our daily trend. I remember another feature of our morning walk which was the sound of cow bells and it was a long time after the first sound that we finally spotted the cattle languidly grazing between trees in the distance. We also had to negotiate a couple of streams that needed the 'extra limb' our trusty sticks provided to safely cross them without getting our feet wet.

John and I are extremely comfortable in each other's company and during most of our longer walks together will, at times, walk apart lost in our thoughts or be side-by-side either in conversation or in silence. There is much we have shared over the years and neither of us feels the need to speak if there is nothing to say. We have similar views on a lot of things, but any areas of disagreement do not in any way affect the affection we hold for each other. We've worked together, studied together, shared the trials and tribulations of being fathers together and no-one has helped and supported me more to overcome the challenges I faced in life than he.

Re-joining the Camino, a small herd of cows are being marshalled across the track in front of us after milking and soon afterwards we are faced with a dilemma with arrows pointing both straight on and towards a turn off to the right. We decide to carry straight on and for a while don't see any arrows and are starting to question our decision, but then stumble across a Spanish pilgrim we haven't met before. He is small and wiry and is lunching in the lee of a gate by the track's side and we manage to discern in conversation that either option of routes is fine, for they will both come together again in a few kilometres.

He later appears at the albergue we are staying in, although we cannot recall him passing us and in the evening he harangues me for over half an hour with his fast and furious Spanish, in a rather one-sided conversation; despite my frequent requests for him to slow down or my many protestations that I do not understand what he is saying. As a result of these characteristics and in the absence of knowing his true name, I feel compelled to refer to him as 'Speedy Gonzales'.

We carry on and although the odd arrow is spotted, they are very sparse and faint. The terrain is at first rather scrubby but then becomes a track between fields of holm oak and we eventually reach Casas Don Antonio, with the other track re-joining us about one kilometre before. Just after the trails link, we see a stork with nesting materials in her large beak and hear what I am sure is the sound of a golden oriole. On the outskirts of the village I spot a buzzard and a larger bird of prey, with an even larger wingspan and wonder whether I've seen an eagle. I later reflect that it is more likely this bird was a griffon vulture.

A small Roman bridge over the river is crossed and we leave the Camino to go up into the village, which is deserted and find a sheltered seat in a bus shelter to eat our oranges before setting off for the last leg of today's journey, around seven kilometres.

Soon after leaving our shelter we observe a man on horseback herding some cattle with the help of a dog. He is not doing a very good job and is shouting as cows scatter in different directions and the dog rounds up part of the herd. A woman is leaning on a wall stoically watching the scene (possibly his wife) and throws a knowing look of contempt in his direction as we pass. We soon leave the road and regain the Camino, although it now hugs the road to Aldea del Cano. We have polished marble square blocks to help us cross one waterlogged area and come to several milarios, each probably around 2,000 years old and cross a second old Roman bridge, and along one stretch, the ancient remains of Roman tiled flooring.

A dense flock of sheep are also negotiated as they are herded in our direction and they part sufficiently to let us pass through their midst. A man is walking to our left on the roadside of this narrow strip of land and a dog hogs the fence-line that runs along the fields to our right. We see a figure ahead, but shortly afterwards realise it is a road sign—we are not going to recreate our 'hallucinatory pilgrim' of the morning walk to Torremejia.

For the last stretch, the Camino crosses a road and we follow it as it veers sharply away from the road towards the village. It is getting cooler as the sky is getting gloomier and we are looking forward to a hot shower and somewhere warm to sit. We have another flock of sheep to negotiate, watched over by a man sat in his car and his two dogs who both bark as we pass. About 200m from the village, the path carries straight on, whilst we turn right along a track which quickly becomes a tarmac road, to find our accommodation for the night. We arrive in the village and the albergue is the first building we spot on our right. We get a pilgrim stamp and a breakfast slip at the incongruously named café Las Vegas and then return to the albergue.

It turns out that there are just six of us in residence for the night. There is a room with a set of bunks in it and a second room which is split into two sections. The first part has a set of bunks and the second two sets of bunks and a single bed. Speedy Gonzales has bagged a bed in the first room. Marie the bottom bunk in the first part of the second room. Andreas the single bed and their Spanish guide has a bottom bunk in the second room. This leaves a set of bunks for John and I and yet again a top bunk for me to negotiate. It is cooler in the albergue than outside as I prepare to have a hot shower. Whilst this starts pleasantly warm, it soon turns cold; not a pleasant experience but an invigorating one! I re-emerge clean but even cooler than before and don my fleece to keep warm. There is a rather small heater which is currently being used to try and dry assorted items of clothing from our party and the towels of those who have showered already.

Marie confides the hot water from the shower seems only to manage two or three before it needs to be left until the boiler heats the water sufficiently again. She had been the third of their 'party' to shower after their arrival. This is reassuring news for John, who can now wait a while before showering rather than have the choice of a cold or no shower. It is worth the wait and soon he enjoys the relief and luxury of feeling both warm and clean again.

It has been a cold and largely overcast all day, with very limited glimpses of the sun. We walked for nine and a half hours today and arrive at the albergue at five o'clock, my longest day so far. Tomorrow will be a shorter day to Caceres and at the end of it we will have a hotel room and facilities with much to look forward to…well that's what we have promised ourselves.

We go out and discover that the local bar doesn't serve hot food until half-past eight, in another two hours. We stroll around the small village and find a shop and return with bread, pate, jambón ibérico, cakes and a bottle of wine, the latter of which is a well-known excellent quality Rioja for which we pay 3 euros. It normally costs around seven pounds at home. Our 3 fellow peregrinos are huddled around the table at the end next to the little heater just finishing a similar feast, having, like ourselves, decided they can't wait until half eight either. They had been to the bar at the Las Vegas and declare it is just as cold there as here. We join them at the table to enjoy our shop-bought homemade feast and as they depart, shuffle closer to the little heater.

The final member of our party, Speedy Gonzales, is full of chatter and stories that none of us can really comprehend. I suppose he may be bored with his own company and this is his chance to wax lyrical. We all play along and laugh at what we think are the appropriate times. We share past/proposed itinerary for the walk and almost have understanding, at which point he continues to rabbit on at an even faster rate.

By half eight, most of our party are in bed. Marie has gesticulated I should bring the little heater into the larger room once everyone has retired. By this time, it is just Speedy and me and it is at least another 15 minutes before his socks and towel are dry enough for his liking and he retires too. My ears readjust to silence after his verbal onslaught and I unplug the heater and head for bed. Marie and I agree the best place to plug it in and I climb up to my bunk. I have three layers on including my fleece and my socks as I snuggle down in the sleeping bag with a blanket over me and try and get warm.

Aldea del Cano to Caceres

(22 km or 14 m) fairly flat
Gradient ascended 40 metres

Sunday 3rd April

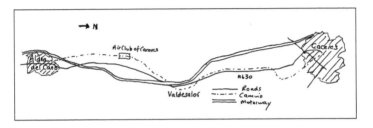

The little heater did take the chill off through the night and I slept from about nine o'clock till four in the morning, then dozed off again for another hour before waking to answer a 'call of nature'. I extricated myself from the sleeping bag and swung my legs and weight over the bunk to locate the first step with my foot. I had completely forgotten I still had my socks on and stepping down onto the smooth metal rung afforded me no grip. I unceremoniously slid down the full length of the steps to the floor below, grazing the side of my leg from hip to knee as I did so. Ouch!

I am writing this some three months later and the mark left by the graze is still clearly visible.

In the kitchen/dining area Speedy Gonzalez is tucking into his breakfast. It is quarter-to six and by six he has left and hit the trail. I return to the warmth of my bunk, making sure I don't lie on the grazed side. Soon afterwards, Ernesto (as I have dubbed him), our Spanish 'guide', wakes and proceeds to rouse Andreas and Marie from their slumbers. I am half-aware of them getting up and ready for their departure as I doze in and out of sleep for a little while. I can hear the hubbub of raised voices in conversation as they gather around the dining table next door, but by seven o'clock all is silent and there are just two Englishmen left in the albergue. This gives us time to come around, sort our bags out and attend to our morning ablutions at a pace we are comfortable with. We had desayuno (breakfast) to look forward to in Las Vegas and then a shorter 22km walk to Caceres and our promised 'luxury' hotel!

Outside it is grey and cool, the Las Vegas is shut and so is the only other café/bar in the village. We set off therefore in the gloom, both literally and metaphysically, to re-find the Camino. After all it is only 15km to the next village (Valdesalor) where there should be a café open by the time we get there.

We soon pass two flocks of sheep and hear the first cuckoo of the day. We are walking now with stands of holm oaks on either side of us stretching out into the gloom as far as we can see. It seems strange that unlike in most deciduous woodland in England, you only get one variety of trees for company. The Spanish oaks, however, are so wonderfully crafted by nature in some magnificent shapes, they provide variety in themselves. We hear more sounds of chainsaws but again have no visual contact of their origins.

The temperature seems to be rising a little and the effect of being back on the Camino, after a good night's sleep and despite the absence of breakfast, seems to be energising. We remark about how towards the end of yesterday spirits were low, it was cold and even colder when we arrived at the albergue. Today it seems warmer. As with the start of each day on this journey of discovery our spirits are higher, and we have high hopes for the day. It is raining slightly and has rained a lot during the night, as the wet underfoot conditions testify. At times we must negotiate flooded areas and large square granite blocks which have been strategically placed to help us across. As a result, we continue to make steady progress.

As well as holm oaks, the first part of today's journey is also characterised by us having the company at times of storks. First one, and then another three, followed by a huge specimen standing guard in a field to our right before he takes off. We watch again as he rises into the air and begins his beautiful and effortless flight. We too are rising steadily now as the path climbs and we can see a Roman castle ruin to our right. We should now start to look out for, according to one of the books we are following, a tall pole. My uncle was six feet three and hailed from Krakow, so I did have previous 'experience'! This pole is described as having distinctive red and white markings—clearly in keeping with the Polish flag!

As we approach the deserted Air Club of Caceres and its abandoned buildings and landing strip, we can see something that might be red and white; it is certainly tall and pole-like, looming in and out of the mist ahead. Leaving the airfield behind we have a further kilometre of uphill climbing before the land levels out and we stop for a drink and a snack of pepperoni, yoghurt-coated raisins and apricots! It is ten to ten. I finally take off the fleece I have been wearing over my two base layers and under my cagoule—the same fleece that kept me nice and warm in bed last night. I get a text from Simon about dates for the three of us finally finishing the Yorkshire Wolds Way and a provisional date is despatched for late May. Another stork glides by and I compare its flight to the best paper plane I ever made, which I was very proud of at the time!

We now have a pleasant stroll across meadows with sweet-smelling tiny yellow flowers as we head towards

Valdesalor. The clouds seem to be lifting but we still can't see the tops of the hills that lie behind the village. We cross a Roman bridge and looking back see that the tall red and white pole is now behind us and for the first time since it entered our consciousness, remains in view for more than a fleeting second. Of course it does, for we are no longer seeking to use it as a directional marker—I might as well have been looking out for my uncle Meitek!

We arrive at the village of Casas de Don Antonio at quarter to 11 and a small market is in progress and after a quick look round go in search of a café or bar. We eventually stumble on one quite by accident, just on the point of giving up and heading back to our 'route'. Breakfast, not for the first time, consists of coffee, toast and jam and by the time we leave it is half 11.

Leaving the village enables us to be reunited for a short while with our friend the N630; sticking with her rather than walking in the wet grass of the Camino which runs alongside the road at this point. We return to the Camino however and go over a new bridge, which was specifically constructed for the Camino and is wide enough for two cars. This takes us over the newly constructed motorway below. After a short while the N630 is re-joined and keeps in touch with the Camino as our route, then goes under the motorway to our left and later re-crosses it to join the Camino on the other side. This stretch also involves a climb and we are overtaken on the rise by three cyclists. Are they just out for the day or are they cycling the Camino, I wonder?

Passing a small village, the sun starts to generate some heat and we see the signs of Roman occupation as we near Caceres. Our entry into this beautiful city is not one, however, that gives that view. We traverse industrial areas and clusters of modern utilitarian flats and numerous sets of roundabouts and roads. Yellow arrows are not to be found and it takes a few attempts at stopping a resident before it is confirmed we are on the right track to find the Plaza Major. It is a long trudge however before the style of architecture and the age of the buildings tells us we are approaching the older part of the city. It seems to take us an hour from the outskirts to finally arrive in the beautiful square that is the fulcrum of what the city has to offer, with its cafés/bars and hotels, municipal buildings and shops.

It is here that one is finally struck by the grandeur and appeal of the place. Finding Tourist Information, we ask directions to a nearby hotel. We are directed to one on the edge of the square and it looks to be what we have promised ourselves. Unfortunately, it turns out to be fully booked and we are directed out of and behind the Plaza in search of a second—and we are assured equally pleasant—hotel.

After spending several minutes following the directions we have been given without success, we stumble upon the Hostal Plaza de Italia and are able to obtain a pleasant, if not palatial room with two beds and a small balcony, on which we put steaming boots and socks immediately for them to dry out, plus a bathroom with a shower. It is 35 euros for the two of us and the price also includes breakfast at a nearby café in the morning. This will be open from six o'clock should we wish to depart very early. It isn't quite what we promised ourselves, but I am sure it will serve us well. We go back downstairs to register in shorts and sandals and decide to go back down to the square for a beer before we shower and change.

This evening we are hoping to link up with Steve and Celeste, who live in Caceres. Steve is 'known' to both John and me, albeit that I only remember meeting him once before, at our mutual friend Maureen's house. Maureen stayed overnight with Celeste when she walked the Camino in 2010. We had alerted them to our arrival in their city last night and once we find a bar for a drink, John rings Steve to finalise arrangements for linking up this evening. Whilst we are sipping our beers, who should appear but Karl and Hermann. They got here early enough to dine in the afternoon and are doing a bit of exploring before they return to the albergue, which is beyond the Plaza Major and off to the left. They join us for a beer and a catch up before heading off. Karl tells me that they saw Inieste earlier in Caceres and that she is okay. She is planning to stay for another day. It is good to get news of another pilgrim who started her journey on the same day as I did.

It is now mostly blue sky with some warm sunshine and the promise of five days unbroken sunshine lies before us, according to all the forecasts we have seen. I notice we have another text from Simon, which must have arrived during the last stretch into Caceres, thanking us for his 50th birthday present. John informs me that we are meeting Steve and Celeste at half-past six outside the town hall, which is at the southern end of the Plaza.

After our very welcome beer, we return to the hostal to shower and change and do a little more washing, to make use of the balcony and the warm sunshine we should have for the rest of the evening. Texts are despatched home and to Maureen confirming both that we have arrived in Caceres and have arranged to link up with Steve and Celeste. We also receive texts confirming our team Bolton have lost again and the reality of their relegation this season is ever closer. We are in reflective mood but freshly showered and changed to go out into the still warm sunshine to meet Steve and Celeste.

Celeste was born and went to university in Salamanca, where we will be in a week and now teaches in a school in Caceres. Steve lived near to us in Shipley, West Yorkshire and had met her through visits to Spain and school exchange visits. They had become friends and kept in touch but had only recently become a couple with Steve having moved out to join her in Caceres some six months ago.

Celeste's grasp of English is impeccable; it is her core subject as a teacher in Spain, and it is pleasant to be able to talk about our journey, their new life together and the wonderful city of Caceres in one common language. We start the evening by having a beer and tapas in a bar overlooking the plaza, before Celeste takes us on an interesting little guided tour of the older parts of the city. It is amazingly beautiful and steeped in history with its winding cobbled streets, ancient stone buildings, including cathedrals, palaces and monasteries, towers and even exclusive hotels.

The old part of the city is a UNESCO World Heritage site. We see the Royal Monastery of Santa Maria de Guadalupe, the Palace de los Golfines de Abajo, visit the old Jewish quarter and look out over the old city walls to the hill where the 'virgin' is brought down from and into the city at Easter.

We are entertained by a peacock and then go to a restaurant, Torre de Sande, where we dine outside and each experience some delicious and original tapas followed by a wonderful fig cake, accompanied by another beer. This is certainly the best food I have experienced to date and isn't too expensive either. We talk about the walk and the highlights to date and Saltaire, which is also a UNESCO World Heritage site, where John and I live and where Steve has previously had a house. Celeste also visited Saltaire and had been impressed by the mills, the architecture and the village.

Teaching, the cultural nuances of Spain and England and building a new life in Spain are also discussed. Celeste tells us about her wonderful home city of Salamanca and the places we must see and where to eat there too. By this time, it is starting to get a bit chilly as the sun has gone down and we retire to a nearby hotel where we sink into wonderfully luxurious armchairs, drink coffee and continue our conversations until it is time to say goodnight. We thank them both for their company, a wonderful evening and wend our way back to our hostal. It really has been an extremely pleasant evening. We promise to keep them both in touch with our progress for the remainder of our trip and I have no doubt we will meet again either in Spain or when they visit England. Steve still has family in the area.

We arrive back at our accommodation late, just before 11, and plan to leave by half-past seven in the morning to get breakfast at the nearby café so that we can starting walking again by eight. I sleep well despite the noise of the TV in the next room, which is still on at one in the morning, when I wake to use the facilities. We are up as scheduled and after ablutions, pack and check out at about eight, half an hour later than planned. This is not before enquiring again about specific directions to find the café, where we are to have breakfast.

We have travelled 132km from Zafra and have a further 233km to go to Salamanca, where we plan to have a rest day to take in some of the sights Celeste talked about last night. Our walking days will need to get longer now if we are to cover the remaining distance to Santiago in the time available to us. However, having spent most of the past five days walking in cool, rainy conditions since linking up with John, the weather now seems set fair for the next stage of our pilgrimage as we make our way towards Salamanca, Celeste's home city.

Plate 5
Ermita San Isidro and fig tree - Day 8

Plate 6
Pilgrim tree - Day 9

Plate 7
Roman bridge on approach to Merida - Day 19

Plate 8
Cross of San Juan - Day 11

Chapter Three

Caceres to Salamanca

***

Caceres to Embalse de Alcantara

(33 km or 21.6 m) mainly flat
Gradient descended 30 metres

Monday 4th April

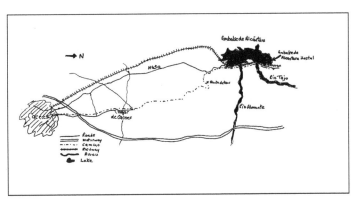

Finding the café didn't prove difficult. We are soon enjoying toast, coffee and orange juice. It is 12 degrees and the sun's coming out to greet us as we leave. We wend our way down to the Plaza again before re-joining the route of the Camino to negotiate through the remainder of Caceres and out into the open country. As we reach the outskirts, we are suddenly aware of

125

(and soon become engulfed by) a thick mist and this keeps us company along the next stretch as we find and keep to the road that will take us to Casar de Caceres—the next and only town or village we will visit on today's walk.

Just before reaching the last roundabout, before the open but mist-shrouded road beckons, a fellow backpacker greets us and asks for directions for Plasencia. It is not on our map and we are not familiar with the geography of places beyond the scope of our route. We suggest, although not with certainty, that he needs to head along the road to Casar de Caceres too. Negotiating the motorway roundabout is a bit tricky but otherwise the next stretch involves us in simply walking along the edge of the road, side-by-side and then in single file as the headlights of an approaching car loom out of the mist.

It is the Caceres half marathon this morning and some of the vehicles have race participants within. The finishing touches to the start/finishing line in the Plaza Major were being put in place as we headed northwards from the centre of the old city earlier. We muse about whether running in this race would provide the perfect excuse to revisit the beautiful city of Caceres and maybe more time to explore Merida, too. The eeriness of the next ten kilometres of road, walking in the swirling mists, is somewhat disconcerting. Sounds are difficult to precisely locate, and we have no real sense of the landscape we are walking through either to the east or west.

The mist is still with us as we arrive in Casar de Caceres and find a café and go inside for what turns out to be a pleasant pause in the form of coffee and cake. We are both covered in dewdrops from the mist and the tops we have tied to rucksacks in anticipation of them being quickly dried in the promised sunshine are probably wetter now than when they were first attached. Alison's directions on how to leave the town and re-join the Camino are useful as there are no discernible arrows.

We have an interesting little stop at a baker's shop to buy provisions for lunch. An older female customer is engaged in heated discussion with a younger female shop assistant over the description of a cake. The older woman is dogmatically insisting it is a chocolate 'something' whilst the younger woman is patiently but soon exasperatedly seeking to explain that it is not a chocolate 'something'. We wait until payment for the disputed cake is resolved. The older woman then turns her attention to us and insists that a specific type of bread is the best one to buy. Partly because we don't want to spend the next five minutes arguing with her (we have seen the ferocity of her capabilities in that department), we agree to purchase the loaf she is indicating and buy a cellophane-wrapped tortilla, which looks good too.

When we vacate the shop with our purchases safely ensconced within our rucksacks, we find that the older woman is waiting outside for us and holds her hand out for some change as a thank you for helping us make our purchase. I decline the invitation to 'grease her palm' and for a while she follows our footsteps before our younger legs garner some distance between us and we reach the end of the village.

Gradually the mist clears, and we find a track that takes us over rolling hills and out onto a plateau, where we can look down, when the mist finally clears, to the main road way off to the right and to the gently rising hills to our left. We pass fields of grazing cows and bulls and have the pleasure of several lavender bushes and an occasional delphinium both to the left and right of our wide track. I spot a siskin and we hear our first cuckoo of the day as the sun starts to emit some real warmth for a pleasant change. The sight and sounds of many a skylark are great company as we stop to take off cagoules. They have effectively protected us from the dewy mist. We can also unzip our trouser bottoms and finally we are walking in shorts; parts of our bodies are exposed to Spanish daylight for the first time this week.

The bread later turns out not to be a very poor choice as it is very dry and from here northwards to Salamanca, the bread we eat is a huge disappointment, being hard, dry and not very tasty.

Larger cows and bulls appear but all are safely contained on the other side of sturdy walls. Suddenly, I become aware of a tremendous buzzing and see numerous bees feasting on the nectar within the lavender flowers and gathering in their pollen. As we approach an opening to our left in front of a gate, we can see that it is occupied by a seated and squatting female figure in her mid-30's. She is deep in meditation and doesn't break from her trance as we approach and pass—nor do we want to disturb her. The countryside we are walking through is beautiful and the greenery and wild flowers are complemented by the presence of many boulders of unusual shapes and sizes in the fields along our walled pathway, which rises and falls in a straight line as far as we can see.

We try and find a good spot to stop for lunch at about one o'clock. At times, walls give way to fencing and there is not a lot of shade, given the height of the sun during this part of the day. Finding a spot is therefore not easy. There are also one or two signs that mark this part of the trail as a former Roman trade route, with the remains of Roman milarios or mile markers. On one of these, I discover a note weighed down with a stone and written in English and addressed to 'Miriam'. It indicates which way the writer is heading and at what time the note was left (about five minutes before we found it). We later discover Miriam was the woman deep in meditation we had passed not long ago and that she and her friend are walking together and are from Australia.

At around ten past one a suitable picnic spot is found, next to another Roman post and we thoroughly enjoy the tortilla, which is moist and very tasty, unlike the bread! It is during the lunch stop that 'Miriam' catches us up and I ask if by any chance she is called Miriam. If so, had she seen the note? She confirms the former but had not seen the note and, thanking us for the information, hurries on to re-join her friend. After a pleasant lunch stop, we are reunited with our rucksacks and set off again.

This really is a very beautiful stretch of Camino, with its rolling hills, an abundance of spring flowers and accompanying birdsong. In the far distance ahead and to our right, we see what looks like snow-clad peaks and debate whether we are seeing snow or whether it is sunlight on very light-coloured rocks. The boulders are still with us and at times come alive as their likeness to living objects manifests and our imagination wanders. Two large rocks to our left are two crouching lizards, another is a lion. A bull's head emerges to our right and we do still have real cattle for company too, although the further into our walk the more sheep and less cows and bulls we see. We spot a beautiful bird with what looks like a deep buttercup-coloured plumage and darts of darker feathers. It must be a golden oriole I suggest to John. It is only the third time I have ever seen one in its natural habitat.

Two huge cranes are spotted to our right, their metal structures rearing up out of the landscape like wild stallions. The huge metal structures seem so out of place in the lush and green vegetation surrounding them. We can see new 'scars' in the landscape as the human intervention of road/rail building cuts through this beautiful landscape. The cranes are there to construct a huge bridge to span a valley rather than to hug the contours of the land as our historical and less intrusive road builders used to do. We spot Miriam in the distance, reunited with her friend.

As more 'scars' appear we are redirected from the 'true' route of the Camino and down a newly excavated track that takes us under a partly-constructed section of the new road or railway. Under the bridge and in the shade, Miriam and her friend are enjoying a drink and some respite from the sun. We exchange greetings and murmur our joint disapproval of the impact of progress on the landscape. The Camino now re-joins its love affair with the N630 and winds up and down beside it as the vista of the expansive waters of the Embalse come into view for the first time. At the earliest opportunity, we drop down to the road itself and follow it for the rest of the day. It is easier underfoot than the rocky ups and downs of the official path. The latter fizzles out anyway shortly afterwards and the only option is to walk along the road.

The last five kilometres of the walk is along the road and it is tough, partly because of the distance we have already walked today, but largely because of the heat of the sun and the lack of any shade. The sun has a double impact as we both experience the direct rays and the heat bouncing off the tarmac beneath our feet. We do, however, have the beauty and majesty of the expansive reservoir to our left. Not all of man's interventions within the landscape leave lasting scars! We cross two double-decker combined road and rail bridges, with the road going across and above the railway tracks. Whilst we are crossing one of these double-decker bridges, a train trundles across below. Looking down to our left, we can see huge carp swimming in the waters and lots of swifts and swallows feasting on the insects as they hover above the blue grey waters below.

A deserted and neglected station is passed on our left just before we cross the last of the double-decker bridges. We eventually find our albergue, which is newly constructed and nestles above and with an unobstructed view of the Embalse below. Our host speaks enough English to ensure that together with our fledgeling Spanish we can communicate effectively. We are allocated the room 'cinqo' and at last, I can bag a bottom bunk, albeit that the design of this wonderfully spacious room means that to reach the top bunks, you ascend a wide stairway to the side of the row to a platform about three metres wide. From here, you merely walk straight on to your bed—no ladders to negotiate at all.

The cost of our overnight stay is 15 euros and includes breakfast in the morning and any washing we want doing as well! All we have to do is hang it out to dry in the late afternoon sun. After leaving our host with some washing, it is time for a shower; quite literally the best and most refreshing shower I have ever had. Changing into clean clothes and going back to the reception and common room area, we have a couple of beers. The first doesn't touch the sides. Then we hang out our freshly laundered clothes in the warm sun.

Sitting outside with the beautiful reservoir as the backcloth to our view and feeling doubly refreshed from the shower and the beer, life does seem rather splendid. The aches and pains in the feet and legs seem to quickly disappear. Marie, Andreas and Ernesto are here too, having stayed at Casar de Caceres last night.

Again, Marie praises the 'scouting' qualities of their unofficial Spanish guide.

An Australian couple is encountered for the first time. They are heading for Salamanca. They started their 'pilgrimage' in Merida, as the woman had previously walked there from Sevilla. They have relatives in Lincoln, England and as a part of their trip from 'Oz', they are planning a visit to the UK, before returning to Spain. They will then fly back home from Barcelona.

Whilst I am writing up my notes of the day's walk, Miriam and her friend arrive, and it appears that they have met the older Australian couple earlier in their walk. It is as it was with the two of us and Marie, Andreas and Ernesto—happy 'families' reunited. During our trip today, I get a text from Steve, thanking us for the tapas, wishing us well and confirming he has obtained a copy of "A Pennine Way Odyssey" and has read the introduction on his Kindle. Spread the word! I text back and let him know we have arrived at the Embalse and are admiring the splendid view.

The other aspect of pilgrimage reunions is that you glean a little more about those who are sharing your journey each time you meet them. In conversation with Andreas it turns out he is only 22, much younger than I had judged. He, like Marie, has set aside several weeks to complete the whole journey and has a specific date at the end of the month when a flight is booked to travel home to Germany; two days before Marie's flight, apparently. Whilst he has some flexibility in terms of each day's itinerary, the pressure is never far away, some days will need to be long ones to ensure he stays on track to get to Santiago in time.

We engage in an interesting conversation about the purpose of walking the Camino. "Maybe you are at a crossroads in your life and for some pilgrims, the need to find some meaning or purpose to that life going forward is their driving force? Or, maybe you just enjoy walking?" he adds.

We both agree that you don't just walk with your feet. Your mind is very active as well.

"It is an ideal opportunity to let your mind wander and contemplate meanings; sometimes triggered by what you are seeing in the landscape, or conversations you have with fellow pilgrims during your journey."

We agree walking the Camino is most definitely an opportunity for self-discovery and to reflect on your own life, on what is good and on what's important. However, walking the Via de la Plata has, thus far, taught me that not all those who search are looking for something.

Still in thoughtful mood, I join John and we go to the bar to order food: a lasagne, glass of wine and bottle of water. We sit down with both Andreas and Marie to eat. It is at this point that Marie confirms their 'guide' is named Jesus and not Ernesto, as we previously christened him. Well, I'm blown! Jesus, though, seems an apt name for a guide along a pilgrimage route.

The lasagne is excellent, and we get bread to mop up the sauce. John orders another glass of wine and seems relaxed as we reflect on a rather splendid day. We both remember spotting frog spawn in a pool today, somewhere soon after leaving Caser de Caceres. Jesus challenges Marie to a game of chess and the sun still beats down. John and I discuss options for the rest of our journey. We agree there will have to be two long days; either tomorrow and Thursday or Tuesday and Thursday, if we are to get to Salamanca on the day our accommodation is booked. We will take stock tomorrow depending on how much sleep we have, the temperature, and how strong we feel!

Jesus has beaten Marie at chess and is wearing a beaming smile. She and Andreas are sharing a hot drink before retiring to bed when I refer to the chess match. She smiles. She calls Jesus 'Gruppenführer' which she explains means 'group leader' in German. It is a term that seems to me to better describe him than

Jesus and for the rest of our time together on the Camino, that is the name he is affectionately accorded by all who come to know him.

There are about 13 or 14 of us in the albergue, which I guess means it is about half-full. No Karl and Hermann, though! It is a truly wonderful spot. I could tell that John's spirits were flagging a little on the long walk today, not helped by a blister on his foot. However, he is full of praise for the beauty and majesty of where we are staying tonight. Our washing is nearly dry in the still warm evening sun. Life is hard, isn't it? I muse.

We watch the wonder of a glorious sunset over the reservoir and finally gather up our almost dry washing and share final reflections on the beautiful day. I log onto the hostel Wi-Fi and delete or respond to several e-mails. We start to get ready to retire and I remember I have the joys of a bottom bunk to look forward to. As we wander down the corridor to room five, passing a weary Miriam and her friend (whose name we still haven't managed to catch), our pace is slow, almost as if we don't really want this day to end.

Embalse de Alcantara to Galisteo

(42 km or 26 m) mainly flat with some ups and downs
Gradient descended 115 metres

Tuesday 5th April

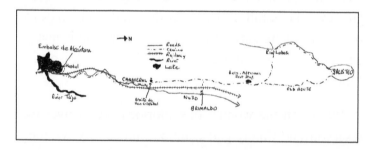

Today will mark the halfway stage of this leg of my journey along the Camino. We have walked 160km from Zafra and have another 170km to walk before reaching Salamanca. We have a room booked in a hostal there in six days, recommended by Maureen, and I am looking forward to having a full day there both to explore, but also as a break from the Camino. I am up and about at seven o'clock, having slept well in my bottom bunk. It is a 'help-yourself' breakfast and I have tea, juice, toast and jam. John bags us a couple of Madelaine cupcakes and a croissant to add to our provisions store. I speak to Marie, Andreas and Jesus at breakfast and they inform us they are heading for Grimaldo today (about 21km and the only other overnight option before Galisteo).

We aren't sure whether we will stay at Grimaldo too or continue to Galisteo. It is agreed this decision will be deferred until later. It will depend on how we feel at the point we would have to leave the Camino to get to Grimaldo. If we can make it as far as Galisteo, we should then have two shorter days walking to look forward to. A Belgian guy arrived at the albergue last night. He joined the Camino at Merida and is going as far as Salamanca on this trip. He also had an earnest conversation with Andreas yesterday evening about the meaning of walking the Camino, great chunks of which I was able to overhear.

He lost both his parents last year in a car crash, which also badly injured his sister. She is currently cared for in a specialist rehabilitation unit. He has devoted a lot of his time since then to working with her and her carers to help her become more independent. His ambition is to see her able to live independently again. He is walking the Camino both to bolster his faith in that outcome and because he never gave himself time to properly grieve. The Camino is helping him to do this. Andreas on the other hand was inspired to walk the Camino by reading an account of it by a German comedian.

Having packed our rucksacks with the few remaining damp items of clothing suitable draped to dry in the morning sun, we finally leave this idyllic spot at half-past eight. Initially, we have the mist for company which persists till about quarter past ten. Our love affair with the N630 also continues as it starts to climb towards the town of Canaveral. A train looms out of the mist on our left, bearing its three carriages of commuters, shoppers and tourists as it heads along the 165km of track to Salamanca. It will probably arrive there around 11. I wonder what time and on what day we will get there and whether it will be as special a place as Celeste described it.

As we arrive in Canaveral, we are following a fellow pilgrim. He turns out to be the guy who asked for directions to Plasencia as we were leaving Caceres on Sunday morning. We leave the Camino and go up into the town and find a very pleasant bar for a drink and cake. After using the facilities there, we make our way to a local supermarket to purchase items for lunch.

The sun is fully in control now and the mist has all been burned away. The narrow streets and little squares provide an adventure playground for what seems to be a rather large population of alley cats. We pause in the shade of a rather splendid church (Ermita de San Roque) to unzip our trouser bottoms, apply sun cream and generally prepare for the rest of the day's walk. It is also an opportunity to stow away the items of clothing that have already dried.

Whilst we are attending to these little tasks we are joined by our Belgian friend. He is keen to view inside the church if it is open, but even keener to find a café or bar for a coffee. We give him directions to the café we just left and leave the splendid little town, nestling as it does in the hills, and head back to the N630. For a little while longer, it is also our Camino route.

A little way beyond the town (two kilometres) and just after passing Canaveral railway station to our right, we leave the road and start what will prove to be a very beautiful cross-country route. Just off the road where our track commences, the very small but picturesque church of Ermita de San Christobal gleams white in the hot sun.

A stone's throw further on is a small man-made pool, teeming with frogs, their croaking forewarning us of their presence long before we get close enough to spot them.

The first cuckoo of the day is heard and the clamouring skylarks with their bouncy flight patterns and soulful songs are resuming their more usual behaviour. Buzzards are also circling high to our left, using the warm thermals to advantageous effect. The flora and fauna are very much a part of our journey again.

The next challenge is to climb a steep fire break as our Camino path takes us up the hillside to our left. This is certainly the steepest section of the walk so far. It is well worth it as the walk now continues in dappled sunlight through a pine forest with pine needles cushioning every footstep and their smell filling our nostrils. The route is still climbing—albeit less steeply —on this stretch before it descends to leave the trees and meets a road near an isolated hotel and club. However, we are soon on a beautiful track, with more open woodland, reminiscent of walking in the Yorkshire Dales.

We walk through old cork woods now until the shade of two Holm oak trees provides an excellent place to have lunch. Shortly after stopping, we are joined by our Belgian peregrino. In exchanging pleasantries, he tells us that he is only going as far as Grimaldo, which he estimates is about half an hour further on. We feel sure we will continue to Galisteo but haven't committed ourselves to our evening destination yet.

After our pleasant lunch stop, we don our rucksacks and continue along the Camino until we see a footpath to our right, which indicates the way to Grimaldo.

There is still much of the afternoon to walk and we are both feeling reasonably OK and without much of a debate, we carry on. Our undulating walk continues in the warm sun to take us through rolling countryside with more holm oak trees for company.

The colours and scent of many wildflowers are all around: cranesbill, saxifrages, wild mustard, hawkweed, scabious, wild thyme, rosemary, poppies, forget-me-nots, gentians, centaury and wild pansies. There are many more whose names I don't know. They all provide a wonderfully vibrant carpet that weaves in and around our feet and fills our nostrils.

A short stop for a drink and a rest is followed by a further stop at four o'clock in the shade of a barn located alongside the track. A short stretch of pavement alongside it provides a seat, with the wall acting as the backrest. It is very quiet and peaceful, and the shade provides a welcome break from the penetrating rays of the sun.

Since our lunch stop, we have crossed flocks of sheep and goats, seen wonderful views across open countryside and really enjoyed the walk. We reckon we have another two and a half hours walking (around ten kilometres) to Galisteo. A herd of goats temporarily separates us as it crosses the track behind me and in front of John.

According to the Gerald Kelly Guidebook, we are soon to come to a disputed section of the route where a farmer does not want the Camino to continue over his land and the alternative route adds a further four kilometres to the route. Given our long day walking and the hot sun, we determine to stick to the original route rather than add the extra distance. We pass the disputed area without even noticing and are suddenly taken down into a village (Rio Lobos), which means we are following the 'new' route. A bar in the village provides an opportunity to take stock and sip a cold lemonade (for me) and a cold orange juice (for John). It is now five o'clock and I enquire how far it is to Galisteo only to be informed that it is nine kilometres further on.

The route from the village is along tarmac roads, with no shade from the relentless sun. We are now both struggling, John with blisters, whilst the backs of my legs are burning from the heat of the sun even though they have been smothered with factor 50 cream. We just try to plod forward. Finally, I am in such discomfort I have to stop. It is about one and a half kilometres further to go. I take on the last of my water and smother more cream on my legs, before summoning up my last reserves to carry on, to catch up with John. Finally, we are on the last uphill stretch before, at last, we arrive in the walled town of Galisteo.

Just before the summit of the hill, there is a patch of scrubby grassland to our left and two horses are trying to find enough grass to stave off their hunger. They both look in very poor shape. I wonder whether they have the energy to look up and take in the sight of two human beings, who probably look in equally poor shape!

The albergue we are heading for is signposted up another hill. It is apparently located behind the Bar 'Los Immigrantes'. At the top of the hill, we can see the bar 100 metres further on and to our left. We finally find our evening accommodation at around half seven. It is locked, although a notice on the door does have a telephone number. I ring and manage to convey and receive sufficient information to understand that 'Amalia' will come along shortly to let us in. She is with us in five minutes along with her daughter. We are the only pilgrims in the 12 bedded hostal. Tomorrow may be different though if everyone who was at the Embalse and who walked as far as Grimaldo today stay here too.

Having signed in and paid our fee, it is time to have a well-earned shower and to hang out some washing in what remains of the evening sun. The shower is sheer bliss. I ring home in response to a text from Sandra to tell her that we have arrived safely and send texts to my daughters, too. I also try to catch up in my journal with the key moments of what has been a long and eventful day. We saw another hoopoe, but only one stork in flight. Others sitting on nests. Thankfully, we should now have two shorter days to look forward to. I estimate that today, because of the 'enforced' detour, we have walked 42km.

I must go, eat and have a well-deserved beer before I fall asleep. We are both very tired after our exertions of the day. Thankfully, it isn't far to Los Immigrantes and having ordered a beer I realise—whilst scanning the menu—I have left my phrasebook back at the hostal and so return to collect it. I am amazed to see a somewhat bewildered 'Gruppenführer' on his own, standing outside the hostal.

"I thought you, Marie and Andreas were staying at Grimaldi tonight?"

"Si, entonces no, devidemos que en su lugar," is his haltering response.

I deduce though this was their plan, they changed their minds and decided to continue. I let him in with my key and ensure he is aware to ring Amalia. He is surprised that Marie's things are not in the hostal. I confirm to him that it is just John and I who are staying tonight so far. He appears even more confused about this. We agree where the key will be left if he goes out for tapas and then I leave him to return to John. I explain the reason for my delay and we use the book to clarify a couple of things on the menu before ordering food. The sun is now setting and casting an increasingly deep red glow over the houses across the street and the countryside beyond.

The food is excellent and clearly freshly made. I have a starter of vegetable stew with a fried egg on top. This is followed by pork, tomatoes and potatoes and finally the best flan I have had in Spain so far. The beers we are drinking are large ones and I can't quite finish the second one. Whilst we are dining the 'Gruppenführer' arrives, still looking for Marie. He stands in front of us for a while and makes a phone call, which seems to go on for a long time. He looks up and down the street continuously whilst doing this. His behaviour is a worry for us too. Surely, the consummate and so highly thought of Spanish guide cannot have abandoned Marie on today's walk? If he thought she should have arrived before him, what has happened to her and what of Andreas? It is now getting dark and we are looking out on a starlit sky. Finally, he seems somewhat satisfied and settles down sufficiently before going inside to order some food. I wonder whether, at home in Saltaire, Sandra will be looking up at the same night sky as us in Galisteo. The walled and fortified town of Galisteo was the last defence against the Christians in the 15th century at the start of the 'Reconquista'. Were those defending it from attack then looking up at similar night skies and seeing the same constellations clearly visible tonight?

We return to the hostal and sort out the bringing in of washing; mostly still wet or damp and fill our water bottles to put them in the fridge for tomorrow. The 'Gruppenführer' is already in his bunk. In conversation, we believe him to be confirming Marie and Andreas are in an albergue around two kilometres away. Reassured, we can settle down to sleep. I am using just my sheet sleeping bag and a thin blanket tonight, a far cry from my experience at Aldea del Cano (just three nights ago). I sleep only fitfully though as my legs are hurting. During the night, I apply some Ibuprofen gel and finally manage to get some sleep before a call of nature wakes me at five—smaller beers may have prevented this, I muse. Having just got back to sleep, I am woken again at six as Jesus gets up and prepares to depart.

Galisteo to Oliva de Plasencia

(33 km or 21.6 m) mainly flat
Gradient ascended 115 metres

Wednesday 6th April

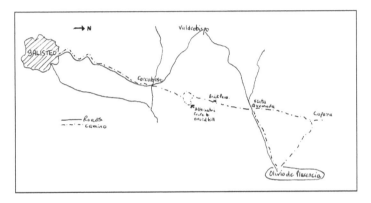

My alarm has been set for quarter to eight, so after a further short nap I am up for the final time before eight and we both take our time in getting ready and return to our nearby café for breakfast. It is around half-past nine before we finally leave the hostal and walk back up to and through the arch into the walled town and then through and out the other side, with me taking the odd picture. Dropping down from the town we bear right over an ancient bridge, where a stork has built her nest on the memorial stone in its centre. Continuing right we now have excellent views back towards

Gallisteo. At a roundabout a misleading Camino sign takes us down a wrong turning, and we waste 15 minutes before retracing our steps.

We then proceed along a quiet country road which leads to the village of Aldenhuela del Jerte. This stretch is pleasant and has some interesting architectural features on several of the barns we pass. Particularly intriguing are the diamond-patterned ventilation holes. The sun is already quite warm, and we are thankful for a stretch of road that provides shade from an extensive line of plane trees to our right. Amazingly, I see some cuckoos—the first spotted during the journey to date. Plenty have been heard, though. Arriving in the village we get some provisions for lunch and enjoy a Fanta in the shade of a bus shelter. Six kilometres covered so far, and it is half-past eleven. Our next port of call should be Carcabosa and then on to our evening destination, which we estimate should be a further 20km or five hours walking.

We continue along the road to Carcabosa and arrive there slightly earlier than anticipated at half-past twelve. Most of this section is on tarmac. About one mile before Carcabosa, we are passed by a bus going towards Galisteo. This is the first bus I have seen since leaving Zafra. Just before the town itself, we pass a large brickworks, before emerging onto the main street that takes us up into town. We sit outside a small café at a small table perched high on two stools and sip lemonade with ice and are given tapas of chorizo. It is exceedingly tasty. We are in no doubt that it is the best 'free' tapas we have eaten so far.

There is not a cloud in the sky and it is now as hot as it has been at any part of any day so far. Over to our right, we have the mountains in view that have been our constant horizon companions for the last two days. It is still a mystery as to whether they are snow-clad or the rocks glistening in the heat of the intense heat of the sun. This mystery, like the earlier one of determining whether we were seeing a pilgrim or a tree on our route to Torremegia last Wednesday, will no doubt get resolved in due course.

Yesterday afternoon and at the sighting of yet another yellow arrow, John suddenly exclaimed, "Leapy Lee", and the mystery of who had a hit record with "Little Arrows" was resolved. What is also a mystery, given the amount of pork and jambón we have eaten, is we haven't seen a single pig or hog at any time since leaving Zafra.

We leave Carcabosa soon after one in the afternoon, after our very pleasant repast and soon leave tarmac again and return to a good track which winds down and along until it divides in two. Here our choices are to take a shorter route which takes us over a small hill, or to take a longer and more meandering route which skirts the hill. We decide on the shorter route and for a while follow a water canal to our right. We pass a farmer fixing his fence and some distance further on I realise the carrier bag with our lunchtime provisions in it, which I tied onto the back of the rucksack before leaving Aldenhuela del Jerte, seems somewhat lighter. On checking, I discover the bag has developed a hole and the only thing left is half our bread supply.

We take off our rucksacks and momentarily stare in disbelief at the virtually empty, torn and sagging strand of plastic hanging limply from my rucksack. I volunteer to go back for half a kilometre or so to see if I can retrieve our lunch. I run for about half a mile and just past the farmer is a bag with the fruit in it. Just past that is half a baton. Running back again with lunch in hand I am reunited with John and we resolve to stop at the next shady spot. It takes about ten minutes of further walking to find such a spot under the shade of a large holm oak tree. The bread is incredibly dry and even with the cheese is not very appetising; a lot of it gets discarded. I am sure the local wildlife will find and make use of it. The bananas need eating straight away but are good. John produces two more Madeline cakes he obtained from the hostal at the Embalse and we enjoy the latter half of our feast and the ability to get some respite from the heat.

A long stretch of the Camino now lies ahead—the Vente Quemada Camino; named because it takes you to a large house of that name which sits on a road crossing the Camino. Here, we will have to make a judgement about whether we carry on and try to find a new private albergue we have seen advertised (albeit not for several kilometres). Our alternative would be to bear right at the road and follow this for six kilometres to Oliva de Plasencia, where we know there is an albergue.

This stretch is pretty, but the path is at times waterlogged and muddy and we also must negotiate a few streams and watercourses, all of which slow our progress. Just past some brick-built pens where a horse is alone in a compound, we pass another building, where a dog is basking in the sun, no doubt guarding a herd of cows and bulls grazing nearby. He is quite loud and aggressive in his barking and he comes quite close behind us. I am glad I have my walking pole which I either tap on the ground or drag behind me to deter him from getting any closer. We leave the area as quickly as possible and once we cross another small stream, he decides not to follow and although his barking continues for a while, we can relax.

Another lone horse is passed to our right and we eventually arrive at the point where the Camino crosses the road and can see Vente Quemada on the other side of it. We have seen no further signs about the albergue at Caparra. The flyer we picked up last night has no directions or location details on it and if we fail to find it, we would need to carry on for a further 24km before there would be another accommodation option. In these circumstances and given the time (half-past five) and our levels of tiredness, we decide our best option is to turn right along the road towards Oliva de Plasencia. However, before doing this we try ringing the number on the flyer in the hope we can communicate sufficiently with whoever answers the call to get directions to the new 'Caparra option'. They don't speak any English and it soon becomes clear we are not going to be able to discern from the call clear enough directions to be able to find the albergue and therefore accept that fate has determined that we will head for Oliva de Plasencia instead.

It is around seven when we finally arrive there, having endured the searing heat from the sun as the road we are on has little, if any, shade. It takes a little while to find the albergue which is of course locked! Whilst we are working out how to contact Monica, the Matradi, two children—a boy I estimate of about eight and a girl, some two years his junior—appear and tell us their mother is Anita and she is not around. The boy proudly tells us in English, "my grandmother is Anita's mother". We call the number provided to contact Anita and from the conversation, I manage to ascertain I am speaking to Anita's mother and that she will come and open up for us in around 30 minutes. She doesn't, however, speak any English. John goes off in search of the bar/shops and returns after about ten minutes not having found anywhere/anything for us to eat.

I go for a wander and eventually find a little bar that sells food and I am just getting back to the albergue as John is ringing to say our hostess's mother has arrived to open up. We manage to communicate sufficiently to understand Anita will not be around until nine and tell her we have managed to find where the bar is to get some food. Once she has left, we leave our stuff and go down to the bar for a beer and tapas. We manage to order two rationes of jambón and queso with bread and polish that off along with a couple of beers in no time at all. We have football on the TV in the bar if we want it—the first leg of Wolfsburg versus Real Madrid.

We discuss our plans for the next few days and today's walk. Tomorrow we will have 24km (we think) to get to Aldeanueva del Camino via Caparra. Today was another day that turned out longer than planned. The sun, the detour and the lost lunch incident had all taken their toll. I worked out that we had covered 33km today and on top of that, I had run one and a half kilometres, too! We agree to have a third and last beer and then head back to the albergue for showers, to be around when Anita calls and to have an early night. Before we leave, we ascertain you can't get breakfast at the bar and we both stow some bread to have with our diminishing supply of mini pepperonis, apricots and raisins in the morning. According to one of our guides, you can get snacks and drinks from a vending machine at Caparra, so we should be able to supplement our supplies there. Apart from that, there will be nothing before we get to our evening destination.

Back at the albergue, we have showers and manage to get the TV working although only on a channel showing netball, so no football to watch. Maybe Anita will be able to resolve this when she arrives! At about 25-past nine and after mooching round the whole of the property and some tedious knob fiddling, I do manage to find out how to change channels and get the football on. Anita arrives about ten minutes later and explains that she was delayed because of problems with a tractor. She explains where everything is for breakfast (we will be able to have something to eat before we set off after all). The albergue was formerly a bar itself and the building has many interesting little features that reflect its history.

We compliment her on the English of her children and explain how they met us outside and told us she was delayed. She says her daughter is nine and therefore I assume her son must be at least ten. There are a couple in the village who visit the UK a lot and are ambassadors. They provide extra private tuition in English to several children in the area. The building might be old and cool now that the sun has long disappeared, with its wooden beamed ceilings and creaking, but the radiators work and keep us warm as the temperatures drop in the clear night sky. I am up at seven to put the coffee on and finish my notes of today's journey.

Oliva de Plasencia to Aldeanueva del Camino

(33 km or 21.6 m) undulating with some gentle climbs and then a descent
Gradient ascended 115 metres

Thursday 7th April

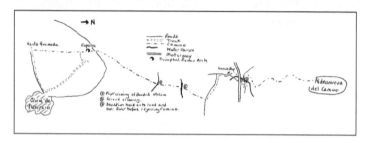

Today is my wedding anniversary and it will be the first of those anniversaries Sandra and I have ever spent completely apart. I left a card and a gift at home and on awakening and after getting dressed and ready for the day, my first thought is to ring and speak to Sandra, wish her a happy anniversary and tell her where to find her gift. We clear away the breakfast pots and make our preparations for departure. The weather again promises another warm day. We negotiate our way out of the village and take the road that will eventually lead us to Caparra, where we will re-join the Camino.

The road soon gives way to a broad track that takes us between open fields with a solitary bull on one side and then a herd of bulls and cows in fields opposite. The track then becomes a lane lined with holm oaks and we soon arrive at some rather elaborate gate posts we pass between. We are now walking through verdant pastures, tracts of which have been corralled within modern and well-constructed wooden fences, around half have been painted white.

There are strategically newly planted clumps of trees too and water troughs, sculptures of animals, birds and more abstract forms. We are walking along a designated Camino—we have a right to be here and yet it feels like I am trespassing on a private estate. It is as if I am intruding within the landscape of an egotist, who has set out to subvert the landscape to his status and wealth. It fills me with a sense of unease. Whilst at one level I feel like an intruder, I feel even angrier that it is he (for I assume it is a man) who is intruding on my pilgrimage walk?

We arrive at the magnificent Roman remains of Caparra and re-join the Via de la Plata, encountering as we do so two Italian peregrinos and our paths will continue to cross for the remainder of the day. Pausing to take pictures, I suddenly feel a connection to previous pilgrims and feel sure many will have found this moment of their pilgrimage a seminal moment too.

We also visit the extensive Roman architectural remains of what must have been a very fine settlement in its day.

The triumphal arch is quite magnificent, given the length of time it has endured in this place and the number of fellow pilgrims who through the years must have passed through. Going through the arch itself is as if you are passing through a narrow keyhole with its own microscopic energy field drawn from all the pilgrims heading onwards to Santiago.

Before moving on time is also taken to apply a fresh Compeed plaster to cover and protect each painful and throbbing blister and to drink water. I have previously found using Compeed plasters, which provide an extra skin to cover emerging or existing blisters, an effective way of being able to continue walking in spite of blisters. There is no sign of the promised vending machines offering the delights of fresh snacks and drinks to fortify our dwindling supplies. Oh well, at least we are now reunited with our spiritual path as well as with the sounds of cuckoos and sightings of storks, chaffinches, bulls and cows, plus much of the flora and fauna that we have grown accustomed to.

I feel at one with myself again and notice how pure the air and light is. The mountains we have in our sights loom even larger in the distance and it is not until the sun gets higher in the sky that the expanse of whiteness near the summit starts to shimmer in the heat. Our debate about pale rocks or snow is renewed. Despite our sore feet and the heat of the sun, our pace is good, and we soon leave our Italian friends behind.

John and I reflect on another walking adventure shared when we flew to Dublin, hired a car and spent a week travelling between all the Irish Munroes. Being able to climb the peaks during the day and then in the evenings being able to enjoy the 'criac' and a few beers had been special to us both. Whilst the McGillicuddy Reeks had been the mountaineering highlights, finishing on the Dingle Peninsula with Mount Brandon and looking westwards across the Atlantic had been a special moment too. We even had time to visit the Dingle races, where some fortuitous betting on my part led to us having a grandstand view and several pints of the black stuff without it costing a penny. I had an unfulfilled promise to take Sandra to see the majesty of the Dingle. I had got her as far as Dublin to support me in running the marathon there.

The air is warm and more humid. Underfoot, there are waterlogged paths to negotiate to avoid getting wet feet. A larger watercourse now bars our way. Crossing it has been aided by the positioning of three or four large granite blocks and other stepping-stones. One or two protrude from the rushing waters but most are well submerged beneath them, showing just how much higher than usual the water must be. The obvious solution at first seems to be to scout the area to find other largish stones which we can add to or place on top of the submerged ones to create a passable route. All the stones I come across seem too small to make any real difference, but I do find two large logs which, with careful manoeuvring, should be able to top off the two most submerged stepping-stones.

The first of these is just too far out of reach to place a log in position, even for John. The plan, therefore, is for him to reach out and gently throw the first log about three feet into position. John takes careful aim, but the log just fails to find its intended target and despite its weight and size, the current catches it and it starts to float away, gradually quickening in pace as the pressure of the flow takes hold. Never mind, we still have a second log to use. Unfortunately, and despite John's careful aim, it soon follows its companion as it bobs up and down before disappearing out of sight. We accept at this stage the only feasible solution left is to take off our boots and wade across to the other side using what stepping-stones we can, submerged or otherwise.

The water is cold and some of the rocks are slimy and the current tugs at our feet, threatening to throw us off balance as we gingerly manoeuvre our way across, hearts racing. With sheer cussedness, we negotiate the obstacle and sit down on the other side to dry our feet before putting our walking shoes on again. As we are doing this the two Italians arrive at the crossing and without pause wade across. They laugh at the sight of two English pilgrims drying their feet and ask with a smile whether they can take a picture of this amusing little interlude. "Of course," we obligingly reply with two sheepish grins to greet the camera. Once our feet are dry and blisters are attended to again, we reboot and are soon on our way. 20 minutes have passed since we arrived at the crossing.

Soon afterwards, however, our mood is completely lifted by the sight of a group of seven or eight magnificently coloured birds; swooping and circling just above a clump of bushes and then settling for a while for us to take in the majesty of their plumage: red, gold, blue and turquoise. They are as vivid as kingfishers but much larger. I am seeing a group of bee-eaters for the first time in my life. This is certainly one of the highlights of my journey to date.

A little further on and we come to another river. Whilst it is shallower than the previous one, it has no stepping-stones, submerged or otherwise. This time we take our boots and socks off without further ado and paddle to the other side. We sit down to dry feet and put socks and boots back on again. This takes a little time but at least we are sitting and resting whilst these operations are ongoing. We now carry on for a further 15 minutes before we arrive at a metalled road where we bear left. Well, at least we shouldn't have any more rivers to ford!

According to both books, this road continues for approximately ten kilometres. About half-way along we catch up our Italian peregrinos. They have stopped for lunch and to take off their wet boots and socks and to dry their feet. They laugh as I indicate that I would like to take a picture of their feet, too! Touché!

We can now see the mountains of the Sierra de Graedos on our right and ahead and yet again have a change of mind about what the whiteness near the tops of some peaks is. We finally agree without a doubt it is snow we can see on some of the higher slopes.

After a short walk along a busier road, we stop for lunch under the shade of a beech tree next to a derelict hacienda. We believe it to be only a further two kilometres to Aldeanueva from here, so hopefully we will be there by half-past two. Our two Italian fellow pilgrims pass us again during our lunch stop and we take our time before departing the shade of the tree. However, it turns out to be considerably more than two kilometres, as we have a further two and a half hours of trekking under the heat of the sun; this coupled with being somewhat footsore makes the rest of the day's journey a challenge.

We get to a point where the 'new' motorway cuts across the Camino route and we are directed off to find the Camino on the other side. This detour should bring us to a dry riverbed but instead, it brings us to another river, too wide and fast flowing to cross. A further detour is required, and we clamber back onto a road that takes us over the river and then drops down steeply to our right. We now have a long, upward stretch of around two kilometres, during which we pass one of the Italians; I will refer to him as the 'apprentice'. The 'master' is apparently some way ahead. We share words of encouragement and he hopes it may be only two kilometres from here to Aldeanueva. I don't tell him I thought that an hour and a half ago!

It turns out to be another seven kilometres from this point until we arrive in the town itself. The day is the hottest so far and the most humid. We took a full one and a half litre bottle of water from the albergue this morning and by the end of today's walk it has all gone, in addition to the one-litre bottles we each had as part of our 'daily provisions'. On this last stretch, I spot a buzzard circling and then swooping to the earth in the direction we came from before rising again some 20 seconds later, having probably swallowed whatever prey she caught. I hoped it wasn't an Italian pilgrim!

We find the albergue with a little difficulty but are finally registered and our rucksacks are safely parked, along with the Italian master, who at this stage seems unconcerned about the whereabouts of his companion. John and I go back down into the town and have a beer as we sit and contemplate the rest of our journey. We both agree it would be a considerable challenge to walk from here to Salamanca and be there for Sunday lunch. Arriving in the town we had seen a road sign that proclaimed: 'Salamanca 95km'. We are both sore underfoot and struggling to contemplate a further two days walking with distances slightly greater than today's, particularly as the route now takes us up and over the mountains.

I manage to elicit there is a bus to Salamanca at 20-past nine in the morning. We now need to ascertain where it may stop on our route sufficiently far ahead, but close enough to the Camino to make it worth catching. John discovers another angry-looking blister on his big toe and the existing blisters have not fared well, despite two layers of Compeed applied at Caparra, probably because their integrity was destroyed by paddling across two watercourses. I too now have Compeed on the outside of both heels to cushion the impact of painful blisters. Whilst the pilgrimage aim is to walk to Santiago de Compostela, doing so needs to remain a pleasurable and reflective experience and not become totally an exercise in endurance.

Realism starts to kick in as we contemplate the distance to Salamanca and the self-imposed time we have left to get there. We have a hotel booked in three days. Given the state of our feet and the contours and distance still to cover and the continuing forecast of hot sun, we start to think about the option of going on to Salamanca tomorrow and giving ourselves some time to recover there. This will, of course, mean returning to Aldeanueva del Camino to continue our journey of discovery. In some ways this seems a preferable option than to be missing out part of the route altogether by taking the bus. We could simply stay here for a day or two, but there is little of interest apart from the view of the mountains and that would also mean cancelling our booking in Salamanca, which we have already paid for.

The importance of reflection and pilgrimage is to know when to take stock and change plans. We both knew we had a room booked in Salamanca on Sunday, but also wanted to spend some time there. Perhaps we should get there early and in good enough shape to be able to see some of the 'jewels' that Celeste has whetted our appetite for? The distances today were far greater than the guidebooks suggested, and the last nine kilometres was not well described at all, hence our confusion at one stage that we may only have a further two to go. The snow on the mountains glistens in the sun and I feel we could be in a town or village in the highlands of Scotland or the Swiss Alps.

Back at the albergue, the shower is the best of the trip so far; warm, refreshing and well worth lingering within the running waters and mulling over the options. Whilst bus stops between here and Salamanca may offer us chance to 'skip' part of the Camino and get to Salamanca by Sunday, is taking a bus to cover part of our route going to detract from my objective of walking the whole way? Alternatively, we may go to Salamanca, spend two or three days sightseeing, resting and then return here.

After my contemplative shower, I sit and write up some notes of the day with John and our two Italian perigrinos for company; the master has been joined by the apprentice and both are lying on their bunks, resting. At least he didn't get eaten by the buzzard! Still wrestling with the options for tomorrow, we walk to a bar that has a good reputation for food according to Gerald.

Arriving there, we realise the phrasebook has been left back in the albergue. John heads back for this and I take the opportunity to ring home and speak to my daughter, Jenny. She has come to our house to have tea with her mum. I then get a call from John as somehow he has managed to get locked in the albergue. I have the key! I go back to affect the rescue and we return together to peruse the menu. I dine on asparagus salad, beef stew and cold rice pudding with cinnamon—all very tasty indeed. We share a bottle of wine to help wash this down and watch Athletico Bilbao play Sevilla in the Europa League, with Sevilla coming out on top two goals to one. During the evening, we make the sensible decision to travel to Salamanca in the morning.

"Maybe I pushed us too hard over the last couple of days, John? Maybe we should have stayed at Grimaldo?"

"Look," he responds, "you didn't twist my arm. I went along with the decisions we took and anyway, hindsight's a wonderful science!"

"Not withstanding that I feel I owe you an apology."

He puts an arm round my shoulder, "Time to head back to our 'digs'."

Back at the albergue, the master and apprentice are already in bed and asleep. I gather in washing, which is largely dry and go to bed. I sleep fitfully from the aches and pains of my feet and legs, although the bed is comfortable. The albergue is bright and modern; it seems such a pity it only houses four pilgrims tonight.

Plate 9
Lunch stop near Roman milario - Day 13

Plate 10
Embalse De Alcantara - Day 13

Plate 11
John and I separated by goats near Grimaldo – Day 14

Plate 12
John fording water crossing with boots in hand – Day 16

Chapter Four

Recuperating and Sightseeing in Salamanca

Friday 8th to Sunday 10th April

The Italians started getting ready at seven o'clock. The 'master' got up and coaxed the 'apprentice' to do likewise. We, however, don't get up until eight, giving us three-quarters of an hour to wash, dress, pack and have breakfast, and then get down to the bus stop for nine. We'd then have time to catch the bus to Salamanca at 20-past nine.

I have mixed feelings this morning. It's strange and slightly surreal not to be packing to walk to our next destination, even though I had completely accepted the logic and appropriateness of our decision.

Were we just tired, we would have taken today as a rest day and then used three days to walk to Salamanca. This would have helped our bodies—primarily legs and feet—recover from their current state. However, we also have painful blisters and a room booked in Salamanca on Sunday. I feel certain we will be back in Aldeanueva del Camino in a few days to continue our journey of discovery along the beautiful Via de la Plata—a route that displays in spades what the Spanish countryside has to offer and what pilgrimage walking is all about.

Will the snow-covered peaks of the Sierra de Gredos Mountains overlooking Aldeanueva still watch over us on our return, I wonder? Well at least we now know beyond all shadow of a doubt it is snow we have been seeing on the mountain tops, particularly on Caltivario, at 2425 metres and on Almanzor at 2592 metres. That snow has been with us since we left Casar de Caceres on Sunday morning. As the mists cleared and the warm sun emerged (and at times slowed our progress) it became our constant companion over the past few days.

The bus arrives on time and we take our comfortable seats for a fascinating and scenic journey over and through the mountains to the highest point the Camino will reach. To start with, there are many twists and turns for the bus to negotiate and we cover the first ten kilometres of the Camino route, but only reduce the distance by road to Salamanca by five kilometres. It takes 40 minutes to get to the city of Bejar, off the Camino route to the right. Parallel to it we would have walked 20km and taken five hours to reach the village of Calzara de Bejar some six kilometres away from its larger cousin, Bejar.

Ultimately, it takes the bus an hour and 40 minutes to make the journey to Salamanca; aided greatly by being on the new motorway for the latter half of the journey. Arriving in Salamanca, I start to wonder whether we will uncover all the jewels Celeste promised us. Before leaving the bus station, we ascertain it is the right place to catch the bus back to Aldeanueva del Camino in a few days. Leaving the bus station behind we head out into the sunshine towards the older part of the city. A temperature figure above a pharmacy tells us it is 26 degrees and it feels cooler than yesterday.

We find the magnificent cathedral and follow the route of the Camino to the Plaza Major. A very helpful young lady in the tourist information office directs us to the Hotel Sara. Unfortunately, they only have room tonight and not Saturday, but confirm our reservation for Sunday. Returning to Tourist Information we are given a list of hotels and decide to head back to Hostal Sara—it is only two minutes away. There is another hostal in the same street, however, three doors away from Hotel Sara, so we go there first and ask about a room for tonight and Saturday. They have a twin room for 20 euros each per night and after having a look around and seeing the room we decide to book in. This will mean we don't have far to go to transfer our things on Sunday. After checking in and unpacking, deciding what is clean and can be worn in the 'city' and what needs to be washed is our next task. The bathroom is small although it does have a toilet and a shower. The sink is in the room itself. The shower is a power one and provides a welcome and refreshing cleansing before we go out to explore Salamanca. However, before going out we take steps to protect our blistered feet.

The next few days are about rest, reflection, nurturing our feet and a little bit of self-pampering. I ring home and speak to Sandra and let her know where we are. She expresses concern that I am pushing us too hard if we need to take some time out in Salamanca. I am not sure my reassurances are taken on board, but I know her concern is genuine. Her support has enabled me to undertake and achieve so much, particularly since my health scare. She was the complete marathon support person, particularly in Stockholm, where I was desperate to find her en-route, to deal with some increasingly painful chafing. It was well past 70 degrees during the race and I had made an impromptu decision to duck under a cooling temporary shower. A decision I regretted almost immediately.

Leaving the hotel, we go out into the warm sunshine and seek somewhere to have a bite to eat for lunch. We find a café that has tables in the middle of the street and after a little wait are tucking into a delicious pizza and salad and sipping refreshing lemonade. A lot of the streets in the old part of the city have been paved and are for pedestrian use only. A lot of the cafés, like the one we are sitting in, have taken advantage of the wide paved areas to provide opportunities for outdoor dining.

We spend a good 90 minutes at the café before heading back towards the cathedral, which is simply stunning and huge. It is apparently two cathedrals in one, with an older and a newer cathedral linked together. Three euros each gets us in and enables us to climb almost to the top of the tower. Different points on this ascent have different views and aspects of both the cathedral and the rest of the city. There is an opportunity to look down into the new cathedral in all its majesty. Higher up, it is possible to have wonderful panoramic views of the whole city and beyond. I am blown away by the architecture, sheer size, and grandeur of the cathedral and of the city that lies around it.

The new cathedral stands on the highest hill in the city, adjoining the old. Work started in 1513 but it was not finally completed until 1733. A major reason for building a second cathedral was the presence of so many university students in the city, many of whom were studying to enter the priesthood. The original cathedral; Santa Maria, was built on the site of the

Visigoth Episcopal See and is believed to have been commenced in 1140, with work being completed in 1289. In the Romanesque central apse is the high altar piece, the work of the 15th century painter, Nicolas Florentino.

Near to the cathedral is the Casa de las Conchas (House of Shells). This is one of the most loved buildings in the city and is distinguished by having over 300 shell symbols adorning its walls. It is the shell which symbolises the journey of pilgrimage to Santiago.

The sense of being in a very special place, gives rise to a further period of reflection for me on both the journey and the pilgrimage of the Via de la Plata. I feel humbled my time on the Camino not only passes through Salamanca, but that circumstance has allowed me an opportunity to pause here. The sense we have reached a staging post on the pilgrimage also prompts reflections on the highlights of my journey from Sevilla, and with John from Zafra—which although of only 17 days duration, seems much longer. Already Salamanca has joined my top ten places one should see or visit at least once in a lifetime.

From the last ten days my favourite recollections, arriving at the paradise that was to be our overnight stop on the 4th of April. Seeing the view out over the

Embalse de Alcantara was pure delight. If you couple this with its cold beer, tasty food, excellent accommodation and wonderful scenery, it had to be a major contender. Caceres and meeting up with Steve and Celeste and being given a short tour of the old city, before enjoying the most delicious tapas, cake and a refreshing beer, was a clear favourite too. The meal in the evening at Galisteo (good homemade food), sitting outside watching the sunset and then star gazing was also memorable. The morning walk last Saturday from Aljucen to Alcuescar was worthy of mention as our route meandered through typical Spanish woodland in dappled sunlight and gave us an extensive experience of the flora and fauna the Camino has to offer.

We walk down to the university and look out over the river at the bridge we must cross to walk into the city. I wonder how many days it will be before I will be taking that walk and how wonderful it will feel to be revisiting Salamanca. A gentle stroll then ensues as we wander around the older parts of the city, taking in the many sites, before returning to our hostal. After a wash, brush up and change, we go out in search of tapas. We make what turns out to be an excellent choice at a small bar between our hotel and the Plaza Major. The deconstructed cheesecake we had for dessert was 'to die for'. A leisurely meal with two glasses of wine and a coffee to finish left us both feeling well-fed and satisfied.

Salamanca is somewhat of a delight for anyone who appreciates the architectural heritage. It has fine buildings, many with glowing orange red pantile roofs, soft golden-brown stone walls—mostly obtained from the quarries of Villamayor. A lot are adorned with unique facades and finely carved reliefs. It is the rich ornamental style which characterises a lot of the major buildings that distinguishes Salamanca. It has its own descriptor, 'plateresque', which sets it apart and gives it a sense of being a 'special' place.

It also has its university and cathedrals, which have drawn scholars and clerics to its midst, over the years. Its strategic geographical significance about the region around it also ensured it became a centre of trading. The Plaza Major is as big and grand as the one in Madrid and it took from 1720 to 1755 to construct. The very fine town hall, which dominates the north side, along with a fine baroque palace and two Corinthian columns flanked by balconies, being one of the final pieces of the jigsaw. On the east side is the Pabellan Real (Royal Pavilion) where in days gone by the king and queen would watch the bullfighting in the square below. At dusk, the whole square is lit up and the majesty of the buildings around its four sides becomes further enhanced. Having soaked in its splendour, a short evening stroll is in order, taking in the night life and illuminated buildings of this beautiful city. Although we couldn't find any 'live' music, we did see a procession of men carrying a figure of Christ into the church near the cathedral. As it disappears into the church, we head back the short distance to our hostal and turn in for the night. I sleep alright, although I am cold at first and not until a blanket is added do I warm up. As I drift off to sleep, my head is filled with images of today's many splendid sights.

I am woken when a TV is switched on loudly in a room down the corridor at six o'clock and 15 minutes later another guest gets up and bangs loudly on the door of the room in question, but the TV persists until about seven. I must drift off to sleep again because it is half-past eight when I check my watch again.

It is my youngest daughter's birthday today and as I am eating my breakfast of toast and jam and sipping coffee, I send a text to wish her a 'happy birthday'. I don't remember ever being away from home and not being around to see her on this day at any time over the past 37 years. I spoke to her two days ago, though.

Our priority after breakfast today is to return to the bus station to check on the times for the bus that will take us back to Aldeanueva del Camino on Monday.

"Why didn't we do that yesterday?" is John's rhetorical comment, when I raise the matter.

The good news is the blisters on our feet are healing well. Gentle tourist walking in Salamanca is not the same as consecutive 40 kilometre stretches along the Camino. A little more sightseeing and some shopping for any small gifts to take back home, are followed by a visit to the university, which is the oldest in Spain. A fascinating couple of hours are spent before we buy some food so we can sit and eat lunch in the square beside the cathedral.

A combination of our sightseeing, walking several miles, the excellent lunch and the warm sunshine mean we return to the hostal for a siesta in the afternoon. It's a hard life being a tourist, just as tiring as being a pilgrim on the Camino. The last two days have been very enjoyable, though. One of Celeste's 'musts' was to eat out at the Casa Casar and so in the evening we treat ourselves to a meal here, sitting at one of the tables that run along the outside of the café. The food is good and plentiful, but in our view is overpriced. We are not used to eating so much and need to take an evening walk after our meal to aid its digestion. This allows us to discover even more fascinating places within the city, including illuminated statues, little squares, musicians and many more tourists who, like us, are soaking up the atmosphere of this wonderful city. We will move to the Hotel Sara tomorrow and on Monday afternoon will catch the bus back to Aldeanueva.

Despite our evening stroll, I still feel full and suffer through the night with indigestion and stomach ache; self-inflicted pain that relegates the feelings of healing blisters to mere discomfort. I resolve to be more frugal in the eating department during our last full day in Salamanca. We check into the Hotel Sara at about ten o'clock. Our new room has a TV that works, a larger bathroom and overlooks the street at the front.

We go out again to soak up more of what Salamanca has to offer and take in the Museum of Modern Arts, a truly remarkable building. The Casa Lis houses art nouveau and art deco pieces and its glassed and dome-shaped art deco roof is simply stunning, particularly when the sun is shining, as it still is, ensuring the beautiful colours of the glasswork are at their best.

We have lunch in the park near the cathedral and indulge in some people-watching in the Plaza Major. There are a couple of wedding parties, a couple of stag parties and several hen parties too. Weekends in Salamanca must be the place for serenading señoritas and marriage proposals. We retire to our 'new' hotel for a welcome siesta.

We buy some small gifts and pay our last visit for the moment to the Plaza Major. On the way back from here and on our way to find a place where we can sit in the early evening sun and enjoy a beer, we bump into the 'Gruppenführer', Marie and Andreas. They have arrived in Salamanca today. After Galisteo they stayed near Capparal; a taxi picked them up and took them to the nearby private albergue—it does exist, then! They then walked to and stayed at Aldeanueva del Camino, Calzada de Bejar and Fuenterroble de Salvatierra. That meant they must have covered about 44km today. Both Andreas and Marie are now back on schedule to get to Santiago within their 'time envelopes'. They join us at our table and we share a beer. Whilst she is inside using the facilities Andreas tells me Marie's pilgrimage, unlike his own, is more spiritual. She lost her father last year after being his main carer for around 18 months and she is seeking to re-establish some connection to faith and some equilibrium and purpose to her life moving forward. He seems proud to be walking with someone who has a 'real' purpose to their journey of self-discovery. He still hasn't worked out why the 'Gruppenführer' is undertaking the Camino, but is glad he is.

Our meeting is like a long-lost family reunion, with hugs and warm greetings and as we go our separate ways we wish them well for the rest of their journey. I wonder whether we will ever catch them up or see them again. Unlikely I think, for having nursed our feet back to better health we need to take care of them going forward. Unlike our French sports journalist we are walking the Camino and are not engaged in a race.

We go off to find our beer in the sun in good spirits though and enjoy pizza and salad before going for the last evening wander in this beautiful city. We find a bar showing a La Liga game and watch the first half before returning to the Hotel Sara. It occurs to me, following the meeting with the 'Gruppenführer', Marie and Andreas once we return to Aldeanueva del Camino, most of the people we have met over the past two weeks will be ahead of us and there will be 'new' pilgrims to encounter in the days ahead. It is with these thoughts in mind I drift off to sleep.

Plate 13
The Cathedral of Santa Maria in Salamanca - Day 18

Plate 14
The stained-glass roof of the Casa Lis – Day 19

Chapter Five

Alduenueva del Camino to Zamora

***

Aldeanueva del Camino to Banos de Montomayor

(10 km or 6 m) continuous but gentle rising Gradient ascended 179 metres

Monday 11th April

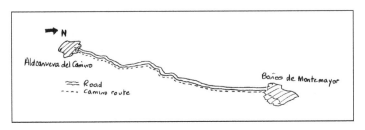

A good night's sleep overall, with the only break being disturbed by the sound of a bed being scraped across the floor in a nearby room. I am up at half-past eight to get a shower and pack. We go off for breakfast and again visit the Plaza Major to sit and enjoy our toast, jam and juice as we watch preparations being made for tomorrow's parade. It is scheduled to do a full circuit of the square before heading towards the cathedral; another sign of how much religion plays a role in the lives of many Spaniards.

Leaving Salamanca is sad, but we are buoyed by the prospect of re-joining the Camino all over again, particularly after our meeting last evening with our three fellow pilgrims, who have all covered the same parts of the Camino during the time I have been here. Whilst we have grown very fond of the beautiful city of Salamanca and its magnificent buildings, friendly atmosphere, parks, squares and vivacity, we will be back this way in a few days. I very much feel alive and at one with myself here.

We head in the direction of the bus station to purchase tickets for our journey back to Aldeanueva del Camino, departing later in the day. This provides an early opportunity to re-test our Spanish and we are proficient enough to successfully complete our mission. Back at the hostal we pack our rucksacks and the bill is settled. The rucksacks are left to be collected later, so we can enjoy more of the delights of Salamanca.

A stroll down to the cathedral and an opportunity to take some pictures is followed by the discovery of a wonderful garden area right next to the albergue and not far from the cathedral. There are views to the south and east and we can survey the route we will be taking as we return to the city in four days. We enjoy sitting in the sun, which is warm when out, but there are also clusters of white clouds around, which make it much cooler when they drift and hide the sun's rays. It is certainly not as warm as the last few days.

We use the time to discuss contingency plans for the remainder of the Camino. Firstly, we agree we should build in some planned rest days between here and Santiago. Options would be Zamora, Puebla de Sanabria and Ourense. We agree to keep the dialogue open.

We sit and have a drink at a café which overlooks the cathedral and whilst there, we observe two pairs of pilgrims pass by. For the first pair—two men—our spot presents an opportunity for them to shake hands and say farewells. One is clearly carrying on through the city, but the other is taking a break to spend more time here - a wise choice. A little while later a second couple —a man and a woman also pass by looking somewhat bewildered by the number of people they must negotiate their way through, as though longing for the solitude of the 'rural Camino' again.

Following in their wake we saunter along to the Plaza Major to sit and eat lunch, having first stopped to purchase it from our favourite 'bakery' in Salamanca. We then visit a small supermarket to buy some fruit and pasties for our lunch. Spending the morning in Salamanca has been a real hardship for us and finally we return to hostal Sara to retrieve our rucksacks and for the last time, make the walk back to the bus station again. We arrive there in plenty of time knowing it is a challenge to work out which stop our bus will come in at. As it transpires our bus is slightly late and by the time it arrives, we have three times enquired from the drivers of other buses which have come into both the scheduled and neighbouring bays about whether they stopped at Aldeanueva del Camino. One of these was an express bus direct to Madrid Airport.

Despite being late our bus makes up time on the journey and we arrive at Aldeanueva at five minutes past four. It takes us about ten minutes to get rucksacks packed and appropriately adjusted, to apply sun cream and get sun hats in place, before we set off along the road that will take us further up into the mountains to Banos. There is still snow on the mountain summits and certainly no doubting its provenance.

It occurs to me as we start walking it will now take us around three and a half days to get back to Salamanca, a journey which the bus we just alighted from took just 90 minutes to complete. Arriving back in Aldeanueva seems to be like yet another homecoming and finally this eagerly anticipated next stage of my journey along the Camino is underway again. The route to Banos de Montomayor is mainly along the road and rises gently and continually for most of the ten kilometres we take to arrive there. In just a couple of places and for only about a kilometre in total, we can get off the tarmac and walk along paths by the side of the road. The mountains provide a splendid vista to look upon as we walk. Around us the broom is in magnificent colour on the hillsides. We come across our first pig, (a wild hog dead on the road-side) and about a further two kilometres beyond him several live pigs in a casa to our right.

A beautiful white horse is being schooled in a small paddock up off the road and the relationship between man and horse is a marvel to behold, as is the graceful flight and circling of the buzzard beyond him. A cuckoo is heard too, closely followed by a second. These familiar sights and sounds of the Camino make me feel so at home. I see, but fail to identify, another bird as it darts into a bush and then shortly re-emerges to skip airily across a field by a hedge.

Banos de Montamayor is a small spa town, which seems to have several café bar and accommodation options. Entering the town, we pass the pretty little church of Santisimo Cristo de la Misericordia, before negotiating several hills up to the right until we find the albergue. This turns out to be pleasant, clean, modern and well appointed. There are three small dormitory bedrooms, with about five or six beds in each. We are both in top bunks but in separate rooms and once more are among peregrinos. Stories of our time on the Camino can be related and shared.

For the first time, there are other pilgrims from the UK—Keith and Susan; they are walking from Seville to Salamanca. They left Sevilla some 17 days ago and will have taken three weeks to get to Salamanca by the time they arrive. They plan to have a couple of days there before heading back to Surrey. They tell us of their experiences of the drastic changes to the weather, which we identify with. They describe themselves as dog walkers not long-distance walkers but have walked the French route to Santiago on two previous occasions. They apparently know Alison Raju, but are strangely unaware of her guide-book. They are using Gerald Kelly's book and are not very complimentary. They have had mixed experiences of Spanish hospitality and of the usefulness of the tourist Information offices.

Their journey to date, like mine, has seen temperatures of 30 degrees in and around Sevilla and cold winds and heavy rain. They have enjoyed walking the last two days in fine warm sunshine. The forecast suggests we should have reasonable weather over the next few days as we head back to Salamanca. There are a Danish couple too at the hostal who are also finishing their walk at Salamanca. They have visited before and are as impressed with it as I am, they are planning to spend four days there before flying back home. I share my knowledge of Denmark, which is based on a working visit to Copenhagen. I did get time to look around and appreciate the beauty of it and I enjoy talking about my experiences with Henrik and Elsa.

Meeting another Danish couple causes me to ponder the whereabouts of Martin and Marian, who I haven't seen for some time. I wonder whether our recuperation time in Salamanca will have given them an opportunity to catch up, or if indeed they are now ahead.

Henrik and Elsa have accommodation booked in Salamanca, but Keith and Susan don't, so we mention our positive experiences of the Hostal Sara, a clean, reasonable, convenient and generally okay place to stay. We also mention the location of the bus station and provide details of the express bus they can get directly to the terminal at Madrid Airport.

A wonderfully hot shower and change follows, plus a little washing, which we can put out to dry in the warm evening sunshine before we go out for something to eat—pizza, as it turns out. The restaurant we find is called Pizza Sandra. I just had to insist we dined there! The pizza turns out to be extremely tasty and freshly homemade, too. It is also not so huge it can't be finished.

We came across several Roman milarios, in various states of intactness along the route today. Where the original milestone was no longer visible, replacements had been erected by 'friends of the Camino'. This is a new feature and I wonder whether it is specific to the area we are now walking in. We also passed the remains of a Roman bridge, where legend suggests a young maiden threw herself to her death to avoid the clutches of a cowboy who was pursuing her—to bed her! A plaque nearby informs the passing pilgrims of the story.

It felt good to be finally walking again, after our recuperation time in Salamanca, and to be with fellow pilgrims. Keith and Susan seemed to have linked up with four other peregrinos and are now more or less walking as a group of six. Erico, from Portugal, seems to be the natural leader. He is walking the whole route and is meeting his fiancée a few days before he is due to arrive in Santiago. They are then planning to continue walking on together to Finisterre to get married. Aah! Romance is alive and well on the Camino.

We return to the albergue and most of our party are already in bed and it is not long before we join them. I am probably asleep by ten but am awoken at two as two of the other pilgrims in the room get up to go to the toilet. I do manage to go back to sleep though and wake again at around six, as other people start to get ready for the day ahead.

Peter Kay

Banos de Montamayor to Fuenterroble de Salvatierra

(30 km or 18 m) rising, steeply at times
Gradient ascended 247 metres

Tuesday 12th April

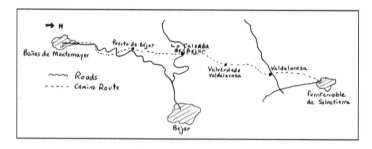

Getting dressed and ready takes a little while, as does packing the rucksack; the routine will, I am sure, get quicker as we get back in the swing of our journey. We have breakfast between seven and half-past and Keith, Susan, Erico and company are off by then. By the time we leave at half-past eight there are just two of the older couples still at the albergue, Henrik, Elsa and a German couple. We spend time discussing our different Camino experiences to date with the Danes and on the off-chance I ask if they have encountered a Polish woman from the UK with a golf trolley.

"Millie," they both chorus.

"But of course," adds Elsa, "she got as far as Zafra with her trolley, having had to make three different stops for running repairs on the way. She eventually realised she could go no further with it."

"I'm not sure if she continued much beyond there, although her plan was to at least get as far as Merida," Henrik informs us.

"I am absolutely astounded she got that far with it," is my response to this amazing piece of news.

"Yes, she is a character," says Elsa, adding, "I don't miss her alarm clock, though."

We laugh and say farewell to the most charming couple we have met on the Camino to date.

It takes a while to find the route again as we head out up the road and then off to the right at a hairpin bend, at which we discover we could have taken a more direct route up through some narrow streets and alleys, as the German couple, who are just arriving there, indicate to us. We now have a steep ascent for about one kilometre and then we flirt again with the N630, before heading down beautiful lanes, along the old Roman road, with plenty of stones from the 'time' to remind you where you are. The route is well signposted from here all the way to Salamanca.

We hear the first cuckoo, see the first buzzard and later our first storks since re-joining the camino. We are in a beautiful valley and can see the motorway on 'stilts' to our right and now behind us the snow-covered peaks. We draw parallel to the peak of Pico de Negro, at 1635m a real mountain and continue our beautiful walk to Calzada de Bejar. Our route now rises steeply again for about one and a half kilometres. The green valley is left behind as the route becomes rockier on this section. Just before arriving at Calzada de Bejar, we are joined on the path by a rather magnificent white horse, which stays about 20m or so behind until we enter the village itself.

On the edge of the village, we pass a rather nice looking albergue and spot one of the couples that were at Banos checking in for the night. We have still quite a distance to walk, but the beauty of our surroundings today makes the long distance seem inconsequential. There are shops in Calzade de Bejar and an opportunity to link up again here with Susan and her five boys. We sit on some chairs outside a little bar, which is unfortunately closed and take off our socks and shoes, unzip and take off our trouser bottoms and take off a top layer, too. Susan and her heroes head off to the sunlit countryside as we continue with our procedures and apply sun cream to newly exposed flesh. In the time it takes to do this the bar opens and we get some water and top up our supplies.

Another eight beautiful kilometres follow as we make our way along the Camino to Valverde de Valdecasa, where we stop for lunch. On this section we hear and spot a warbler, a lizard runs across our path and we reminisce about previous sections of the walk and of similarities this stretch has with some of our favourite sections from last week. We also see a field in which a herd of steel grey cows are lazily munching on the sweet meadow grass. We have our first water crossing of this stretch, negotiated by hopping from one rather unsteady rock to another, with a crude handrail to one side for balance. This is certainly not a handrail any occupational therapist would have signed off as suitable in a hurry. It is also another justification for carrying a stick; balancing is certainly made easier.

The shelter for the Consulto Medico opposite the cross and church in the village provides a seat and a place to hide from the hot sun. I use the opportunity to catch up on writing my notes. We set off again at two and hope to be in Fuenterroble by five at the latest.

As we leave the village, we spot some rocks in a field that look remarkably like pigs and continue to enjoy the scenery and birdsong that keeps us company as we walk. Another steep section follows, this time on the road, for about three and a half kilometres before we arrive in Valdelacasa, almost 1,000m above sea level. Leaving Valdelacasa, we pass up the opportunity to stop at a bar but do stop for a slurp of water before carrying on for a further two kilometres. A quarry can be seen over to our left and ahead. At the junction of tracks, I realise it is important to take the left track, keeping the quarry on our right for about 400m before clearer signage guides us to turn right at a junction. Our route carries on again slowly gaining height, but we now have the quarry on our left.

A final stop of the day is taken at around half-past three for a break and a chance to air feet and socks, have some dried fruit and a drink. The remnants of our blisters are thoroughly padded and protected and there are no new areas of concern. We are about four kilometres from our resting place for the evening. The refugio at Fuenterroble is famous for its Camino welcome, its host the local parish priest, and it is virtually the half-way point of the Via de la Plata. Both Alison and Gerald indicate a stop over here is almost a must for any pilgrim. Maureen was also insistent this should be one of our overnight stops. Carrying on after our short break we arrive at the wonderful Refugio at quarter to five, greeted warmly by Antonio and then

Maria (both volunteers who are helping at the hostel). We will meet Don Blas, the parish priest, later.

There is also a warm welcome from many people, including a number we met with last night. The refugio at Fuenterrable is a 'denotivo', where peregrinos donate an appropriate amount for their stay. According to Gerald, ten euros is acceptable. There is an opportunity to eat a meal together with fellow pilgrims at half-past eight and this opportunity seems to be a splendid way to meet and get to know some of our new group of fellow travellers. We are also promised we will be able to meet with the hostel's patron and benefactor, Padre Don Blas, who is the local parish priest. He will dine with us.

A welcome shower and change are followed by washing and finding space on the crowded criss-crossing of washing lines—already full of fellow pilgrims clothing and towels. There are still a good three hours of drying left in the day, so it is well worth the effort. The lines are attached to several trees that stand sentinel over a little grassy courtyard, one of many interesting features of the grounds of the refugio. Most of the other peregrinos are housed in a rectangular single-storey structure at the back of the hostel. It has space for about eight sets of bunks, a couple of showers and a toilet and washroom area. We have been offered accommodation in the main building, however, up a steep flight of stairs in a room with five beds, which we have to ourselves for the evening.

As well as the grassy courtyard, the grounds of the refugio are full of interesting artefacts and there is even a dedicated room for North American peregrinos, and a garden area. At the entrance to a field, that also belongs to the 'commune', are some wonderfully decorated wooden carts, several bales of hay and an unusual assortment of old farm machinery. There are sheep lower down the field and the whole demeanour of the place and its surroundings portray images that are a cross between a hippy commune and an arts and crafts retreat. It becomes clear over the years that many volunteers have stayed here to assist Father Don Blas. Most have left their marks and helped to create the many facets that make up Casa Parroquial refugio. The insides are more Spartan, basic and utilitarian, but the place clearly functions well and apparently has no shortage of volunteers wanting to stay and help.

It is no wonder the refugio is something of a legend on the Camino and certainly not just because it is almost at the half-way point of the whole route. It was also a great favourite with Spaniards who, in modern times, have spent time and money in regenerating interest in the Via de la Plata as a pilgrim route. One of the leading lights in promoting the route and a former president of the Sevilla 'Amigos' (friends of the Camino) was Jose Luis Salvador and his ashes are apparently buried somewhere in the building. All the volunteers who are present during our brief stay are very helpful and pleasant at all times.

Having freshened up and attended to our laundry we go out and find a nearby bar for a well-earned beer, before returning to dine with our current Camino family. Before visiting the bar, we find a little supermarket to buy some provisions for tomorrow's journey. The bar has low ceilings and a very rustic feel and four elderly Spaniards are propping it up and putting the world to rights. We sit at a nearby table; greetings are exchanged, beers purchased and they return to their conversation. I muse at the incongruity of the disco glitter ball hanging from the ceiling and the large TV in the corner, on which motorcycle racing is showing—a meaningless backdrop to those present. We have a little time to reflect on our day's walk and ponder whether the reason you see more bulls in Spain and more cows in the UK is simply a reflection beef farming is the norm here whilst dairy farming is the norm back home.

Back at the refugio, we retrieve our mostly dry laundry from the now largely empty maze of washing lines. Five of our fellow pilgrims, including Keith and Susan, have opted not to join us for dinner and are already tucked up in bed. There is a large rectangular table laid out for our feast and most of us help to ensure there are enough chairs and cutlery in place for our party. At the meal there are two fellow pilgrims from Austria who live in Salzburg, Enrich and Georgina, Erico from Villereal in Portugal, Stuart from Ontario in Canada, Guivanni from Italy and a younger man, Paul from France. In addition, we are joined by six volunteer helpers and eventually by the Padre himself. Stuart is an interesting guy and we will spend time with him over the next couple of days. Erico will become a member of our Camino family for most of our onward journey. He is the acknowledged leader of a small Camino band that includes Giovanni, Stuart, Keith and Susan.

The banquet consists of soup and bread, lamb on the bone, or to be more accurate (for it has been cooking for so long) lamb 'off' the bone, salad, flan, followed by oranges, with water and wine also available. The wine is a rather rudimentary local red, which most drink, but I stick to the water. We are kept waiting until about nine, before we can start eating as we must await the Padre's arrival and following this his saying of grace before we eat. The soup has been on the table steaming in earthenware bowls for at least five minutes before Father Don Blas arrives and we start to regret not eating out earlier and envying those in our party who have already gone to bed by the time he arrives to kick off our feast. The hubbub of conversation, camaraderie and the sound of hungry peregrinos tucking into what's laid out before us soon diminish such thoughts. The Padre is a lively and convivial character, not that I expected anything less. In conversation with him, we discover amongst the pilgrims who stayed here last night were two German men and a Danish couple, in all probability I surmise, Karl, Hermann, Martin and Marion.

After we have eaten, we help to wash up and eventually retire to our rather chilly dorm and I consider what I might wear to keep warm in bed. I don a pair of lightweight skin-tight long johns and keep a base layer on and in addition pull a blanket over my sleeping bag for extra warmth. I don't sleep well and during the night I discard the long johns, which is not an easy manoeuvre as it is now too hot, and I feel restricted with them on. Eventually, I get some sleep but am awake and up at 14 minutes past six, beating the alarm by 60 seconds and have a wash and use the bathroom. There is no hot water, but this helps in the waking up process.

Fuenterroble de Salvatierra to Morille

(30 km or 18 m) rising, again steeply to the highest point of the Camino and then descending again Gradient ascended 185 metres and then 241 metres of descent

Wednesday 13th April

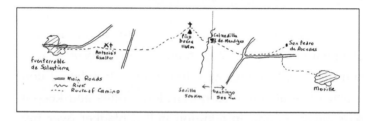

Having freshened up, I set about sorting and repacking my rucksack and getting dressed for the day ahead—a 30 kilometre trek to Morille. Today will see us pass the actual half-way point and ascend and descend from the highest point of the Camino, certainly a day to look forward to!

We have breakfast with Keith, Susan, Bernarde and Jean, from France, all of whom missed last night's banquet with Father Don Blas. Our French couple set off about ten minutes before John and I are ready to depart. It is ten minutes to eight when we are leaving the friendly haven of the hostel and heading for the open road again. After about two kilometres, the road gives way to a long, flat and grassy Camino path and at about 25-past eight we catch and pass Bernarde and Jean. There are vast open spaces on either side of us and we soon hear the first cuckoo and then it is cuckoos and skylarks for company all the way.

We stop at a cross and a shelter devoted to Antonio and this gives John a chance to find cover and deal with a queasy tummy! Our stop allows our French couple to almost catch us again before we continue through an undulating and scrubby wooded area, prior to the vista opening again. We are walking on a high plateau with valleys and mountains beyond and to our right. A straggly line of wind turbines can be seen on the hilltop skyline ahead.

We arrive at a sign after we have been walking for exactly two hours which tells us Fuenterroble is ten kilometres away and behind us—we have certainly maintained a good pace for the first part of today's walk. According to Gerald, we have an option of two routes about 13km beyond Fuenterroble, which split just before the high point of the Camino. Despite me looking out for this and pacing the next three kilometres, we never find it and looking slows our progress somewhat. However, this may be more to do with the terrain climbing steadily and steeply at times. We catch up with and speak to Stuart and then carry on, vowing to have a break at the point where the paths divide. The whirring of the turbines provides an audio backdrop to our climb and is loud enough to drown out any birdsong.

Just below the summit, we think we find the division of the paths and stop to take off our boots, have elevenses and a well-deserved rest. Only later do we discover what looks like a second path merely arcs round and re-joins the main one about 400m further on. As well as the noisy turbines, circling honey buzzards have kept us company for the last two kilometres—at times up so close that you can clearly see their wonderful mottled brown, fawn and dark grey plumage and their wing span, with apparent outstretched fingers, in all its glory.

Stuart passes while we are enjoying our first real stop of the day. Setting off again we are soon at the rocky summit and have time to take in the rather magnificent cross marking the highest point of the Camino. Pico de la Duena stands 1169m above sea level and we have splendid long-distance views in all directions. Despite the cross itself being cordoned off with barbed wire, I can still clamber high enough to enjoy the views.

The Camino route passes below and to the right of the summit rocks and the cross. According to Alison it is now six and a half kilometres to the pig farm, which is the actual half-way point of the Camino. I continue my pacing routine and reckon it is barely five kilometres. Calzadi la de Mendigos is certainly a spectacle. Most of the pigs are lying in somnolent posture. There isn't a blade of grass to be seen in the main enclosure. Passing it, we can see Stuart ahead and think we now have about ten kilometres before arriving in Morille. A stop for lunch at around one o'clock is agreed. A long straight stretch now ensues and ahead, as well as Stuart, we can see Keith and Susan too.

For the next half an hour their presence fills our horizon and allows us to muse on the life stories they have shared with us already. Stuart we know is, like me, walking the whole Camino in one go and is using the experience as a buffer between two major phases of his life—employment and retirement. He has had health issues to contend with over the last few years and views each day on the Camino as fitness readying for the next. He plans to stay for several days in Salamanca and we have shared our knowledge and appreciation of it with him. He has a flight home on the 12th May and has allowed time for a number of rest days throughout this trip, although to date he hasn't used any. Salamanca will be a real recharging of batteries for him. He has felt well supported by Erico at times, however, like many peregrinos, he likes to walk alone at his own pace, although he enjoys the company of others at the end of the day.

Keith and Susan have both been married before and it was their connectivity to a local church where they live in Surrey that brought them together as a couple. They claimed to know Alison—but strangely had not seen or been aware of her guide-book. They were using only Gerald as a guide. They were warm and pleasant in the company of others, however, they clearly each had idiosyncratic ways which at times grated against the harmony of their relationship. Keith liked to walk at a faster pace than Susan and I got the impression at times he was itching to forge on ahead and leave her behind. Susan was a steady walker and had been impressed with her ability to complete some of the daily distances they have achieved on this trek.

They both agreed it was a lot tougher than anything either of them had done before. They were walking as far as Salamanca on this visit and hoped to return next year to complete the Camino. Like Stuart, they were planning to spend a few days recuperating in Salamanca, but in their case it was a return to Surrey that lay beyond. I have also the opportunity to wax lyrical to them about the jewels Salamanca has to offer; including the oldest university in Spain, the two cathedrals built (one inside the other), the House of

Shells, the splendid Plaza Mayor and so much more. I feel sure they will enjoy the city, too.

As if to prove a point about Keith's desire to break free, we see in the distance he suddenly accelerates up the hill, leaving Susan behind. We watch as Stuart catches her up and the two of them exchange words. Stuart then carries on and Susan appears to be searching for something in the grass at the other side of the road. After a short while, she sets off again up the slope. We are about 200m away at this point and suddenly see Keith heading back down the hill at speed. Maybe he has come to assist his beloved up the steepest part of the hill?

However, he walks straight past and continues towards us, scanning the ground as he does so. He is so intent on his searching that, despite waving to him, he hurries straight past us on the other side of the road, completely oblivious to our presence.

At the crown of the hill is a bend to the left and some trees where there are bushes and rocks, which represent a reasonable place to stop for lunch, particularly as it just turned one o'clock. I quickly abandon the first rock I sit down on due to several rather large ants crawling around my feet and up and over the rock. A second and more suitable rock is found and a leisurely lunch of cheese and biscuits, pepperoni and a banana are enjoyed. Whilst we are lunching, Keith begins walking more slowly up the hill this time. He sees us and waves. His demeanour suggests he has not found whatever he was looking for, though.

We depart our lunch stop after about half an hour and calculate we should be in Morille by around half-past four. This morning we started out at around 950m above sea level, dropping down before beginning our steady and at times steep climb up to Pico Duena the highest point of the Camino at 1169m. We then descended again to arrive at the Arroya Mendigos, just before the pig farm.

Our route now takes us on or alongside a road in an open stretch of upland. The breeze gets up, blowing from our right in the east or in our faces from the north. A spot is now found where the Camino divides with the left-hand fork going to San Pedro de Rocades—a number of our overnight party are headed there. The right-hand fork, however, is our route as it leads to Morille where we will stay tonight.

We arrive there at half-past four as predicted and find the albergue. Just before it, there is a community centre and in front an interesting metal sculptured figure of a woman seems to be welcoming us to the village. Just past the albergue is the bar from which we can get the key to the albergue, which has one room containing three sets of bunk beds with a separate shower and toilet to one side. There is a small space to hang out clothes in an alley between the back of the bar and the entrance to the accommodation. Already in the albergue is a Portuguese peregrino, Jose, as well as Keith and Susan. The rest of their gang have decided to stay at San Pedro.

The tableau of events we witnessed with Keith and Susan now becomes clear. After a bit of a tiff, Keith had flung his phone away and then subsequently been unable to find it. He had then walked on in a pique. Susan subsequently retrieved the phone but had not let on to this fact when they passed each other on the hill and it was only when an apologetic Keith re-joined her later in the walk (having searched in vain), that he and his phone were reunited. All was calm and well again now between them, but one wondered whether Susan would always tolerate Keith's acts of childish petulance?

We take it in turns to shower—surprisingly hot and refreshing despite the small cubicle and the spartan nature of the facilities. The opportunity is taken to undertake some more laundry and socks—underwear and towels are hung out to dry on the line outside. The sun is as hot now as it has been since we returned to the Camino on Monday.

A little stroll in the warm sun reveals there is no other hostelry than El Bar de Isa in Morille and so we return there to have a drink. We sit with Jose, who doesn't speak any English and, despite him being Portuguese, his Spanish is only a little better than ours. Keith and Susan are having a lie down before dining. We have arranged to all meet and dine in the bar later. They will be in Salamanca tomorrow and are looking forward to that. We may have even talked Stuart into spending a second day there! He is recognising at his current rate of progress he will be in Santiago with over a week to spare before he flies home from Porto to Canada.

A second small beer soon follows, and I buy a beer for Jose too. We have a conversation in pigeon Spanish. Two drinks soon turn into three and its only seven o'clock—a good job they are only one third pint measures! During beer number four, I receive a phone call in response to a text, which confirms I am going to be a grandfather again—my daughter has been for her 12-week scan. All is well and I have a short conversation with my five-year-old granddaughter, Bella, who is very excited about the prospect of having a baby brother or sister. I am struck with the importance family plays in one's life and how whilst walking the Camino as a peregrino, one creates a transient but close family of fellow pilgrims.

Bella was the first grandchild to be born. As well as Maureen now having a grandson, John now has six grandchildren. This gives us yet another topic of conversation to share. It is strange how the developmental milestones of grandchildren seem to be acutely observed, whilst similar milestones of one's children become more subsumed within the processes of parenthood and work.

Our meal in the bar is good—soup with noodles and bread and a slice of festival pie to start with—followed by entrecote steak and chips, finished off with flan and cream. The whole meal is accompanied with some very drinkable local wine. More information is shared between Keith, Susan and ourselves, including my email address and a promise to keep in touch.

Back in our accommodation, washing having been gathered in, evening ablutions are undertaken and I am soon asleep. I sleep well until a more fitful period prior to the alarm going off at half-past six. By seven o'clock everybody is up and about, although Susan is going to delay her departure, she says, to "let Erico and the boys catch up". Their plan is for Keith to go on ahead and await the group's arrival in Salamanca. It is John's 67th birthday today and I plan to take him out for lunch in Salamanca to recognise the occasion. We have options of either staying there and then having two 30+ kilometre walks on the following two days, or of walking 33 kilometres today with the promise of a shorter day's walk tomorrow. Can we pass up the opportunity of spending more time in Salamanca?

Morille to Salamanca

(18 km or 11 m) mainly gently downhill
Gradient descended 92 metres

Thursday 14th April

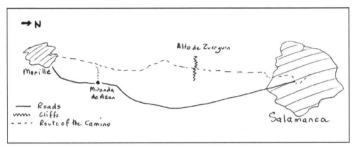

Setting off at half-past seven it is still a little chilly, but we are both in shorts and prepared for another warm day. Jose departed 15 minutes before us and our brief acquaintance with him is at an end—as our paths don't cross again for the remainder of our walk. Both Keith and Susan are still at the albergue as we leave, and we say our farewells to them both, too. Our route takes us north out of the village of Morille and then once more into open country. A field of solar panels adorns a field on our right and for me is reminiscent of leaving Almaden de la Plata on the third day of the first stage of my journey along the Camino with Maureen. That seems a very long time ago.

The sky wears a red-pink tinge to the east and to our right, as we walk out into a vast open plain that stretches before us. The sunrise that follows is quite magnificent, but we lose it for a while as we drop down and go through a wooded area, where the temperature seems to reflect how it is still awaiting the impact of the rising sun. We start to gently climb and before long we are finally reunited with a now fully risen sun. Arriving at a farm, two horses suddenly appear, and trot nonchalantly forward to greet us. It is as if they wish to exchange comments with us on the majesty of the dawning of another warm day.

Making our way through the farm, I spot a huge grey dog sitting languidly in a small paddock to our right. He seems to sense we are no danger to the livestock he is guarding. He doesn't bark or move towards us, despite being un-tethered, but seemingly studies us with his big dark eyes. It is a pity all Spanish guard dogs can't so easily assess we are not a threat and watchfulness doesn't have to be appended with hostile barking and often aggressive manoeuvrings.

Once the farm is behind us we are once more in rolling country and the first cuckoo of the morning emphasises this to us. Following a left turn and a short climb we get a first glimpse of Salamanca nestling on the horizon.

It remains within view and gets ever closer for the rest of the morning. We deviate off the Camino into Miranda de Azan, looking for a bar in which to get breakfast, but nowhere is open until ten. As it is only 25-past nine, we stop but make do with a feast of yoghurt-coated raisins and a pepperoni stick from our dwindling provisions stash, using the opportunity to take our boots off, before setting off again at quarter to ten to reconnect to the Camino.

As we get to the junction, we spot Keith and Susan approaching about 100m away and allow them to catch up. We exchange warm greetings once more and take pictures, before they head down to Miranda de Azar, where very soon the bar will be open, and they will be able to enjoy their last Spanish Camino breakfast. Are we envious? Concerning the breakfast yes, but about it being their last one before returning to the UK, definitely not!

Heading on, our route meanders for a while and the sun is lost behind a stubborn cloud that seems to wilfully prevent its escape for a good while. Crossing a road, we climb up to and then on to the cliffs at Alto de Zuergurn. It was here on the 22nd July 1812, where Wellington met General Pakenham to give him the order to advance towards Miranda de Azan. This order led to the battle of Los Arapiles as the Spaniards know it, or the battle of Salamanca as it is known to historians in the UK. On that day the Anglo-Portuguese army under Wellington's command defeated the French infantry—their biggest defeat in battle since 1798.

The battle occurred during what was known as the Peninsula War. A Spanish division was present but took no part in the battle, as they were positioned to block French escape routes. Around 11,000 soldiers died or were wounded in the battle, the majority (6,000) on the French side and 7,000 French troops were captured. As a consequence, Wellington's army was able to advance to and liberate Madrid and the French were forced to abandon Andalusia permanently. I'm not sure whether the bar in Miranda de Azan was open for breakfast or not that morning!

From here nothing further will obscure our view of Salamanca, rising as it does out of the landscape and filling the horizon ahead. The last five kilometres of approach though is across open, scrubby ground and even when we finally reach habitation. It continues to be rather dull, although the looming towers of the cathedral are never far from view and drawing ever closer, giving rise to an increase of adrenaline as once more the magnificent city of Salamanca awaits our arrival.

Finally, we emerge on to tarmac again and are soon crossing the Roman bridge we had looked down on a few days ago. Across the bridge we climb up to and alongside Salamanca's wonderful twin cathedrals once more and find a seat on which to sit and take stock.

After a brief discussion, it is agreed we should end our day's walk here and once more sample Salamanca's delights, even if this now means two longer days of walking ahead. We determine we can rest a little this afternoon as well as enjoying the variety of opportunities the city offers us. Had we gone on we would have arrived at a small village, with little to offer by comparison in the way of cultural diversity. Appropriate justification or not at the time, with hindsight I don't think there was ever any doubt given the choice, staying in Salamanca again would have always come out on top. This debate about location and surroundings is one that seems to be increasingly resonating in my head in relation to where we should live going forward and I wonder where Sandra's thoughts are on the issue of, 'should we stay, or should we go?'

Another night at Hostal Sara is negotiated, this time we have a different room at the back, rather than overlooking the street. There is no balcony either, but it is ten euros per person cheaper and still very comfortable. A hot shower is enjoyed followed by a change into 'going out' clothes, to find a suitable lunch place to celebrate John's birthday. It is two o'clock and his preference is to eat a 'proper' meal now and maybe have a lighter snack in the evening. This will also mean we are not eating too late in the evening and then going to bed on a full stomach, as we will need to be up for an early start in the morning.

After a little exploration a restaurant that looks like it has reasonable options is located just across from and behind our hotel. It is an excellent place and we enjoy the main course of lamb cutlets, chips and asparagus, followed by an elegant fruit cocktail for John and a flan for me. The latter is a better offering than last night, but still not as good as the flan I had at the Bar Immigrantes in Galisteo.

Walking through Salamanca again provides a sense of comfort, wellbeing and peacefulness, as though the two of us have been joined by a close third friend too! The Plaza Major is again a bustling scene, through which most people within the city seem drawn to pass through at some point as they go about their business. Just as we are leaving the square, who should we encounter but our German peregrinos, Karl and Hermann. They had arrived in Salamanca yesterday and decided to have a rest day today. Another opportunity to catch up on our respective journeys, which had not coincided since our beer together in Carceres.

They had stayed in Casa de Caceres and Grimaldi in addition to our overnight stops, so had been a day ahead of us when we returned to the Camino four days ago. Huge Anglo-Germanic bear-hugs are exchanged and we bid them farewell. They confirm it was indeed they and Martin and Marion who stayed in Fuenterroble the night before we did. Martin and Marion were also planning to be in Salamanca by today, Hermann wasn't sure whether they were staying one or two nights here though. As we go our separate ways again it is four o'clock, and an afternoon siesta is agreed upon and subsequently enjoyed.

Returning to the streets of Salamanca, socks are donned under sandals, partly to protect our feet and because there is a cooler feel to the evening, maybe a portent of a change in the weather? We have set ourselves five tasks to complete during our evening stroll.

Provisions are purchased for tomorrow's trek. Secondly, the route for our departure from Salamanca is also researched and found. Our third task is to identify somewhere that would be open from seven in the morning where we might purchase breakfast; in this task we fail, but are sure something will turn up tomorrow. We also identify where in the city we should get our pilgrim's passports stamped, albeit we later get these stamped at Hostal Sara. Finally, we source somewhere to have a snack and a beer and then return to our Hostal to leave our provisions there, before venturing out again.

We bump into Stuart again and find out after a bit of searching, that he has found somewhere comfortable where he can stay for 20 euros per night. He seems tired and a little weary today. He also informs us all of Erico's group were feeling it after yesterday's walk. He wasn't sure what happened to Keith and Susan and so we were able to reassure him. He isn't convinced they will still be together next year when they plan to return to complete the Camino. The incident we witnessed yesterday wasn't the only time Keith left his 'beloved' behind. He did this on the approach to Merida and it led to the pair of them having a heated exchange in the middle of the Roman bridge.

We find a lovely little square off the Plaza Major where we enjoy a couple of hours with two small beers and two tapas followed by coffee. The bar is showing a reprise of last night's Atletico Madrid versus Barcelona quarter-final second leg tie, which Atletico won to progress to the semi-final. Whilst we are sipping our beers, I spot Inieste crossing one end of the square and dash off to catch her and she returns to join us for a drink. I introduce her to John, and we talk about Karl and Hermann, who informed us she was in Caceres at the same time we were. She is still comfortable with socialising at the end of each day's walk but prefers to walk alone during the day.

Whilst John is ordering drinks from the bar, I ask her whether she has found some comfort or at least some self-forgiveness since our last meeting in Zafra. She smiles and tells me she has come to an accommodation with herself but is still keen to visit the town near Barcelona where he lived with her mother. I fully understand and tell her my first memory in life is of getting onto a cream and red trolley bus in a city centre. When I had spoken to my mother about this memory, she told me this was in Newcastle, where my biological father lived. She told me I would have been about 18 months at the time. My mother worked in the Civil Service in Newcastle where she had met him. She had also made other friends in the area and was visiting them with me when the trolley bus journey took place. She smiles at my story, but as John returns with our beers we move on to other matters of mutual interest.

She was as surprised as I was Millie had made it to Zafra with her golf trolley and not surprised she had carried on from there without it. It is good to catch up again and maybe our paths will cross again over the coming days. Returning to Hostal Sara it is time to pack, ready for an early start in the morning, before retiring to bed.

Peter Kay

Salamanca to El Cubo de Tierra del Vino

(34 km or 20.5 m) gently undulating
Gradient climbed 38 metres

Friday 15th April

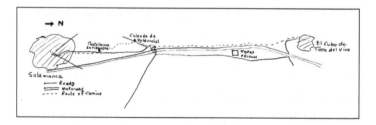

We are up at quarter-past six and ready and out by seven. We eat some apricots, small cakes and have a drink of water to keep us going until we can find a proper breakfast stop. It should certainly keep us going for a couple of hours. A false start ensues as it is raining outside, and we return indoors to don waterproofs and pull rain-covers over the rucksacks before leaving the hostal at last. We meet a fellow pilgrim; this later turns out to be Bernhard, who is also leaving the hostal at the same time. Following the directions on the map provided by the tourist office we sourced yesterday, our footsteps of last evening are retraced. It is still dark as well as wet. We stop for a coffee on the outskirts of Salamanca but they haven't started serving breakfast yet and so we leave and carry on in heavier rain. We have the N630 for company for five kilometres until we arrive at the first village beyond Salamanca, Aldeaseca de la Armunia.

With the rain coming down in stair-rods, at this point walking is just a matter of putting one foot in front of the other and propelling ourselves forward. We are wet and silently lost in our thoughts. We meet and pass Erico and Giovanni under a bridge, readjusting their gear to maximise protection from the elements. The rest of his 'group' have all stayed over in Salamanca. On entering the village, we cross the main road and then skirt the church before leaving the road altogether and returning to Camino tracks again. Soon afterwards Alison's directions are again disrupted by the presence of the new motorway, but the arrows are reasonably clear, and we are soon heading on a track under the motorway and then carry on across at first flat and then gently rolling terrain, before the route flattens out once more before it reaches our second village of the day. Just before getting there, I spot an animal darting across the Camino and judging by its size and the way it moves I believe it to be the first hare we have seen on this leg of our journey.

In Castellanos de Villiquera, according to Alison, there are two bars and a shop. After searching in vain we meet a resident who informs us the last of these two bars closed two weeks ago! There is a shop where we buy some bananas. The rain has eased by this point and we find a bench to sit on and take off our boots to let hot and steaming feet cool down. A banana and a madeleine cake and a drink of water are taken on board as fuel for the next leg before our lunch stop. We still have around 20km before we reach tonight's' resting place at 'El Cubo'. Whilst in Castellanoes we meet Giovanni who was walking with Erico earlier, but no sign of Erico himself. Giovanni is a jovial giant of a man, who tells us he is feeling so blessed to be walking on the Camino.

He has suffered two heart attacks during the last three years, the last one some 11 months ago. He had sworn to God if he survived the second one he would make a pilgrimage of thanks. He had undertaken a little research and the Via de la Plata seemed to fit the bill for him. He was very apprehensive about walking such a distance, but since his chance meeting with Erico, has grown in confidence. Like Stuart, he views each day's walk as training for the next. He likes the solitude of walking alone but enjoys the camaraderie of meeting other pilgrims at the end of each day.

A stretch of three and a half kilometres now follows to the village of Calzada de Valdunciel, where we had originally planned to stay last night. The last two kilometres is walked in heavy rain again. As we suspected, the village does not have a lot to offer and would have taken another four hours walking from Salamanca to get here. It does, however, have a church with a large porch area and we seek shelter here to let the worst of the rain pass. The church of Santa Ellena certainly provides good refuge for pilgrims in wet weather. It also has an altar which is apparently dedicated to Santiago pilgrims.

Giovanni catches up. He is very tired and weary and is going to stay here tonight. He believes Erico, like us is going on to El Cubo de Tierra del Vino. It seems like within the space of 24 hours Erico's 'band' has completely disintegrated and he is now walking on his own. We watch as what we think is a female peregrino goes past wrapped up in her cape to protect her and her rucksack from the rain—it is only her gait that gives her gender away. After about 15 minutes in the porch the rain eases a little and we find a nearby bar in which to enjoy some hot coffee and toast!

It is noon when we leave the comfort and warmth of the bar and we still have about 20km or four and a half hours walking to do. It is still raining and carries on for a while, even getting heavier again, before slackening to be replaced by genuinely light rain. About three and a half kilometres beyond Calzada de Valdunciel, we arrive at a further point where the presence of the motorway has again changed the Camino route and spend a little while walking along the N630 again, before we are diverted back on ourselves to swing underneath the motorway and continue along an undulating track which runs parallel with the motorway for what turns out to be 13km. It is the most boring and uninteresting stretch of the Camino thus far. We stop for a foot rest and have some water and a madeleine and then after a further four kilometres, almost an hour, stop again for lunch.

The rain stops around half-past one and it is threatening to brighten up. This improves our spirits and following our lunch we have a new spring in our step as we continue our march alongside the motorway, now looking out for and eventually spotting the watchtower of the high security Topas Prison, which is on the other side of the motorway. The weather is improving all the time now and we eventually leave our parallel route to join a disused road, which may have been the road route prior to the motorway's arrival. This eventually joins a junction where our destination for the night, 'El Cubo' is signposted as one and a half kilometres ahead.

We arrive in the village in bright sunshine. There are two albergue's, both opened about three years ago. We check them both out before deciding on the first one. As we are approaching, we see two women coming away from it, minus rucksacks. We assume therefore we will not be the only peregrinos staying at albergue Torre de Sabre tonight. Greetings are exchanged and we ring the bell and meet the lady of the house, who speaks only Spanish, but we manage to get by. She provides us with a refreshing glass of water and shows us to our room, which has two single and two bunk beds. Beds are yet to be claimed so we bag a single one each. A small tour of the house and grounds follows as we are shown the bathroom and where to wash and peg out clothes.

John goes off for a shower and I prioritise getting some washing done to maximise what drying time is left in the day. I then catch up on my daily notes, before John emerges refreshed and rejuvenated. Our hostess confirms there are indeed two señoras staying as well as ourselves and the accommodation has been open for three years. The only miscommunication seems to be after checking my passport, she puts me down as Irish. Breakfast can be taken at seven in the morning and so we should be able to leave by half-past seven. The room cost is 12 euros and it is a further three euros for breakfast. We talk to her about where we might get a meal tonight and the local bar. It isn't clear from the response whether we will get a meal there or not.

It is now my turn to enjoy a refreshing shower and ponder on the day's walk. It was late morning before we heard the first cuckoo today and whilst we did see a hawk, some crows and of course the hare, there were no buzzards and no storks. I wonder whether the female figure in the poncho was Inieste and why the thought didn't occur to me at the time! I think about the conversation with Giovanni and my health scare and reflect it was self-determination and a very supportive family, not God, that called me to the Camino. I dry myself and after getting dressed re-join John and we meet the two señoras, who are in the next dorm to us. They are not English and appear a little shy.

Exploring 'El Cubo' we find the shop, by asking a local, and obtain water and top up our food supplies. The village takes its name from the area immediately to the south of it being rich in vines, whereas beyond it to the North, the fields are mainly given over to growing corn. We have now moved beyond the province of Salamanca to the Province of Zamora. Indeed, tomorrow we will have around 30km to walk to get to the principal city of Zamora. It would certainly be good to get there early enough to enjoy what the city has to offer.

Back at Albergue Torre de Sabre we discover the two señoras are both Spanish, but they do not speak any English at all so our conversation is limited. It seems however they are eating here this evening and we revisit the conversation we had with our hostess about dining this evening and wonder whether that was what she was trying to explain. If a meal arrives for us all well and good. If not, we will adjourn to the local bar for about half-past eight. The girls are not staying for breakfast as they want to get an early start to get to Zamora. They are retiring to bed soon after eight as we are setting out to the bar. "Buenos nochas, señoras" is the last exchange we will have with them.

An interesting experience follows at the bar as again there is no English spoken or understood, so we negotiate what we want entirely in Spanish and by consulting the handwritten menu options and our English/Spanish phrase book. I fair very well and have a wonderful lentil soup, followed by a passable meat dish in a tomato sauce with mushrooms. John unfortunately ends up with a limp salad, followed by chips and a lot of tasteless and rather bland meat croquettes. We do have pleasant wine to help it go down and are back at the albergue by quarter-past nine and in bed by half-past.

There is a little heater in the room and as we had switched this on before we went out, the room was warm on our return and some of the washing placed strategically around it was dry. The remainder of our laundry is arranged over the end of one of the bunk beds in the hope this too will be dry by morning. This turns out to be pretty much the case with only two items needing further airing.

El Cubo de Tierra del Vino to Zamora

(29 km or 17.5 m) gently descending
Gradient descended 188 metres

Saturday 16th April

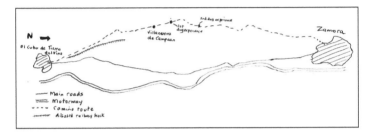

Up as planned at ten to seven. I check outside. It's dark and dry but chilly. Breakfast is toast and jam, madeleine cakes, water and very strong coffee. Two more slices of toast arrive as we are finishing the coffee and we decide to wrap these in serviettes for later. After cleaning our teeth and finishing packing, we are ready to set off as planned. During breakfast however, it has started raining again and like yesterday we must adjust our attire before we set off. This means it is nearer to quarter to eight by the time we get going. We are informed by our hostess the two señoras left about an hour earlier. As we leave the village, we spot four peregrinos, who must have stayed at the other albergue, and after a further two kilometres, we pass them. Greetings are exchanged; neither Erico or Inieste however are part of the group. We then have a rather pleasant walk in the rolling countryside alongside a disused railway track. I spot another and what turns out to be one of several hares seen during the day's walk and it isn't long before we hear the familiar and reassuring sound of our first cuckoo.

The rain is light and doesn't stay with us too long, but there is a cool breeze. The walking, however, is much pleasanter than yesterday. At about the same time I spot the second hare of the day a hen harrier is seen over to our right. Our route takes us up to a fine wooded area where there are Java plants and broom in plentiful supply. As we descend from our lofty little paradise with the main village of today's walk on the horizon, the underfoot conditions return to cloying mud again. Reasonable time has been made during our morning walk, with five kilometres per hour for the first two hours and a further two kilometres in the following half an hour. All of this means we arrive in the village of Villanueva de Campean at quarter-past ten, having covered 14km already. We can't find anywhere in the village to sit and have a boots-off pit stop, except some steps in the small porch of a building that could be a social centre, former bar or even a very plain church.

The opportunity to get out of the cool breeze and to take our boots and socks off is very welcome, with a little to eat from our stash and a drink of water. A short way from our resting place the first of what will become an increasing number of commemorative plaques about the Camino is spotted. According to Alison we will, and indeed do, see more of these whilst in the Province of Zamora.

Leaving the village, the route takes us out into open fields again as we enter a rolling terrain. A pair of goldcrests are spotted frolicking in a hedge, their bright and distinctive plumage and their flirty flight patterns easily giving away their identity. We now have pleasant walking again, although at times cloying mud hampers our progress. At the approach to a farm in open country, a dog (it turns out to be two) barks to let us know he is around. As we approach, he heads straight for us, snarling as he does so—his teeth bared and his saliva hanging off them and leaving almost a visible trail as he leaps into the air, hurling his huge frame in the general direction of our throats. His leap, however, is halted in mid-air as the leash he is on doesn't quite stretch to the middle of the path. Hearts beating faster, we leave the farm behind us with the sound of angry and frustrated barking ringing in our ears.

This is our second dog encounter of the day. Earlier and again whilst we were passing a farmstead a barking dog, not tethered in this case, snapped at our heels for the whole time it took us to get beyond. He was belatedly called to heel by his owner, who doesn't welcome peregrinos crossing his land, despite the Camino passing through. We had certainly quickened our pace and I used my walking pole to hit the ground behind me frantically as we sought to escape from the aggressive hound. Interestingly, the footprints of the two señoras we had seen at times up until this point disappeared after this farm and we surmised the dog may have eaten them for breakfast. However, about a kilometre beyond the farm the imprints of their boots return, and we can stop considering such thoughts. Maybe it had more to do with the slightly firmer ground between the farm and the resumption of their footprints.

After these two incidents it takes a while for our heartbeats to return to normal and a further half a kilometre beyond the resumption of the footprints, we stop at a right fork in the Camino for a lunch stop. It is ten to one and two hours and five minutes since our last stop. I am hungry and devour some cheese and bread (saved from Salamanca), a banana and two little cakes. Boots and socks are removed whilst debating with John whether a threatening black cloud is heading in our direction or not. Five minutes later it is, and it starts raining. Hurriedly, things are packed away, socks and boots restored to aching feet and anoraks put on as the rain whips hard into us at our luncheon stop. Ironically five minutes later, and just to be perverse, it stops as quickly as it has started, and it doesn't return for the rest of the day's walk to Zamora. However, it remains overcast, grey and cooler, so we remain as we are, prepared for the elements, for the rest of the day, too.

Larks and finches featured on today's walk as does a second hen harrier, soaring on the thermals just before we arrive in the city of Zamora. There are storks along the river bank as we approach. Their presence is a welcome reappearance of wildlife creatures that have played such a part of our Camino experience. As we reach the city, we cross the pedestrian Puerta de Piedra bridge across the Rio Duero and follow the signs for the Camino which climbs into the old part of the city past the albergue.

We decide to find a hostal this evening to enjoy a little bit of extra luxury. The Tourist Information office we locate is closed until half-past four. It is by this point quarter to three and after consulting the map we have of Zamora, obtained earlier in Salamanca, we head for the location of two-star hostals and find there are several in the same street about half a kilometre away on the north side of the old city. The old part of Zamora looks as interesting in many ways as

Salamanca, but maybe not on such a grand scale. The temperature gauge outside the formaccia informs us it is only 16 degrees though and the chilly breeze makes it seem even less.

Following the map takes us straight to the street with the hostals we had identified and the first one we try, Hostal Chiqui, only has one remaining room with two beds and as a bonus a young female receptionist who speaks very good English and is both very obliging and helpful. The room is 40 euros, 20 each, which is fine and the shower which follows is lovely, hot and mightily refreshing.

Our hostess informs us in response to our question we can book a hotel for two nights in Puebla de Sanabria and offers to help us to book in advance via her laptop if this would be helpful. John has been worrying about confirming rest day arrangements and given the positive progress we have made over the past few days, we have agreed to stay the one night here, on the proviso we do have a rest day in Puebla de Sanabria, so we gratefully accept her offer. She takes our payments for the room and pilgrim passports to stamp and once we are showered and changed these are returned to us. It is about half-past four by the time we have attended to all our chores and are ready to go out.

Three hours of sightseeing and perhaps a meal is now on the cards. However, before we go out Sara, our very obliging hostess, books two night's accommodation for us in the Hostal Carlos V in Puebla de Sanabria for Thursday 21st and Friday 22nd April. This will give us another five days walking from here before we can enjoy the rest day we have promised ourselves. We also discuss and agree to have an extra day in Ourense, too. With one of John's biggest anxieties resolved we can go and enjoy the rest of our time in Zamora. It will be good to have more time to look around the historic city of Puebla de Sanabria. John has already had texts from our friend, Steve in Carceres to tell us it is worth seeing and promising details of an excellent restaurant to have dinner at whilst we are there.

Sara, our helpful hostess, also gives us recommendations about where to eat in Zamora too. It is time to go out and have a wander. It is still chilly, and we are a little tired, so it is important not to get too carried away in our sightseeing and we restrict our meanderings. An extremely enjoyable cake and a cup of tea in a café near the Plaza Major is very welcome. We are so impressed with the food we purchase bocadillos for our lunch tomorrow whilst there. We then retrace our steps to the Tourist Information Office, where a helpful young man provides a map of Puebla de Sanabria and gives us directions to find our hotel there. Zamora is a very friendly place.

Approaching it from the south you can see the rocky hill the original settlement was built on and the castle still stands impressively woven into the fabric of the cliffs. The city has expanded over time, but within the older parts is full of many Romanesque style churches, which date from the 12th and 13th centuries. It is said to have more examples of such churches than any other city in Europe. As a strategic fortified settlement, it unsurprisingly has a history of battles and fierce fighting either to capture it or to defend itself. None more so than in the 15th century conflict and battle for the control of the city that took place between the supporters of Isabella and those of Juno la Betraneja. Because of the fierce and prolonged fighting that raged for many months, there is now a Spanish proverb which means—'Zamora wasn't won in an hour'; equivalent to the British proverb, 'Rome wasn't built in a day'. Just beyond the Tourist Information Office, a beautiful square has within it on all sides architecturally entwined plátanos falsos trees that are currently bare and austere, but I am sure in summer will provide wonderful colour. A short walk beyond is the Plaza Major in one corner of which stands the cathedral, again dating back to the 12th century and remarkable for the fact it only took 23 years to build.

We find the tapas bar Sara had given us details of and sample the skewers of meat she recommended and a very smooth red wine. Today is far too cold for beer. Another wander enables us to locate and purchase some more Compeed blister prevention salve. We have been applying this to our feet at each two-hourly foot-stop since leaving Salmanca the first time and so far, it has worked well. Another bar and another tapas and glass of wine are consumed before we head back to Hostal Chiqui. It is still chilly out and we hope for a warmer day tomorrow. Texts are sent back to our partners in the UK to say all is well. The weather forecast suggests two cooler days with the possibility of some rain, before we should have three warmer days before getting to Puebla de Sanabria—we will see!

We never caught up to or saw any more of the two Spanish señoras, but later discover both Erico and Bernhard, (the peregrino we saw leaving Hostal Sara in Salamanca) had encountered them and declared them to be 'speed-merchants'. I don't think they would have moved any faster than we did through the two farmsteads with the dogs, though! Reflecting on today I have decided whilst Salamanca is the beautiful city, Zamora can certainly lay claim to the title of the friendly city. My thoughts drift back home to Sandra and I know I want to return to Spain to share with her

the delights of Salamanca and maybe we could spend a
little more time here in Zamora, too.

Plate 15
Followed by a white horse – Day 21

Plate 16
The summit of Pico de la Duena – Day 22

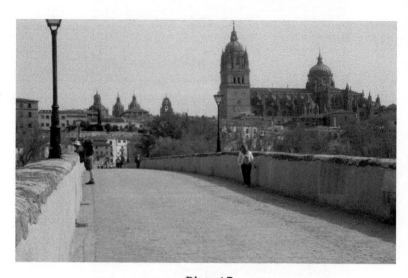

Plate 17
Crossing the Roman bridge back into Salamanca – Day 23

Plate 18
Commemorative plaque on a wall near Zamora – Day 25

Chapter Six

Zamora to Puebla de Sanabria

***

Zamora to Riego del Camino
(34 km or 20.5 m) a day of gentle ups and downs
Gradient descended 23 metres

Sunday 17th April

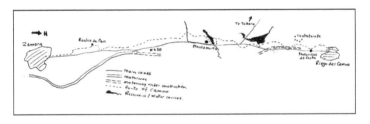

We are up and out of our hotel by half-past seven and the directions provided by our hostess to find the Camino route from Zamora prove extremely helpful. Whilst we are negotiating these, a cycling peregrino— a young woman in her early 20's, possibly Japanese— approaches us from the opposite direction, looking lost and bemused. I ask if she is searching for the Camino route and she is happy to join us as we continue, following the directions we have been given until we once more find the familiar yellow arrows to guide us. Her relief is clear, and she thanks us both, mounts her cycle and slowly ascends the road that winds up and out of the city, along which we will soon find open country again.

We are at a small square and we have small café bars on two sides and stop for breakfast at the one to our right, which proves to be a splendid choice. A wonderful toasted bun and jams, fresh orange juice and coffee are truly enjoyed and will certainly set us up for the morning walk. Too often in Spain, the toast is rather dry and tasteless and often cold. The buns were fresh, flavoursome and still warm. The toasting did nothing to take away from this experience. This is one of the best breakfasts to date.

On our way again before eight, we are soon caught by another young woman, also Japanese, who is walking the Camino on her own. She is wearing trainers and has a very lightweight and small rucksack that makes even my 20-litre sack look big. Our tracks will remain connected for the next 20km as we head northwards on our journey to Riego del Camino. The terrain is at first rather scrubby and only on the descent into Roales de Pan after six kilometres does it improve. In the village, it is once more the church that provides an opportunity for a rest. We sit on a form outside and take off our boots and socks to apply more Compeed foot balm to any tender areas.

Near to our resting place is a small shop and I put on my boots before meandering across to buy some bananas. There are a group of around six peregrinos gathered near the shop—five men and one woman, all 60 plus in age. From snatches of conversation I overhear, I determine they are from France and I exchange greetings in French as I return with the bananas to John. A couple of minutes later they are on their way and snake past with the one at the rear still trying to get his rucksack properly in place. They seem to be carrying much more than we are.

Our Japanese 'amigo' has caught up again and sitting on the next bench, taking a sip of water as I re-join John. I take off my boots and socks again just to provide some fresh air to them and watch as the young Japanese woman takes off her walking trainers to air her feet, too. Apart from a swaddling bandage tightly bound round each foot, she is wearing no socks. Her feet are pale and wan in the greyish morning light. Her backpack looks even smaller once she has removed it, but apart from the airing of the feet and the sip of water, her deliberations are rather brief compared to ours and, despite arriving some ten minutes after we did, we are only putting our socks and boots back on when she departs. We remain between 100 and 200m behind her for the next 14km.

As we leave Roales de Pan, our route opens again and there is little, if any, shade. It is still cool, though and neither of us has yet felt the need to shed any clothes. We are both wearing a base layer, walking shirt and our cagoules, as much for protection from the wind rather than as a waterproof, (although at times during the day it threatens rain, we don't see any at all during our long days walk along the Camino).

About six kilometres out of Roales de Pan there is a junction of tracks and our group of French peregrinos are resting here, taking a break from the biting wind as we pass. We and the young Japanese woman carry on and the route is clearly visible for quite a distance ahead. A fellow pilgrim seems to be walking about 400m ahead of the Japanese woman, who is about 150m ahead of us at this point. My attention is, however, suddenly with a peregrine falcon as she takes to the air to our right and soars into the sky in characteristic flight; her long and pointed wings fully extended and her long tail in evidence as she heads up and directly north-eastwards with rapid wing beats. Her steely blue-grey colouring and barring to her feathers is at first clear and then a blur as suddenly, she engages in a spectacular dive and is lost from sight.

As my attention returns to the track ahead, I can see a car approaching. As it nears the first pilgrim it stops and two people get out and have a conversation with him, before getting back in. He then resumes walking and the car moves closer until it draws alongside the Japanese woman, when the same sequence of events occurs, as it does when it gets to us. The driver is a man and the passenger a young woman. They tell us we are on the wrong route and should go to our right to find the correct one at the earliest opportunity, at a junction ahead. We thank them for the information. However, this proposition is clearly at odds with both guidebooks and the signage on the ground, which though in short supply along this stretch, suggests we are on the main Camino route. After a further two kilometres we come to a road. The Camino seems to clearly cross this and continue along a track. We watch as both the first pilgrim and then our Japanese peregrino turn right along the road at this point.

Contemplating our options, we decide to break for a moment to take stock, have a bite to eat and debate whether following our intuition to carry straight on as per the sign, or to turn right as per the couple's advice, presents the best way forward. Whilst we are in the throes of our deliberations, the French group catch us up and without a moment's hesitation turn right. Is this because they know this is the right way or because they have been influenced by the couple in the car? As we are getting ready to depart, still not entirely sure of which direction to go, a local man approaches and we converse in Spanish sufficiently to determine we can go either way, but if we want the albergue or shops in Montemarte, we should go right. As we are walking beyond Montemarte and don't need the shops, we resist the general flow and carry straight on.

We are caught by another car after 400m and a different man and young woman seek us to deviate to the albergue or to go for food. We politely explain we have eaten and are heading beyond Montemarte to Riego del Camino. They seem to understand and indicate we are indeed on the correct route, then. A second peregrine falcon seems to confirm our decision as he appears from behind, but then heads northwards towards a ridge before he disappears. The jara plants here are plentiful and adorn the hedgerows but are nowhere near as big as the ones I saw further south, and their flower heads are yet to fully develop.

Two kilometres beyond the junction, we enter and then skirt round the north-western side of Montemarte and have a short stop before continuing to follow yellow arrows. They lead us down to a path that crosses a reservoir, which is probably dry in summer. It is well-stocked today, however, and an alternative path is followed that takes us briefly back on to the N630 road bridge, crossing the reservoir. On the other side we pick up the Camino again and connect to the point we would have arrived at, had we been able to cross directly. Above this point on a hill and across the water from Montemarte sits a chapel, the Ermita de la Virgen del Castillo. It has a small graveyard to one side and the ruins of a castle are also visible.

Our route now meanders between fields and fincas and we have two further encounters with dogs, thankfully not as frightening as previously and we also meet and greet a donkey. However, none of our earlier companions are seen, and we can only presume they were all prevailed upon to stay at the albergue in the village, or maybe they were only intending to walk as far as Montemarte anyway.

After a short and pleasant, but slightly undulating trek along the Camino, we now arrive at a stretch where the construction of the new motorway has both blighted and diverted the Camino and our new route takes us firstly over the motorway on a bridge constructed especially for the Camino. After about one and a half kilometres of walking alongside it, a second newly constructed bridge takes us back to its left-hand side.

Just prior to the second bridge, we stop for our lunch, a needed rest and an opportunity to let our feet 'taste' fresh air again. Continuing beyond the second bridge we are back on the original Camino route. The path winds round and through grasslands and we start to anticipate the ruins of the former Roman settlement at Castrotarafe, which was inhabited until the 18th century. Its 'castillo' was apparently the seat of the Knights of the Order of Santiago.

The ruins of the old walled town are suddenly upon us and are indeed a spectacle to behold and an opportunity to ponder the lives and roles of those who lived here from Roman times until about 250 years ago. Although the land around is gently rolling, the town would be on a slightly higher level and therefore able to command good views of anyone travelling along the Camino route. They could determine and 'police' a visitor's intentions.

A further two kilometres on from here, the village of Fontanillas de Castro, is a welcome return to current day habitations. The village holds another plaque to celebrate its connection to being part of the route of the Camino. We pause and take our boots off for a while alongside a pleasant fountain, which sits in the middle of a square opposite the church. Refreshed but still somewhat weary, we continue the final leg of the day's journey to Riego del Camino. The last four kilometres seem to take an age, but we finally arrive at Riego and pass what looks like a bar on the main road. There is no sign of life, however. This applies to the rest of the village. We cross the road into the main part and most of the houses seem to be empty. We do eventually find the albergue and as a very pleasant surprise, Erico is waiting outside to greet us.

He explains the lady who is responsible for the albergue lives in a house further up the street and he accompanies us there and introduces us to the señorita, who takes five euros payment, stamps our passports and informs us we can buy bread, ham and cheese from her for tomorrow's journey. Erico has also arranged for the bar (the one we passed on the way into the village) to open this evening and provide us with a meal at seven o'clock. Wow! Later we are joined in our rather spartan albergue by a Swiss peregrino; the very person we saw leaving Hostal Sara in Salamanca three days ago. His name is Bernhard and his arrival ensures between the four of us we will probably increase the population in the village tonight by between five and ten percent.

After showers, a change and a chance to write up some notes we link with Erico and Bernhard and head towards the bar. We have had nine hours hard walking today with some sunshine in the afternoon, but it has mostly been a grey and chilly day. It was well into the afternoon before a layer could be shed. Tonight, I will be grateful for my sleeping bag. It turns out I will also need to use a blanket.

At the bar we dine on a rather thin noodle soup, which is hot and well-seasoned with bread to dunk. This is followed by a rather plain entrecote pork steak and chips and we have an apple for pudding, which all of us take away to have for the following day. We drink two bottles of wine between the four of us during the meal and the camaraderie of being peregrinos, coupled with the wine, mean the conversation flows well. Bernhard's motivation to walk the Camino is to meet girls from Vienna. Twice on previous pilgrimage walks this has happened and on one occasion, this led to him and the Viennese señorita becoming partners. They lived together for two years. Erico is walking the Camino to get married. His wife to be will meet him in Ourense and they will then walk to and beyond Santiago until they get to Finisterre. Here, they will swear their dying love for each other and be married before God. They will then return to Portugal and have an official civil ceremony with family and friends present.

Our elderly host and hostess at the bar would like to sell up and leave so they can join their children and grandchildren, who all live on the north-east coast of Spain. However, no-one wants to buy a bar in Riego del Camino, where three out of every four houses are unoccupied, there is no work, and the community are struggling to keep going in what is increasingly a ghost town. There are over 200 houses but only 40 people live here. Ironically, an Englishman has recently astounded the couple by buying a house in the village.

"In order to commit slow suicide," suggests Erico, "and become yet another of the Riego ghosts."

Bernhard informs us the albergue in Zamora, which we walked past on the climb up to the castle, was completely full. It might have held two Spanish señoras, Karl, Hermann, Inieste, six French and two Japanese pilgrims, I surmise.

We take a further two bottles of wine back with us to the albergue and through the course of the remainder of the evening, these are consumed. We discuss routes for tomorrow as we are all headed along the 'Sanabres route' and plan to stay at Tabara tomorrow night. Both Erico and Bernhard believe there are two places where you can take short cuts, which will chop six and a half kilometres off the day's journey. The first involves a turn off two kilometres before Granja de Moreruela. (We followed this route and it didn't save us any distance). The second is achieved by turning right at the bridge over to the other side of the Embalse we must cross.

Erico makes some interesting comments about Keith and Susan and their relationship, which he has witnessed at close quarters for around three weeks. He clearly does not intend to have that kind of relationship with his new wife. We talk about shared Caminos. This is Erico's ninth and Bernhard has walked several, too. It is his second attempt to walk the Via de la Plata. Blisters and bad feet cut short his first attempt and he only got as far as Caceres.

"Blisters nearly did for us," I interject, agreeing with his reason for cutting that attempt short. "Luckily, we were able to take three days out in Salamanca to recover."

Bernhard has until the third of May to get to Santiago. His mother has a place there where he can stay. He has visited the city many times. Erico trained as a doctor there and so they both know Santiago de Compostela very well indeed. Erico believes it has its dark parts but doesn't elaborate. Bernhard's mother apparently, when travelling to and from her apartment, likes to take the bus between Santiago and Austria over a 24-hour period.

They both go outside for a smoke, Bernhard lights a cigar and Erico a roll-up and on their return the subject turns to religion. Erico has one God derived from studying many religions. He has wanted to do this Camino since he was seven. Bernhard believes in many Gods as he believes if you study Greek or Roman history, they all have many Gods. Erico is trained as an oncologist (a job not without its challenges) but one he loves dearly. His fiancée is also a doctor and he is certainly not going to follow in the family business of wine production. He now, as he has for a four-year period, specialises in identifying and using natural remedies to counteract and mitigate the impacts of cancers. He is committed to his profession.

John and I change the mattress on John's bed, which has a broken spring poking through, for another from the larger dormitory room. it will be empty tonight. John and I have bottom bunks in a room boasting two sets and Erico and Bernhard have a similar arrangement in a separate room. I wonder what they make of our mattress routine before we are due to turn in for the night. They are still swapping stories as we contemplate retiring. It appears Erico is having to listen to Bernhard's life story, in particular all those times when things went awry, the poor decisions he made, or a wrong turn taken. They both conclude walking the Camino is very special in some ways. Maybe Bernhard is ahead of his time!

The conversation is certainly getting deep as the wine departs the bottles. Bernhard has fought depression for around 25 years. Yoga and meditation have been the most effective ways he has managed his condition and prevented a return to some of his previous dark places. The world in general—politics, the Camino, egotism, having children and having a happy death—all get covered before we retire to bed just before ten o'clock. Erico is a guy you can't help but warm to. Bernhard is clearly still struggling to work things out for himself.

Where am I on this continuum? I'm not afraid of death, feeling there are still lots of things I want to do. I'm happy with who I am and who is in my life, but maybe still searching for a final piece of the jigsaw before I can share and know the complete picture of my life. I do know, I am now absolutely sure moving to a new house will be the best option for both Sandra and I and yet again wonder if she is reaching similar conclusions. Tonight's conversations have, at times, been deep, but then there will always be times on any long-distance walk when critical self-examination and the meaning of life are the mind-dominating questions.

Riego del Camino to Tabara

(32.5 km or 19.5 m) a relatively flat walk as we arrive at the point where the Camino divides and we take the Camino Sanabres route to Santiago Gradient descended 5 metres

Monday 18th April

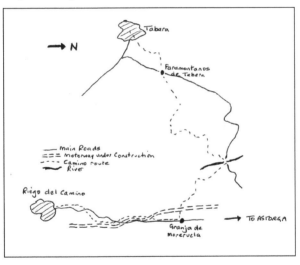

I didn't sleep well. In the middle of the night I got up to pull a blanket over the sleeping bag. My dad would have been 96 today. I wonder what he would have made of my journey of discovery. As we start to get ready, Bernhard is first to depart at around seven o'clock, followed half an hour later by Erico. We are finally on our way just before eight and negotiate our way out of the ghost town that is Riego del Camino to pick up the route again. We shortly arrive at another stretch that has been blighted by the arrival of the motorway, which is not yet open. It feels a little weird passing a service station yet to be fully commissioned. Maybe there may be employment opportunities there for a few local people and Riego del Camino could yet be saved?

Granja de Morreluela is where the Camino divides; the Via de la Plata continues northwards and the Sanabres route goes north-westwards. The latter will be our route with four more days of walking before we get to Puebla de Sanabria, where we have arranged to take an extra rest day. This will leave us around nine days walking on the final leg before we get to Santiago de Compostela. Granja de Morreluela is where we plan to have breakfast, although we had some yoghurt-coated raisins, an apple and a madeleine cake before setting off. I find the church which stands at the junction of where the two Camino routes divide and continue along the main road, trying to find an open bar. Eventually, I double back to John and on the opposite side of the road we find a community centre, bar and café all rolled into one. We have coffee, juice and toast.

The television is on and some mindless Spanish game show is on, which I am only vaguely aware of.

However, suddenly, I hear the music of Monty Python's 'Always Look on the Bright Side of Life'. It is in Spanish, but I am immediately reminded of my sister who died last year, aged 49, after a prolonged battle with alcohol addiction. It was the song she chose to have at her funeral and summed up my little sister perfectly. She was the apple of Dad's eye and I was so glad he wasn't around to see her struggle with the physical and emotional consequences of her prolonged drinking.

We set off again soon after ten and retrace our steps to where the Canabres route splits from the Via de la Plata. About one kilometre along the route we go under the new motorway again and have no more diversions to contend with for the rest of the day. The scenery improves and we can see the hills of the Sierras we will be walking in the distance. A buzzard is spotted at close quarters before he takes off from the branch he is perching on and climbs into the grey-blue sky, demonstrating a range of his flying and gliding skills.

There are lots of jara plants along the sides of the Camino and some broom too. The sun occasionally appears but just when we are thinking of taking a layer off, it goes behind a cloud again. About eight kilometres beyond Granja de Moreruela, we can see ahead a bridge and get glimpses of a river snaking around the lower curves of the hills we are now descending. Beyond, we can see tree-covered hills with rocky outcrops puncturing the vista at random. As well as the river running south to north, a green valley runs westwards, with the highest of the tree-covered hills being to the north. In the far distance we also get the occasional glimpse of higher mountains with snow-capped peaks.

Our view is ever-changing as we wind our way downwards, finally arriving at the picturesque bridge that takes us across the river Esla.

At the other side of the bridge there are two options, a rocky and meandering route over rougher terrain or a route that keeps to the road for a little while before joining easier tracks through more open countryside. We decide to take the road route and a further two kilometres beyond the bridge stop for something to eat and for a rest. The sun is out again and finally one layer can be removed. After another kilometre we leave the road and pick up the Camino path again. We have a very pleasant walk to the next village Faramontas de Tabara. This gives us about six and half kilometres still to walk until tonight's resting place. We buy a Fanta orange and some 'chips' from a shop in the village and carry on to the church in the village centre where we can sit on a form to eat our lunch, homemade jambón crisps and 'queso bocadillos'.

Soon after leaving the village it starts to rain, so we quickly tog up and carry straight on, walking into the prevailing and strengthening wind. At one point the rain turns to hail and the size and speed of the hailstones hurling themselves at our stooping faces forces us to shelter under some trees. By the time we set off again, we are wet and cold. We encounter some sheep, a dog and a farmer just before we cross under a bridge that will carry the new TVE high speed train line north to the French border and southwards towards Sevilla.

We arrive in Tabara soaked and shelter in the porch of the church as we seek the right way to find the accommodation (for which we got a discount voucher last night, courtesy of Erico's negotiating skills at the bar we ate at in Riego del Camino). We have a lot of wet and dirty clothing and hope we can do some washing and drying tonight. There is, however, enough dry stuff to put on after a hot shower. We meet Bernhard who is off to the bar and are informed Erico has negotiated for us to dine at eight this evening in the restaurant close to the hostal. The restaurant and bar also own the hostal we are staying in. In our room I am still cold, even after a shower, and climb into my sleeping bag, then pull some blankets round me to get warm so I can write up my notes from the day's walk. It is only six o'clock and there are still two hours before we will eat. My pen is malfunctioning, and my notes are barely legible. As a consequence, my scribbling is cut short.

I was aware Tabara, though not particularly memorable in terms of what it has to offer architecturally, is famously the birthplace of, arguably, one of Spain's greatest poets, Felipe Camino Gatiea de la Rosa or Leon Felipe as he is more commonly known. Felipe was born in Tabara in 1884 and is chiefly known for his anti-fascist writings about the Spanish Civil War, although his first book was published in 1919, 'Verses and Prayers of a Traveller'. He left home to travel with a group of poets and performers who entertained people across the length and breadth of Spain. He fought in the Spanish Civil War and left Spain in 1938 after the defeat of the second republic, for Mexico, where he remained until his death in 1968.

His writings inspired several generations of young people including my father, as they sought to overthrow and tackle what they saw as the social injustices perpetrated by the ruling classes in both South America and Europe. Several of his poems were found in a notebook Che Geuvara was carrying at the time he was captured by the Bolivian Army and CIA. It is strange, though, three times today memories of my father and sister have been at the forefront of my mind.

Remembering my father reciting translated poems of Leon Felipe and one of his other great inspirations, Pablo Neruda seems to bring inner warmth, even if I am shivering on the outside. I am certainly feeling too cold to go searching for any references within the town to Felipe.

Instead, we go to the bar and sit with Bernhard, Erico and three German men, who are all walking on their own, but like many on the Camino like to link up with others once the evening's resting place has been decided. I find out Erico has saved a week's holiday for the past two years and added time to this year's holiday allocation, so he is able to take the time he needs to complete the walk. Bernhard is 43 and has taken all this year's leave and worked his journey around bank holidays. Erico is 39 and his wife-to-be is also a consultant, but she specialises in kidney transplants and infections.

The evening meal is a pleasant affair taken in the restaurant upstairs from the bar. The youngest of the three had been bitten by a dog just two kilometres beyond Carcabaso and had to summon emergency help. He had an hour and a half wait before emergency services found him and was in hospital in Plasencia for 24 hours. He then had a week recuperating in a hostal before feeling able to continue his walk along the Camino. He shows us the wound, now healing well, but the teeth marks are still visible. The wound, he tells us, was weeping for 15 days after the attack but has now dried up. He has a bandage over it to keep it clean and prevent the risk of getting any further infection. The dog in question came at him from the side out of the entrance to a finca, possibly because it was early morning and not on a leash.

Had he been passing the place later in the morning it may have been tethered. In the dining area are a group of four who we believe to be German and Japanese, an older man and woman and a younger couple, two pilgrims who keep themselves very much to themselves and a band of four Camino cyclists who don't seem to mix with those of us walking the Camino. This is the largest group of pilgrims we have seen at the end of a day's walk for some time.

Despite our efforts during the evening, we cannot get all our clothes washed and dried and each of us will have a bag of wet stuff within our rucksacks on tomorrow's walk. It is to be hoped our boots, propped up against the small radiator in the room, will be somewhat drier by the morning. A trip to the shop results in re-stocked provisions.

With Erico and Bernhard we have two bottles of wine between the four of us. The accommodation and meal costs us 15 euros, partly because of the voucher we were able to produce from the bar in Riego del Camino. Erico assures us all there will be no more rain for several days and with that thought in mind, I don't sleep too badly. I'm up once in the night, during which time I rub some Ibruprofen gel into my left knee as it pains me, and I feel sure will prevent further sleep without such treatment. It works and within 15 minutes, I am back asleep.

Tabara to Santa Croya de Tera

(22.5 km or 13.5 miles) undulating with some hills
Gradient ascended 15 metres

Tuesday 19th April

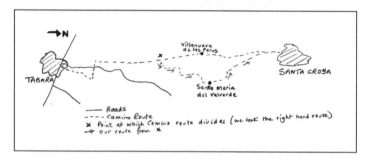

We're up at seven o'clock and do most of the packing before we go for breakfast; a pleasant change to be doing this and then to be able to set off walking without being on the lookout for a breakfast stop. Breakfast consists of the usual tosta and jam, juice and coffee, but is good and sets us up for the first part of today's walk. We see Bernhard and the three German men but no other pilgrims before we are ready to depart at quarter-past eight, backtracking to where the Camino both enters and leaves the town.

There is a stork nesting on the church as we pass by.

John says, "That looks old," quickly adding, "the church, not the stork".

We leave Tabara behind and start to walk along a tiera path that soon takes us back across the route of the incomplete express railway. We can now see a line of pilgrims stretched out in front and are also soon passed by the four cyclists. We catch and pass, with the usual pilgrim greetings, the foursome of German and Japanese origin we had seen in the dining room last night. The breakfast is clearly spurring us on and we eventually pass another pilgrim and are within touching distance of a second, before we stop for a footrest and a drink of water. This is at the rise of a steep climb six kilometres beyond Tabara. There will be more hills to climb before we get to Santa Croya.

Carrying on and about nine kilometres beyond Tabara, we arrive at a junction and after consulting both Alison and Gerald determine both straight on and right will take us to the same place and neither route is any shorter than the other. We decide to take the route to the right, which is the one Alison describes and is the one Gerald refers to as the 'purist'. We decide to rest at the junction and have something to eat and a further footrest. Whilst we are there, three pilgrims arrive individually within about five minutes of each other and they carry straight on rather than turning right.

As we are preparing to depart, rested and re-energised, the group of four arrive and stop to exchange greetings. The guy who seems to be their leader, is from Munich. He tells us he will be visiting Cornwall and Wales in June. We share information about the route choices. There is a village part-way along both routes before they come back together again. I explain we are taking the route to the right, which is described in our guides as the 'purist'. We have an interesting conversation about just how few stretches of the Camino are now entirely consistent with the original. He believes the stretch from Banos de Mayor to Salamanca is probably the longest continuous stretch of the original route. Now, there are many ways to Santiago; there is no longer a singular specific route.

We say our farewells and head right along our chosen 'purist' path and after a little while, we arrive at the village of Santa Maria de Valverde but can find no shop or bar and therefore there is to be no luncheon options other than from our existing stash of food. The sun is now a welcome companion and makes our onward progression all the more pleasant. We have travelled 14km from Tabara and only have a further eight and a half kilometres before we get to Santa Croya.

Soon after leaving Santa Maria de Valverde we, at first, hear and then see a magnificent golden oriole as he flies across the Camino in front of us to a cluster of trees on the other side. He gives us a burst of his beautiful full-throated fluted yodelling song. The golden yellow of his plumage is made even more vivid by the shimmering rays of the sun. Ahead, a group of poplar trees seem to be joining limbs in an array of solidarity. At the edge of this plantation there is a trig point and glorious views of the mountains ahead stretch before us, with snow on at least one of their summits.

As we arrive on the outskirts of Santa Croya, we catch up with one Spanish pilgrim and are caught by the young German who was bitten. John and I decide to stay at the albergue in Santa Croya, as does our Spanish peregrino, however our German 'amigo' carries on. We are all aware there are two other villages with accommodation ahead—the first in one kilometre and another a further ten kilometres beyond. My feet are hurting today and I need to apply a Compeed plaster to my heel where a blister is threatening to break out. Despite our best preparations and regular stops, the Camino is hard on the feet and getting them wet yesterday and starting today's walk with slightly damp boots will not have helped.

The albergue in Santa Croya is beautiful, as are the two young Spanish señorita who seem to oversee it. We can have lunch at three o'clock. It is quarter-past one when we arrive. Dinner is at eight. We agree to both. What's more, our washing will be done for us and we can then peg it out to dry in the warm sun. We should have everything dry before nightfall. The showers are spacious and the water hot. I take time in letting the water flow over me and feel thoroughly cleansed once more. There is a sheltered garden behind the albergue where we sit and enjoy the sun, keep tabs on our washing and at three o'clock precisely, welcome the arrival of lunch which is brought to us by one of our young señorita. She sets it down in front of us, throws us both a huge smile and with a toss of her glossy dark hair, walks back into the albergue. Our eyes don't leave her retreating form until she is gone.

There are specific days and times that are rather magical on the Camino. Today we seem to have found a little bit of paradise, witnessed the flight and birdsong of one of nature's wonders, experienced wonderful scenery with the promise of more to come, and had our warmest day for some time. This more than made up for the eight kilometre walk along the motorway, the rain and hail and dark coldness of yesterday. My feet may be sore, but I reflect I am indeed very happy today. Two long days to come and for the first time, I start to think about how I will miss the Camino when I eventually have to say goodbye.

Lunch is freshly prepared, including an extremely tasty sandwich of cheese and tomato on newly baked brown crusty bread. Also enjoying the garden area, warming sun and lunch are our German and Japanese quartet and our Spanish pilgrim. I can now see the quartet are all of a similar age. Maybe the way one dresses on the Camino can make some people look younger? Either that or today's walk has significantly aged half of the group! These thoughts are soon lost as the second señorita appears to inform us our washing is done. She too has jet-black hair and a winning smile. She is also happy to oblige by taking a picture of us, a rare opportunity for us both to appear in front of the camera together.

Never have I enjoyed pegging out washing more and I calculate I must have washed about three-quarters of all my clothing, judging by the amount of line space needed. There is plenty of drying capacity as the line stretches along three sides of the garden area, however within the next 15 minutes all of it is in full use as a variety of German, Japanese and Spanish freshly laundered items of under and outer wear create a multi-coloured and fluttering array of drying. The German guy from Munich is called Johan and he wants to get to Santiago by the third of May and to be back home by the fifth as on that day, it is his wife's birthday. The Japanese pilgrim is Sekido from Tokyo and she first met Johan on the Camino five years ago. They arranged to meet the following year to walk together again and during that visit met the other two members of their party, who are Spanish. This is the third year the four of them have walked together.

It appears all our other Camino comrades of recent days may now be ahead of us, but we may reconnect with some at the end of our long days walk to Mombuey tomorrow. Will we yet link up again with Karl and Hermann, who were behind us prior to our three rest days in Salamanca but must surely now be not more than one or two days adrift? Getting to Mombuey tomorrow is now a walk we are committed to as Catriona, the first of our two Spanish hostesses, has kindly pre-booked a hotel there for us. We shared our need to get to Puebla de Sanabria in two days and discussed options for tomorrow. After a discussion, we accepted Mombuey was probably the best destination if we were to balance out the distances to be covered each day. She was concerned accommodation there may be restricted and now, at least, we know in advance we have a bed for the night there.

For the first time since Salamanca, we have three nights of accommodation ahead of us already resolved. We go for a nice stroll along the road by the river, recommended by Catriona, and then head back into the village and find a bar. This is full of about 30 Spanish men playing cards and apart from dialogue with the barman to obtain a beer, the rest of the room carries on as if we aren't there.

All the washing is dry when we get back and after gathering it in, we sit outside to enjoy the last rays of the warming sun before some darker clouds arrive and obscure it from view. Despite this, there is a beautiful sunset over Santa Croya as we near the end of a rather special day, but not before enjoying a plentiful meal of pasta followed by a segundo of chicken and a postre of yoghurt, served to us by Catriona and Amelia, the second of our two hostesses. There is even time for a short walk to the bridge over the river to catch the last of the sunset as we reflect on how long ago it seems since we left Aldenueva del Camino for the second time, and just how far I have walked! We also reflect on how helpful and obliging the señorita in the hostels north of Salamanca seem to have been. Today was the last day in which we were walking virtually due north; from now on we will predominantly be walking west.

Santa Croya de Tera to Mombuey

(40.5 km or 24 miles) steadily rising with some steeper undulations)
Gradient ascended 45 metres.

Wednesday 20th April

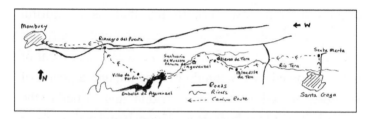

I have my best sleep yet on the Camino and am in the middle of a beautiful dream in which I seem to be running in slow motion through fields in glorious sunshine, with lots of familiar and smiling faces urging me on. Then, the alarm goes off! After getting dressed, we take our stuff through to the main hall to pack to minimise any disturbance to the only other person in our dormitory—Antonio, the Spanish pilgrim.

We have a breakfast of coffee and cake from the vending machine before setting off around quarter-past seven. It is still dark but we are on the road for the first kilometre, so should be OK. It will be the longest day of this section of the walk and tomorrow will be the last day's walk before we can enjoy another rest day.

We say final farewells before we depart to those fellow pilgrims who are up and about, which includes Johan. He is paying more to stay in a studio apartment above the hostel. These days he prefers such arrangements to dormitories, and he confesses he likes his creature comforts, too.

None of our fellow peregrinos at Santa Croya are planning to go as far as us today, so we are unlikely to see any of them again... at least not until Friday. Arriving in Santa Marte, the village one kilometre beyond Santa Croya, we find the 'tiera' route of the Camino and are now heading almost due west.

We skirt a wood and then cross a field. Looking back, the sun is coming up behind the trees and I stop to capture the beautiful sunrise.

As I am doing this, I notice a fellow peregrino crossing the field behind us and we wait whilst Bernt, the German with the dog bite, catches us up and we walk the next stretch together. He stayed at the hostel in Santa Marte last night, which sounds to have been equally as pleasant as our accommodation in Santa Croya. I can't imagine it would also boast two warm and friendly señoritas like Catriona and Amelia though.

We share thoughts about our respective journeys along the Camino and the places, experiences and people that have made the most impression. Our earliest first cuckoo of the day introduces herself at around quarter-to eight after which we fall silent as we enjoy the beauty of our surroundings, with the Camino taking us along river banks, canals and through woods. As well as hearing the cuckoo we see a woodpecker hard at work.

Just before a short section of road that will take us through the next village a second cuckoo is not only heard but seen, a rare but magical moment. At the village we go in search of a café bar for a drink and maybe some toast, Bernt is keen to press on and we say goodbye, convinced our paths will cross again later in the day. We waste fifteen minutes looking in vain for the mythical café bar before heading along a canal to the next village, Olleros, where again after a wander round almost the whole village, we find the albergue and discover it has a bar and café and is open for business. It is quarter-past ten and we have been on the Camino for three hours and have covered 14km; plus at least one more wandering around two villages. Bernt is sitting at a table in the bar enjoying breakfast. He too had a wander around the village but then met a local who informed him of the nearest place to get breakfast and pointed him in the direction of the albergue.

It is time to briefly catch up with my notes before we leave and return to sun-filled streets and then out into open countryside again as our route takes us past an isolated, but rather stunning, church, the Santuario de Nuestra señora de Agavanzal. It appears to be a shimmering white in the sunlight, sitting as it does in fields alongside the banks of the glistening and gurgling waters of the Rio Tera. The building is considered a shrine and locals still undertake a devout procession here every September, in honour of Nuestra señora de Agavanzal. There is an outstanding heraldic coat of arms above the doorway.

We continue along a stretch that takes us on a winding path up to and then down to a dam which crosses an 'embalse'. The road across the dam not only provides views to the west and of our way ahead, but also to the east showing the route we have taken; the white church glistens far below us in the trees, with the ribbon of winding silver that is the river getting ever thinner as it disappears over the far horizon. The sweet aroma of the jara 'rose' is very noticeable here and seems to permeate into my clothing. I can still smell it as we stop at the other side of the dam and yet there isn't a jara in sight.

After our stop, we continue for about three and a half kilometres, hugging the shores of the Embalse de Nuestra señora de Agavanzal, a delightful lakeside section, with several small beaches that beckon us to stop and go swimming. The vistas here must be photographed. Eventually, leaving the lake, we arrive at the small village of Villar de Farfon, now home to a mere 14 inhabitants. The floods caused by the creation of the nearby Embalse destroyed all the mills in the village and robbed the villagers who owned and worked in them of their livelihood. Our enjoyment of our lakeside walk is therefore tempered somewhat by the knowledge of the unintended consequences of its creation. It seems strange, in light of this, to have named the reservoir after a religious icon still recognised and revered by local people.

We take time to lay out a picnic banquet of bread, purchased from the hostel last night; pâté, cake and water. Whilst we are enjoying our feast, Antonio (the Spanish pilgrim who shared our dormitory last night) catches up and stops briefly to exchange pleasantries and then is on his way again. He set off an hour after us and is clearly able to make timely progress. He took a shorter and more direct route up to the dam, which veered right near the church. We have covered 26 and a half kilometres so far today and according to both Alison and Gerald, we have another 15 before Mombuey.

Setting off again around quarter-past one, the sun is at its highest and the temperature must be around 21 degrees or so. We leave Villar de Farfon along a walled green lane, which then turns into a track between bushes with jara plants in abundance and climbs upwards for three kilometres and then down again to Rionegro del Puente, where we had originally planned to stay. Whilst this would have shortened today's walk, it would have meant covering around 45km tomorrow. We have the company of some beautiful wild flowers in yellows and purples as we climb to the high point and can see the snow-clad mountains that surround the hilltop town of Puebla de Sanabria, our resting place tomorrow and for two nights.

The village is located on the banks of the river Negro, a tributary of the Tera and is the birthplace of Diego de Losada, the founder of Caracas and lies between two valleys. The palace where Diego de Losada was born was recently restored and now provides a cultural centre in which a library, Tourist Information Office and ethnographic museum are located. The sun is still warm, so we sit on the shady side of a church and have another welcome foot rest. We have maintained about a 200-metre distance behind Antonio for the last six and a half kilometres. He is planning to stay in Rionegro this evening, as is another pilgrim we haven't met before, who arrives at the church and exchanges greetings. We have about a further two hours walking to do and should be in Mombuey by five o'clock

A difficult eight kilometre stretch now follows; for the first quarter of this we are by the motorway and then are walking across an open plateau with the sun blazing down without shade. Along this stretch there is also an eerie silence which I can't quite work out at first, until I realise it is the absence of birdsong. Maybe all the birds are having a siesta to avoid being out and about in the heat of the sun? We eventually arrive in Mombuey, hot, tired and foot sore, but the hotel Catriona booked us into is clean, modern and well-equipped. Once in our room, I sit on the bed and check my feet. I now have Compeed on my left heel and on the ball of my right foot to protect those areas. After a half hour rest and following texts home to family, we go down to the bar for a thirst-quenching beer. We meet a French guy who lives near Paris and has been walking for 31 days since leaving Seville. It is 29 days for me, including the three days we spent in Salamanca.

Whilst we are enjoying our beer and to my utter amazement, a rather fresh-looking Johan and Sekido emerge from the doorway to the bedrooms. Surely, they cannot have set off after us, walked all the way and got here before us? It turns out they travelled by bus from Santa Croya to Mombuey along with their

Spanish 'amigos' who are apparently currently having a siesta. It would have taken us between ten and 12 hours to walk here, explains Johan. Having walked large sections of the Camino in previous years he no longer feels compelled to complete every day on foot. He is not sure how many more years he may be able to do any walking and enjoys the creature comforts at the end of a day too much to risk spoiling these by being too worn out.

I think of the experiences of Erico and Giovanni, Marie, Andreas and Jesus, Bernt, Inieste, Karl and Hermann, Martin and Marion and Bernhard and the many other peregrinos I have met during my journey to date and realise you should never judge the journey of another, as you are unlikely to have travelled the same way. For all of us, the Camino will provide a different set of experiences, influenced by our own histories and the reasons for each wanting to walk its 600 miles. Experiences in themselves are the essential ingredients of a fulfilled life. Whilst it will be a different journey, I feel sure the memories and the comradeship it provides along the way will remain special to every one of us. I am jolted from my thoughts by John, who has discovered the restaurant at the hotel doesn't start serving food until nine o'clock. It is a kilometre further into town to the next bar and the prospect of adding another two kilometres is not appealing, so we retire to the room for another lie down. Feeling peckish, we eat some bread and pepperoni from our now depleted ration stash.

Tomorrow night we will have the restaurant recommended by Steve to look forward to, dining in the full knowledge we won't have to do another day's walking the following morning—it won't, therefore, matter if we eat later. Rather wearily, we return to the restaurant which is on the ground floor through the bar area and are ushered to a table and handed two menus by the waitress. In no time at all she is back to take our order. I hurriedly decide on a lentil broth, pork loin and chips and flan. The broth is excellent, but I can't finish it. The main course is not too bad, and the flan is passable but certainly not the best I have eaten thus far. We have a glass of Vino tinto to wash it down and retire to bed. It is difficult to get to sleep so soon after a meal, but eventually tiredness takes over and I sleep until about two. The room was cold when we turned in and so I had kept a tee-shirt on and all the covers on the bed, but by two it is very warm and the shirt and most of the bedding have to come off for me to get back to sleep. I sleep fitfully until half-past six and am up at quarter-to seven to get ready for our last day of walking before our now much-needed rest day.

Mombuey to Puebla de Sanabria

(40.5 km or 24 m) gently rising with several ups and downs—and wrong turnings—during the day
Gradient ascended 69 metres

Thursday 21st April

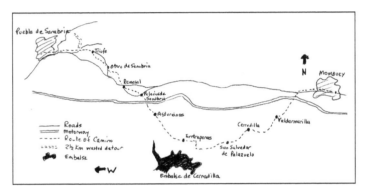

The air is still chilly, but the day promises to be warm again. It takes a further one and a half kilometres of walking along the road and 20 minutes before we leave Mombuey and for the following 20 minutes, we walk beside the new motorway again. However, once clear of this, we start walking along undulating narrow lanes between stone walls and encountering picturesque small villages every two to four kilometres, with scenery very reminiscent of the Yorkshire Dales. Between the route from leaving the motorway to finding the right lane to follow, we are momentarily lost as we take a wrong turning before quickly realising our error, backtracking, and following the signs to Valdemerilla, which has a small church and a fountain and some very pretty houses and a profusion of spring flowers growing along the grass verges outside of most of the houses.

We have our first foot-stop here and Antonio catches us up; he left Mombuey ten minutes after us. In conversation it becomes clear he is in fact French and not Spanish. He is fluent in both languages and speaks a little English, too! He reckons because of the new motorway we should add another one and a half kilometres extra to today's distance to Puebla de Sanabria, which makes it 35km today.

By the end of the day I calculate we have walked more than five kilometres further.

The next two pretty villages of Cernadilla and San Salvador de Palazuelo come and go and we get glimpses of another large embalse to our left, before we get to Entrepenas, the fourth village of the morning where another stop is needed. As we are leaving this village, we are faced with confusing signage again and can see Antonio ahead. He seems to be following the road heading northwards. We also meet a married French couple who are walking the Camino and who we have not encountered before. They ask our help to find the right route and with a combination of consulting guidebooks, geographical logic and luck we find a route in the right (north-westerly) direction, albeit it is a good while before we finally have the reassurance of a Camino sign to indicate we are on track. The French couple are about 200m behind us when we find this path and at my beckoning start to follow, but before long, it is clear our faster pace means they can no longer be seen in our wake.

This route takes us alongside the motorway but at a lower level. We are walking on a path that has the high banks up to the motorway on one side and a barbed wire fence on the other. There are fields and at times woodland behind the fence and once more we have occasional glimpses of the reservoir, which must be around four kilometres to the south. It is clear from Alison's guidebook we should have found an opening to cross over or under the motorway by now if we are going to re-join the original Camino route. Our progress, however, remains constrained to the path we are on for a good three kilometres before we finally arrive at a bridge and can at last cross over the motorway. It is clear when we arrive at the outskirts of Asturianos, another kilometre has been added to the anticipated mileage of the day.

I earlier assured the French couple the route we were on would eventually bring them to Asturianos, as that is where they are staying this evening. I am mightily relieved therefore for both their sakes and our own this assurance proves correct. At the entrance to the village is a large and well-preserved church and by its side a seat—a perfect spot to stop for lunch. Antonio approaches and we again exchange greetings. I think he is as surprised to see us ahead of him as we are, and to discover we got to Asturianos before him. After an enjoyable lunch stop, feeling refreshed, we set off and as we are doing so I notice the French couple approaching. We wave and give them the thumbs up. They probably have another half a mile to walk to get to the albergue they plan to stay in tonight. After another pleasant walk, we arrive in Palacios de Sanabria where a form near the church at the top of the village awaits. I walk down the 200m to the main road and purchase two chilled Fanta orangeades from a bar on the corner before returning to join John on the wooden seat for a refreshing drink.

Whilst we are sitting on the bench another peregrino appears and we get into conversation. His name is Sergio and he is from Spain, although he is currently living in Portugal. We point out where I got the Fanta from and he bids us farewell as he goes off to get one.

It is very humid today and after our long walk yesterday, the heat means it is taking us a little longer to cover the ground today. The scenery is completely different on today's walk, at times reminiscent of the Dales and at other times it is just like walking along one of the many chemins near my brother's 16th century farmhouse and smallholding in central France. It also feels a little strange because we are further north and around 900m above sea level, spring is clearly much later than any part of the Camino I have walked to date, despite it being later in the year. It is more like walking in early March than in mid-April. Some of the lanes we are walking along would have a lot more shade once the leaves on the trees are out. We are surrounded by bare branches, however, so less protection from the sun. There are still wild flowers and herbs and surprisingly an abundance of butterflies, both big and small.

We hear cuckoos periodically during the day, the first one just before Valdermerilla and the last one about a mile beyond Palacios de Sanabria. We reflect on this during another much-needed stop and John is convinced the last cuckoo was mocking the weary efforts of two mad Englishmen out in the hot midday sun. Setting off again, we find ourselves soon walking beside the motorway, this time below us and to our left. We hope this will not be for too long; it is half-past two and I reckon we still have another two hours walking before getting to Puebla de Sanabria. Whilst we are enjoying a banana and a drink both Antonio and then Sergio the Spanish peregrino walk past and smile at our bare feet 'steaming' in the sun. Carrying on, we arrive at the next village which is supposed to have lots of 'grumpy' dogs, according to Alison. We encounter two older ladies as we pass through, neither of whom is grumpy and we don't have any sight or sound of dogs, grumpy or otherwise. Not that I am complaining! At the far end of the village, Sergio has stopped to take off his boots and have a rest, too.

Beyond the village we come to a junction with a more major road and our yellow arrows seem to indicate we should cross over and carry on down a tiera on the other side. There is what looks like a variety of buildings that could be a town about two kilometres away downhill and to our right, which we convince ourselves must be Puebla de Sanabria. The path at first is clear but starts to become less distinct as we drop downhill and lose sight of the buildings we seemed to be heading for. We start to doubt we are on the right route and eventually I concede we are not, but not before a fair distance has been covered. We trudge back uphill. retracing our steps until we reach the road again; an unnecessary detour which adds a further two and a half kilometres to the day's walk. I spot Sergio over to our right, clearly walking along the road and suggest to John we cut across the corner and head in his direction. "No more unscheduled detours," he firmly asserts, and we keep to the track until the road is regained, by which time Sergio has disappeared.

The road drops and twists and turns before it starts to climb again, going under the motorway, which sits on concrete stilts above our heads. Beyond the motorway, it bends sharply left and continues to rise until finally we can see Puebla de Sanabria below us with the mountains beyond it, many of which have pockets full of snow dotted near their summits. We have a long descent to the outskirts of Puebla, before a final climb up to the old town and our hotel, royally named 'King Carlos V'. From the point we could see the town a further three kilometres has been covered. With all our detours, including the unfortunate two and a half kilometres near the end, I estimate we have covered 40.5km today; a lot more than either Alison or Gerald suggested it would be.

We take our things up to the room and have a quick freshen up before going out in search of a bar to have a celebratory beer prior to getting showered and changed. Who should we meet at the first bar but Erico, which leads to warm handshakes all round. He explains Giovanni is here too, but he has gone to the pharmacy to get some glasses as his have broken. It isn't long before Giovanni joins us, complete with new glasses. It is quite astonishing he has made it this far, given where he was when we last saw him in Calzada de Valdunciel, on the day we walked to El Cubo de Tierra del Vino, some 20km beyond Calzada. He stayed there that night and has effectively been at least a day behind us for the rest of the Camino, until he arrived in Montemarte, intent on staying there only to find the albergue was closed. He had carried on walking and eventually got to Tabara, meaning he covered 50km (30 miles) that day. For an overweight man in his late 60's, who has experienced two heart attacks in the not too distant past, this is some feat of endurance. Whilst I hold Erico in high regard, it is quite clear he regards Giovanni as his 'hero'.

Before he returned from the formaccia, Erico had been waxing lyrical about this man who eats two menus at a sitting and has a figure to show for it, who is not in the best of health and yet when the chips are down, he walks 30 miles in one day. The four of us enjoy catching up and Erico also updates us on the progress of Bernt and Bernhard too. When I go to pay for the beers we have all enjoyed, it turns out Giovanni has beaten me to it—the guy is truly amazing, as Erico would say! We retire to the hotel and get showered, changed and empty the rucksacks. We each have a bag of dirty washing and one of our main tasks tomorrow will be to get as much of this washed and dried as possible.

Today has been a very undulating route with many ups and downs, more so than any other day on the Camino thus far. I reckon we have climbed about 600m today and descended around 350 over the course of some 38km; not counting our last detour. My feet are certainly tired and a little sore. I think I would struggle to do a full day's walk tomorrow and am so pleased we have a rest day. Both of us are really in need of the break.

What else have we seen or not seen today? No birds of prey or storks. Lots of rabbits, particularly on the stretch beside the motorway after leaving Mombuey. It is the first time I have seen rabbits on the Camino, though rabbit does appear on the menu in lots of places. We encountered an amorous pair of chaffinches on the outskirts of one of the villages and white broom and periwinkle beyond them, but otherwise the flora was less plentiful than on previous days.

A leisurely wander up to the old town and the castle, built into the hilltop and from where there are expansive views in all directions. We also locate the restaurant Steve has recommended and later in the evening return to await it opening so we can not only be the first diners, but also select our table. This gives us a wonderful view over the countryside to the east, from which we can view the last three kilometres of our walk into the city.

The food is so well presented it demands to have pictures taken before we eat, and it doesn't disappoint. We have a very nice Rioja to slowly help the digestion, as we recognise the long days have taken their toll, but at least we now have a rest day to look forward to, to better enable us to start the 'homeward' stretch of our journey along the way to Santiago. It is dark by the time we are wandering back down the cobbled streets to our hotel. We can take breakfast from any time after eight in the morning. On other days, we would have been walking on the Camino for an hour by that time.

Plate 19
The ruins of Castrotarafe – Day 26

Plate 20
Bridge over the River Elsa – Day 27

Plate 21
John and I at the albergue in Santa Croya – Day 28

Plate 22
Beautiful sunrise greets our early start – Day 29

Chapter Seven

A brief Interlude

Friday 22nd April

The historic city of Puebla de Sanabria is quite something, with its churches, castle and narrow steep lanes. It looks out to the north and east over the Sierra de la Cabrera and the Sierra Segundera where snow is visible in the mountain gullies. To the south-west, it is only around 15km to the Portuguese border and to the south-east, are the plains and rolling hills we walked over to get here.

I have a good sleep and lie in until around quarter to eight. After breakfast, we have more time to reflect and take things easy. Today is, we agree, most definitely a day of rest, with a little exploration of the city, too. After washing some clothes and pegging them out on a line in the courtyard at the rear of the hostel, a rest is in order. First, we give some necessary attention to our feet. Blisters are well-covered, and any tender areas get smothered in Compeed balm. Socks are then carefully placed on each foot and sandals (not boots) are the order of the day.

It is around 11 o'clock before we venture out and the plan is to be back at the hotel by two at the latest.

Outside, it feels strange to be walking without the weight of the sack. We retrace our last steps on the Camino from yesterday to go down to the river, walking along for a little while, then climb the 370 steps that lead from the bridge over the river and up to the castle. This is certainly good for the heart rate.

At the top we look down and see some pilgrims coming over the bridge and wait to see whether it might be anyone who has been a part of our journey, appearing along the designated route. We spot nobody, but then realise these peregrinos are climbing up the 370 steps as we have done. However, they have their rucksacks and will have possibly walked for two or three hours today already. The group turns out to be Johan, Sekido and friends and we take snaps of them and applaud as they achieve the last few steps. They may have taken the bus to Mombuey two days ago, but today are demonstrating their commitment to walking the Camino. We share warm greetings before saying our goodbyes as we go for tea and cake in a pleasant little café at the bottom of the main cobbled street.

It feels alien to have time on our hands and not to be walking to our night's destination. This does, however, allow the mind to wander and I start to think of returning home again and of the best future option for Sandra and I, which (I now firmly believe) is to seek a move to a new home. One in a location we are happier with, which can (or has the potential to) deliver the practicalities of daily living we will both benefit from in the years to come.

The other major topic of conversation between us relates to fellow pilgrims and our efforts to try and work out where those people, who have impacted on us the most upon the Camino, are up to on their journeys. Who is in front of us, who is behind and who are we most likely to meet again?

Erico and Giovanni are a day ahead of us now, so it is conceivable we may see one or both of them again, possibly not until Santiago. A lot will depend on whether they take another rest day as we plan to do. Andreas, Marie and the 'Gruppenfuhrer' could be three, four or even five days ahead of us, unless they have taken several rest days since leaving Salamanca. It is therefore extremely unlikely we will catch up with them. Both Bernt and Bernhard are two days ahead of us now according to Erico, and therefore we probably won't see them, either.

Karl and Hermann, Martin and Marion and Inieste present the biggest conundrum. We last saw the Germans in the Plaza Major in Salamanca eight days ago and know from them Martin and Marion were also in Salamanca. We saw Inieste on our last evening there. We were both convinced at the time we would be sure to meet all five of them again over the coming days. At least we know they all planned to take the Sanabres route too.

John and I now spend a splendid and amusing half hour using our best reasoning, inspired guesswork and cross-questioning of each other, before we write down three possibilities of where we think they are today. "You first!" says a smiling John.

"I reckon they will all get here today," I confidently assert.

"I think it will be tomorrow before they get to Puebla," is John's assessment.

We return to Hotel Carlos V for our agreed afternoon siesta and it is almost six o'clock in the afternoon before I wake, somewhat disorientated from my slumber, certain I can hear Karl and Hermann whispering in the bunk below me and I will soon be getting up to start another day's walk. It takes a couple of seconds to realise I am in a single bed and John is sitting on his bed reading 'Gerald' and it is late afternoon.

We go out for a stroll up to the castle and consider the menus outside various bars and restaurants where we might eat. We also buy some provisions for tomorrow and do a little people watching as we walk down to the bar where we met with Erico and Giovanni yesterday, half expecting to see Karl and Hermann or Martin and Marion enjoying a beer, but there is no-one there we know.

John asks whether I may consider returning to Spain to continue the walk from Santiago to Finisterre on the north-western Atlantic coast, as Erico, Karl and Hermann and Martin and Marion plan to do. This sounds a splendid idea and I ponder inviting my brother to join me on that stretch. John is interested, too. It is, after all, what many of the early pilgrims did, believing where the land met the sea, was the 'end of the world'.

"We could also explore the option of travelling to the Port of Cadiz and negotiating our way back to Sevilla on foot, in a comparable way," I add.

Returning to our hotel, appetites sharpened by our evening stroll, and our musings on extending the Camino at both ends, we sit outside and order food and a beer. Just as the beer arrives, a familiar female figure approaches, and to our pleasant surprise it is Inieste; she arrived today and like us is planning to have a rest day here. She is staying in a small hostal about 100m away from the castle. We say our farewells just as our food arrives, a rather wholesome and very tasty Cocido madrilène for me with butter beans, bacon, chorizo and black pudding, accompanied by some chunks of warm and flavoursome bread. John has an equally satisfying paella and we both savour the food and the atmosphere as the sun finally disappears.

The platters of food are so plentiful postre is declined and as the cool of the evening settles, it is time to go inside. The first half of the big game is watched in the bar of the hotel—the second upstairs, having retired to our room as tiredness rapidly sets in. I am probably asleep within five minutes of the end of the game and bedside lights being switched off.

Plate 23
Castle at Puebla de Sanabria – Day 31

Plate 24
Looking down on the new town from the old – Day 31

Chapter Eight

Puebla de Sanabria to Ourense

***

Puebla de Sanabria to Padornelo

(31 km or 18.5 m) including 8 km unplanned detour! Steadily rising for most of the day Gradient ascended 350 metres

Saturday 23rd April

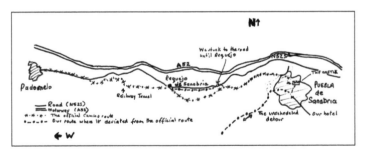

I am up, showered, and down to breakfast just before eight o'clock. The day dawns with a clear blue sky and sunshine as promised, albeit the weather is supposed to change, and we are likely to have rain every subsequent day until our arrival in Santiago. Breakfast is thoroughly enjoyed, and we are also able to obtain a packed lunch for later, which means the provisions we bought yesterday can remain as part of our stash.

There is another peregrino staying at the hotel, but he is a Spanish cyclist and is given clear instructions on which way to go by our host, who doesn't speak a word of English. He helpfully affords us the same privilege, explaining in gestures and descriptions of the route we should take to regain the Camino. It is quarter-past nine when we are finally underway. We set off in high spirits, having deciphered most (if not all), of the route we have been instructed to take. Getting used to carrying a rucksack after a day without, is one of the immediate trials, making sure it is sitting right and the straps are tightened to distribute the weight evenly, so the back (and not the shoulders) is taking the brunt of the strain.

The tricky first stretch our host has shown us is carefully negotiated and takes us down out of Puebla de Sanabria and across a small bridge over fast running water, then between houses along a minor road. There are some rather faded yellow arrows at intervals, which is encouraging. After about a kilometre we arrive at a crossroads where there is no indication as to whether we should bear right or left. According to our host, picking up the yellow arrows or 'signs' as he referred to them should guide us back to the Camino once we find the road between the houses. We decide to fork left and soon come to a T junction, where turning left will take us back to Puebla, so we head right. Our decision is made more certain by consulting Alison's guide, which refers to turning right along a road that in two kilometres will bring us to a junction with the N525, which the Camino route follows for a while.

The road rises gently but continuously, and it isn't long before the first cuckoo is heard, shortly followed by two more; it is a reassuring sound synonymous with the Camino. A colourful Spanish jay sweeps down from a tree to our left, crosses in front of us before alighting on a holm oak tree beyond. He is quickly followed by two more jays, the azure blue of their plumage sparkling as it catches the warming rays of the morning sun. There are taller plane trees, poplars and broom. A stork is spotted sitting on a tree top nest to our left and not long afterwards a second stork sweeps across the road in front of us—familiar sights and sounds returning.

What we haven't got though are any visible signs to indicate we are on the right Camino route, no yellow arrows or shell markings that would enable us to completely relax. After about half an hour and at a junction with a dirt track coming from our right, we stop as there is a car slowly descending the track to join the road. As it stops, I enquire with the driver if we are on the right road for the Camino, adding we are heading initially for Requejo de Sanabria, which should be around five kilometres beyond Puebla de Sanabria.

He indicates we should continue for about three kilometres until we arrive at a bridge and then we must make a right turn to follow a track that will take us to the Camino. I am pleased I've been interpreting and understanding his directions thus far, but he then continues with a longer and more incomprehensible explanation as to the route we must take before he drives off. At least the first part of his explanation was clear, and we decide to press on to find the bridge he referred to.

After a further one and a half kilometres we do arrive at a bridge on the outskirts of a village, Lobeznos. We have walked for an hour since leaving Hostal Carlos V, covered at least four kilometres and are not on or near to the N525. A stop to take stock, have a drink of water and re-consult both guide books convinces us the only sensible option is to turn around and head back to Puebla de Sanabria. We are not on the right route and have no confidence following the directions we had been given would take us there.

Retracing our steps is painful but relatively speedy and by the time we pass the Hostal Carlos V it is quarter-to 11. As we pass the hotel, I reflect so far today we have walked eight kilometres and made exactly no progress along our proscribed route. Following the cobbled street back up to the castle at the high point of the town is the plan. We know there is a Tourist Information Office there. With our knowledge of Spanish and the likelihood the guide will have some knowledge of English, we should be able to get sufficiently clear directions to pick up the right route. A good plan but unfortunately the Tourist Information Office doesn't open until 11 o'clock. This provides an opportunity to take off our boots and socks for a little while and to survey the land and roads around us from our vantage point. I work out which road is the N525 and therefore which road we need to go down to join it.

Just to be on the safe side we wait until Tourist Information opens and obtain a map of the area for ten kilometres around the town and confirm what I have previously worked out. Our host at Hostal Carlos V had set us off completely in the wrong direction—had we continued to walk beyond Lobeznos we would have been increasing the distance between ourselves and our Camino. Chastened but not undeterred we set off again, now confident the road we are following will take us to the N525 and we are on the right route. Soon clear yellow arrows appear and offer further reassurance and we can relax.

We see and catch two fellow pilgrims about three kilometres before Requejo, who amazingly turn out to be Martin and Marion. I last saw them during my final day walking with Maureen. I tell them we knew they were probably close by from our meetings with Karl and Hermann. It is great to catch up and to introduce them to John. We share our respective knowledge of who else we both have met along our journeys. I confirm we saw Inieste last night, but she is planning a rest day in Puebla de Sanabria today. They haven't seen her for over a week. They are also aware Millie made it as far as Zafra with her golf trolley but are not sure how much further she walked.

Marion is also able to clarify Bertrande and Cecille, the French couple who also started on the same day as I did, made it as far as Salamanca. They were, however, planning to go back to France from there and return next year to finish the whole pilgrimage route. Like us, they have periodically bumped into Karl and Hermann and are on 'more or less' the same schedule. Marion tells us they have also gone wrong this morning and got wet fording a river after missing the designated crossing point.

I express the hope they will remain a part of our 'family' along the rest of our journey. Where we bump into them is at a junction between the road and a track which veers left at a 30-degree angle from the road.

They are debating whether to take the track or the road. I am clear after our earlier faux pas, we are sticking to the road to Requejo, to make up a little time. About ten minutes after our farewells, I look behind me and can see them some way off, but also sticking to the road.

Along this stretch I spot between 40-50 little lizards, none of them more than four inches long, all basking in the sun and darting for cover as we approach. Just before the village itself, we pass a rather austere and drab building on the right-hand side of the road. It is a nightclub called 'Club Romantica'. I cannot imagine taking a loved one there for a romantic evening, though!

We have a well-earned second 'foot-stop' in Requejo de Sanabria, climbing a short rise to sit in the shade of a church. Socks and boots are discarded and laid out in the sun, whilst we apply protective balm to our feet and enjoy our lunch.

There is a strikingly marked black and white snake curled up on the cool stone seats. He is about six inches long but is clearly deceased. The black and white pattern looks a little like a miniature football scarf and I wonder whether he was discarded there by a disillusioned Newcastle fan.

A café is spotted down in the village and we leave the sanctuary of the church and the company of the dead snake and head to the left of the Ayuntamiento building to it. I ask for and get a tea, which is a strange infusion (a tea bag in hot milk), certainly not the best cup of tea I have ever had. A solitary pilgrim is sitting at a table inside, enjoying some lunch and a beer, a huge rucksack perched on a chair outside giving away his 'credentials'. He studiously avoids eye contact when we go in to order our drinks.

The route from the village follows a lane past houses with verandas with stone steps up to them and garages and what would have been places for animals at ground level. This is a construction that will become very familiar to us over the remainder of the Camino. Judging by the fast-flowing water in the drains and nearby streams, it would be easy to see the narrow twisty lanes and the ground floors of the buildings being prone to flooding. I surmise the design of the buildings is deliberate so it offers some protection to the inhabitants of the houses and their possessions at first-floor level and above.

Beyond the houses and past the village the Camino returns to the road and climbs steadily, heading for a pass over the mountains, which we can see ahead in the far distance. After following the road for a further four kilometres our route bears left and now follows the old road as it continues to rise and twist and turn as it reaches up to the high point of the pass. There are lots of butterflies on this stretch, although the scenery on either side is rather bleak. It may be late April but as we are high up in the mountains very few trees are in leaf and the remnants of the cold and long winter are still dominant, the ground littered with dead leaves and twigs as well as moss and lichen-covered boulders and stones.

Reaching a bend to the right with a sheer drop to the left we can see three huge bridges that span the gorge. Our path continues relentlessly upwards and now takes us under the first of the bridges. The huge arches high above us enabling the N525 to reach the high point of the pass. Two more bridges span our path as both the north-west and south-east lanes of the new motorway rise and fall from and to the pass ahead. Our route now bends in a huge horseshoe, hugging the hillside and now crossing a bridge where on one side the water tumbles down from the mountains high above and on the other cascades into the gorge below.

On the other side of the horseshoe, we again pass under the motorway and can see high above us where the route to the north-west disappears into a tunnel, boring through the mountains to progress towards Galicia and Spain's northern seaports. Once more under the N525, our path continues up an even steeper trajectory, negotiating S bends until the high point of 1260m is reached. Here there is a modern cross and an opportunity to pause and take in the views before we continue down into Padornelo. At a bar there we enjoy a cold, if expensive, glass of orange.

According to Gerald there is supposed to be a hotel 500m beyond the village and given the time and that we have walked over 30km today, including the eight unscheduled ones this morning, we debate whether we should stop there or not. Lubian, our planned overnight resting place, is a further seven kilometres beyond Padornelo. We conclude if there is an open hotel which looks reasonable and we can get an evening meal there, it would represent the best option. If there is also a TV where we may be able to watch some football, that would be the icing on the cake.

There is a hotel, which is hopeful, albeit finding a way in is tricky. Once we have negotiated this, the inside is clean, has a bar, a dining room, a TV and available rooms. It is quarter-past five in the afternoon and we agree to stay put here for the night. We have a small beer to celebrate our decision and completion of our first days walk on this final leg of our journey. A twin room costs us 20 euros and the dining room opens at half-past eight to serve food. Breakfast isn't included but there are plenty of suitable supplies we could stock up. Alternatively, we could stop at Lubian for breakfast. The bars there should just about be open by the time we arrive tomorrow. The sun is still beating down and we have been walking for eight hours, which is long enough. My feet have held out well but my shoulders and back ache from carrying the rucksack.

The stop gives me time to write up the notes from today's walk before we need to get ready, do some washing and make our way downstairs to eat. The forecast is still for rain tomorrow and for a steep drop in temperatures from Friday onwards—oh joy! However, once we are over and through the mountains and we get closer to Ourense, the warmer it will get. Although, it won't be anywhere near as hot as the 23-degree temperatures we have been walking in today.

At times today, the route was a bit like going over Shap by the M6 motorway with the Lakeland fells on the left and the Howgills on the right. Although, I think the high point of Shap is less than a third of the height of the pass (1260m) we climbed today. I text home to say all is well before we enjoy a pleasant meal with water and a beer, whilst watching a La Liga game on TV. Outside there is a reddish sunset, which may suggest fine weather in the morning, but the forecast is still saying rain. We are back up to the room and in bed before 11 o'clock. The alarm is set for seven o'clock to make sure we can be off by eight.

Padornelo to A Gudina

(32 km or 19.5 m) initial descent followed by steep climb and then further descent
500 metres of descent and 300 metres of ascent in total

Sunday 24th April

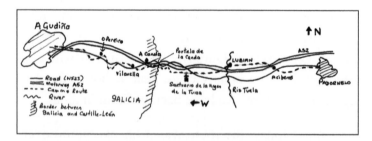

I slept well to start with, then woke in the night with what felt like the weight of the world pressing on me. Getting out from under the cover and a blanket makes a significant difference, but it is a while before I drift off to sleep again. The noise of the alarm eventually wakes me once more. It takes an hour to get up, washed, dressed, packed, and then to make our way downstairs to the bar. We have coffee and share a large pain au chocolate and stow a madeleine for later. The weather forecast still states rain, but it seems the north of Spain is faring better than the south, where some places have experienced flooding. The weather system, however, is travelling northwards in our direction.

We start walking again at 25-past eight and continue for a little way along the N525 before we bear left onto an earth track. This is welcomed as virtually all our walking yesterday was on roads. I am suddenly spotting and scenting flowers again, which is a portent of much more to come. A solo pilgrim is passed, and greetings are exchanged. He is from Brazil and is also hoping to make A Gudina today. Our paths cross several times during the rest of the day.

Before we get to Lubian, the route drops down and then turns sharp right as we first go under the railway and then the motorway. High above our heads, we hear the noise of rumbling traffic competing with the morning birdsong. There are some cleverly engineered little bridge crossings beneath our feet, as we cross cascading streams and tumbling watercourses. The path is, at times, wet and boggy. We pick our way along these stretches, managing to negotiate the driest way through until the outskirts of Lubian are reached. More stone buildings with their verandas and steps start to appear on either side, some are derelict and in a poor state of repair, whilst others are well maintained. Lubian is a very picturesque place and its narrow streets seem to guide, wrap themselves around and draw us into its main avenue. Here, brightly painted windows and doors and an abundance of colourful and scented flowers greet our arrival. A plaque commemorating the Via de la Plata is given pride of place and a swathe of some rather beautiful bearded irises overlook the lower part of the village and the mountains beyond.

Another warm welcome is found at the bar and soon we are sitting outside and enjoying toast, marmalade and coffee for breakfast. We are served by an engagingly pleasant barmaid and we also buy (on her recommendation), what turns out to be a moist and tasty slice of Spanish tortilla to have later for lunch. She provides us with some large chunks of bread to accompany the slabs of tortilla. These are 'on the house', she tells us, or at least that is what I understand! Whilst we are having our breakfast, three members of the local gendarmerie arrive at the bar for their morning coffees.

As we are preparing to tear ourselves away from our breakfast, I become aware of two other pilgrims (a man and a woman), maybe in their 40's setting off from another hostal and bar about 20m beyond where we are sitting. It will be two days before our paths coincide again but then they, like most others on the final part of our journey, will continue to cross paths with us until Santiago de Compostela is reached.

After leaving Lubian in dry but greying skies we have a further stretch of weir and stream crossings and our route rises 300m over some five kilometres. We are walking over rough and rocky terrain and are climbing steadily as we head higher into the mountains. Yet again we go under the motorway, high above us, great concrete pillars stretch up above the tree canopy, holding their travelling cargo of cars, lorries and coaches.

About two kilometres beyond Lubian the Santuario de la Virgen de la Tuiza is reached. It is still used for romeríos four times each year. The church dates from the 18th century and replaced a former ermita on another site not far away. Soon after leaving it behind we find ourselves going under the motorway again. The Santuario was built in a lovely, quiet yet idyllic and peaceful spot and it seems such a shame it is now sandwiched between two flyover bridges of the new motorway—progress on the move!

There are now some fine stretches of green lanes before we have yet more water courses to contend with. The sound of running water is never far away and vies with the wind playing tunes as it stirs the branches of the trees that seek to bar its progress. There are plenty of cuckoos and skylarks to serenade us too and for now no sight of, or sounds from, roads. Our steep ascent requires a short rest and it is a relief to briefly shed boots and socks before we push on to the summit pass.

We now leave the region of Castille y Leon and the Province of Zamora and enter wonderful Galicia and the province of Ourense. Whilst Alison's guide book had suggested we would be able to spot the pass in the distance by the presence of another red and white pole, this is not seen until we arrive at the summit and can now see the splendour of Galicia laid out in front of us. Maybe this is because along the ridge a plethora of electricity pylons and wind turbines now vie with the pole for visual attention. A glance back over the treetops and downwards shows us just how steeply we have been climbing.

As I take in the Galician scenery it seems almost at once to be greener and as we make our way into the region there are far more way-marked Camino signs to aid our journey. It is almost as if there is a big but invisible sign at the summit indicating "Galicia welcomes pilgrims". Even the greetings from the locals we pass seem warmer and I feel special and privileged to be walking the Camino here. I could never have imagined a few years ago after my health scare to be undertaking a walk of such magnitude. I feel like bursting into song and say as much to John.

"Steady on now," he says, "we don't want to jeopardise our welcome into Galicia."

Although there were a few spots of rain at the summit, we have so far managed to avoid the forecast rain. I am amused to find my initials are carved at the bottom of a stone at the high point of the pass. The stone displays the route from Puebla de Sanabria to Santiago de Compostela. There are some fine long-distance views, although it certainly appears to be raining way ahead on the next range of mountain summits.

It isn't long before the first drops of rain fall and for the rest of the day we are accompanied by light showers. At one point, the rain increases in intensity and we pause to put on cagoules and protect the rucksacks with their covers. I am still walking in shorts, a single base layer and a walking shirt and am perfectly warm enough. A short stretch back on the road again is followed by a return to an earth track as we drop under the railway line. Here we take the opportunity of the shelter provided to stop and apply more Compeed balm to our feet. We don't dally long though, as although we are dry under the railway bridge, the ambient temperature feels at least five degrees lower. Walking across the pass into Galicia feels like a significant milestone as we get ever nearer to Santiago. We leave our shelter and carry on in the spitting rain and are glad to be moving again to warm up.

I almost tread on a snake before it slithers away through the green grass and up the bank. It is about 18 inches long and is brown, much bigger than the dead snake we saw yesterday. Just after this encounter, we enter the small village of A Canda, about one and a half kilometres beyond the pass.

A lunch stop is made at a bridge crossing that provides a perfect stone bench for us to sit on. It is here we discover just how delicious the slab of tortilla is and how well it goes down with the hunk of bread provided 'free gratis' for that purpose. We follow this with a sweet and juicy apple left from yesterday's packed lunch and a chunk of chocolate coated raisins. These have been welded together, warmed in yesterday's sun, then cooled overnight and again during today's walk to form two more or less equal clumps. I feel blessed to be sitting here enjoying such a veritable feast, surrounded by such splendid greenery. Feeling refreshed and energised we set off again and I am further rewarded as I spot my third golden oriole of the pilgrimage (this one a female) and point her out to John as she darts into trees ahead. Her original resting place was a tree blighted with a bright orange fungus, covering the gash where a bough has been previously torn away from its trunk in a storm.

The scenery is much greener for a while and there are splendid views ahead and all around us now. Soon after leaving our lunch stop, we arrive in the village of Vilavella and have two gates to negotiate, the first has a gap to its right, but the second requires to be open and then shut. There are so few such obstacles along the Via de la Plata its presence and the barrier it presents momentarily flummox us both. As we are in this moment of suspended animation a group of four Spanish jays take off from our left; their colourful plumage and raucous cries seeming completely at odds with each other. As I round the next bend two more jays screech and fly away bemoaning the impudence of our intrusion. Now it is the turn of a pair of bullfinches to entertain us and a tortoiseshell butterfly flits amongst a cluster of potentillas, as if pointing out one or two early flowers that are just starting to bloom.

Vilavella has an impressive little outdoor gym with all the equipment painted in bright blue and yellow. It also has a spa hotel according to Gerald. However, we do not see any sign of it as we pass through and beyond the village. At the end of the village is a large stone, which is a good place to stop and enjoy the luxury of taking off our boots and socks for a short while. As we are airing our feet, Sergio (now walking alongside our Brazilian peregrino) catches up and warm greetings are exchanged. We are never far behind them afterwards until we finally get to A Gudina much later in the day. The buildings in the village have lots of interesting architectural features and most seem to be occupied. Indeed, there are much fewer derelict buildings between here and A Gudina than we had seen over the past two days.

Yellow arrows are plentiful here, too, as we leave the trees behind and are now walking through open moorland. There are lots of naturalised flowers with pinks, blues and yellows predominating in a colourful —and at times aromatic—canopy that runs either side of the path. Our way now takes us through a landscape strewn with large boulders and stones that are reminiscent of Ilkley Moor, back in Yorkshire. We have wonderful all-around views. There are one or two crosses along this open stretch with depictions of the crucifixion upon them, reminding us we are on a pilgrimage trail. A solitary crow sedately flies past as if checking on our progress. The wild flowers are certainly colourful and their various scents tantalise our nostrils and enhance our mood as we start to leave the moorland behind and re-cross the railway before arriving in the village of O Pereiro, where we enjoy the last stop of the day. It is a further eight kilometres from here to A Gudina.

Our route finally re-joins the N525 and a rather unsightly and unimpressive entrance to the town mars slightly what has been a wonderful day's walk. A large cement works to our left typifies this last stretch and we are passed and sometimes overtaken by a constant stream of cement mixers arriving to fill up and then depart to deposit their contents. No doubt, I surmise, at some nearby motorway or high-speed train construction site. Beyond the cement works is a stretch of grey road, which matches the darkening of the sky and the rain we are walking through.

Reaching the hostal on the edge of town, initially, we turn down its rustic charms and go off in search of something more salubrious, as John is worried about the state of his feet. Being in a larger town he has promised himself there must be a quality hotel somewhere to be found. After a fruitless search, which at one point involves me going off alone, I return to find John waiting at a junction. The road off from the junction leads down to the albergue, another accommodation option, but one John may be keen to avoid tonight.

I do, however, persuade him to have a look before we discount it. The usual premises are closed for refurbishment, but a nearby building is being used as a temporary base. Inside is a large dormitory with 24 beds, all but three of which seem to be taken and only three top bunks remain unused. There may be one or two familiar faces within the midst, but John is clearly unimpressed and doesn't dally long enough to warrant any introductions to any of the occupants. He is adamant he needs the space and time to sort his feet out properly and so we return to the main street. Whilst John was waiting for me at the road junction, he had spotted a bar across the road and so next we check out this option, but the rooms are cramped and look grubby. We backtrack to the hostel we saw first, and which John categorically rejected in favour of finding something more luxurious.

Three-quarters of an hour after arriving in A Gudina we are finally checking in to the Hostal Madrilena, initially after being told there are no rooms. It transpires there are no twin rooms available and our only option is a three-bedded room, but we will only be charged for the use of two beds and at 17 euros and 50 cents, this is a reasonable compromise. On our earlier travels through the town we also spotted a pharmacist and stopped to purchase two further tubes of roll-on blister prevention salve, which hopefully will keep us going until Santiago. There is a restaurant, recommended by Gerald, about 200m away and another bar before it. After showers and foot ablutions, our evening's dining and entertainment appear well mapped out. I take the opportunity to write up some notes about today's experiences. John's feet are paining him, but the blister prevention precautions he has taken and our routine of two-hourly stops has paid dividends and his feet, despite his earlier misgivings, seem to be holding out.

It may, though, be prudent to have a shorter walk tomorrow, although the only place with the possibility of accommodation before Laza is a good 20km away. According to Gerald, there was an albergue there, but he believes it closed in 2013. Let's hope it, or another, has re-opened since then, otherwise it is a long 34km walk to Laza. Just as we are preparing to leave to go out for dinner, a wet and bedraggled German pilgrim arrives to check into the hostal. He looks utterly whacked and confirms the rain is now heavy. It may be only 200m away, but waterproofs will be needed to go out to dinner and remain dry.

A trip to Gerald's recommended eating place is a huge disappointment; it only serves tapas, is small and cramped and full of Spanish men so there is nowhere to sit and eat anyway. We backtrack to the Bar Castro where there is a restaurant, not yet open. There are already several peregrinos within the bar waiting for the restaurant to open at half-past eight. It is 23 minutes past eight when we arrive, so we don't have long to wait, just long enough to enjoy a small beer. In the dining area are about eight or nine tables of differing sizes.

On one table are a group of three English-speaking pilgrims, who we will meet again in a few days and discover to be a New Zealander, an Aussie and an American, who was born and brought up in Spain. At a table next to them is the Brazilian peregrino, dining alone and beyond him a table with four pilgrims—German we suspect. At another table a quartet seems at times to be using English, but it is difficult to gauge their nationalities. Later in the week, we will discover one of them is Francuesca, a French woman and two of the others are the couple we spotted earlier in the day at Lubian. They turn out to be German too and along with Francuesca will become a part of our wider 'pilgrim family' on the last stretch to Santiago.

The final diners at the start of the evening are another couple but they are too far away to discern what language they are using. I imagine most, if not all, of the group will be staying in the albergue. There is, however, no sign of Sergio, Martin and Marian or Karl and Hermann. Our dining experience is finally completed by a group of initially five and eventually six Spanish men, clearly locals and not pilgrims, who converse loudly and enjoy a beer or three! The meal is good, the flan I have for postres, particularly so—certainly one of the better ones I have had. We return to the bar to watch some football, albeit we leave before the game ends. There is a terrific downpour whilst we are in the bar and it is only when the downpour stops, we make our way the short distance back to our hostal, where I set the alarm for seven in the morning before we turn in.

A Gudina to Campobecerros

(20 km or 12 m) largely road walking on the level with some uphill and downhill stretches
Total descent 85 metres

Monday 25th April

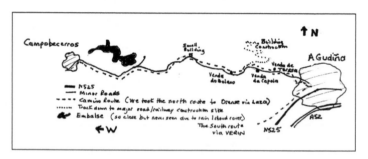

The morning dawns grey with steady rain falling, in sharp contrast to the past few days. A reasonable night's sleep is followed by the usual attention to our feet and togging up for the day's walk. Today will be the first day I start walking with waterproofs for some time, although I am still in shorts with my over-trousers accessible at the top of the rucksack. A couple, who I believe to be Japanese, are checking out as we leave. The bar in our accommodation is not open and therefore we return to last night's eating place for breakfast. No toast though, so we make do with a couple of madeleines and a coffee. Before leaving the town we find another bar that provides us with bocadillos to take out for lunch and where we also enjoy some toast and marmalade whilst these are being prepared.

We finally leave A Gudina well fed and stocked up with food for the day ahead, should it need to be a long 34 kilometre walk to Laza. It is now about nine o'clock and we take the northern route out of the town. This should take us through the village of Campobecerros, where the possibility of a shorter day may lie in store. It is raining persistently as we leave and at times during the day, the rain falls heavily. There are several small hamlets spaced at irregular intervals along the narrow rain-lashed roads we walk along.

For what seems an age we also must contend every other minute with the drenching spray, rotational clanging and back draft from passing cement mixers, each one adding further torment to our sodden progress. As each hamlet looms into view we dream of somewhere to shelter from the driving rain and the churning machines but nowhere offers up such an opportunity. At the second of these hamlets, we see a couple of fellow pilgrims ahead and are wished good morning by the owner of a house, who is standing in his doorway surveying the rain. Our responding— buenos días—seems to lack the conviction of exchanged greetings of the last few mornings.

It isn't long before we catch the fellow pilgrims ahead and re-establish contact with Martin and Marian who tell us they are planning to stay in a bed and breakfast place they believe to be about two kilometres beyond Campobecerros. I reckon we have walked six kilometres beyond A Gudina and probably had to dodge the spray of around 50 cement mixers by the time we pass a turn to the right and down below can see a construction site. Although we don't see one of the heavy lumbering vehicles take this route with its churning load of cement or concrete, once we pass it we only have the occasional car to contend with. A 100m beyond the turn-off a momentary lifting of the gloom allows a view of the site that requires such a continuous supply of concrete. A viaduct that will take the new high-speed railway across the valley below is starting to take shape. At the third hamlet, a fierce dog barks and bares his teeth at our approach, but luckily for us, he is behind a fence and therefore doesn't pose a physical threat.

Despite continually looking for somewhere to stop to momentarily get out of the rain, nothing suitable is found. There are not even any trees big enough to be able to share their leaf canopies either. At one point a small building the size of a bus shelter appears to our right, but it is so dilapidated it does not warrant more than a cursory glance. Negotiating our way through another of the small hamlets, we are faced with three big dogs all of whom bark fiercely and are wandering freely, but thankfully they don't make any threatening moves towards us. The road continues to climb, and the rain continues to pour. At a summit, there is a glimpse of the views Alison describes and for a moment I think it is going to clear, but then the mist and rain descend again, as do we, our road now winding downhill. A fleeting glimpse is presented of an embalse down the valley to our right and a picture is taken when the rain is at its lightest, as much to prove to myself in times to come I did walk this stretch.

The rain increases in intensity again as we arrive in Campobecerros, it is only one o'clock and we have covered the 20km in just four hours, largely because we found nowhere at all to stop on the route. I spot a sign that suggests there is an albergue here and we beat a path to its door, initially locked, but there are fellow pilgrims inside who open the door for us and at last, we get some relief from the rain. The albergue is rather cramped. There are nine sets of bunks giving 18 beds in total. However, all the bunks (bar two) are butted up to each other, which means you are sleeping immediately alongside the person in the next bed, whether in a top or a bottom bunk. There are still three bottom bunks free but sleeping in any of these will mean effectively sharing a bed with a stranger. John and I can sleep side-by-side in a top bunk though and opt for this option.

Getting out of wet things and finding somewhere to give them a chance of drying is the next challenge, followed by trips to the shower and bathroom to freshen up. There is one shower and toilet for men and a similar arrangement for ladies. The showers are good, roomy and have plenty of hot water. In the albergue already are seven people, four of whom were dining in the restaurant last night. The German couple and another woman, who we later come to know as Francuesca—who were all dining together—and the guy from New Zealand. The other three include our long-lost comrades, Karl and Hermann, and there are more man hugs and warm greetings as we catch up on each other's news. The lady who runs the albergue arrives whilst we are getting sorted and stamps our pilgrim passports and collects the eight euros, we each pay for our night's accommodation.

A group of four South Koreans arrive and initially after a short conversation depart again, clearly put off by the prospect of having to sleep close together in top bunks or next to strangers in bottom bunks. It is not long, however before they return, realising in terms of accommodation tonight, this is the only show in town! We discover later they are called Moon and are all related, being a brother and a sister, each with their respective spouses. In such circumstances sleeping 'together' in top bunks is perfectly acceptable.

John and Karl are in deep conversation. Karl is from south-east Germany not far from the Austrian border and has a son who lives in Newcastle, who married an English wife. Both John and I have family connections with the area, too, so have geographical anecdotes to swap and pass the time as the steam rises from drying clothes. The windows mist to block out views of the pouring rain and most people are lying in their bunks to keep warm, keep dry or to do a little reading and reflecting on their journeys.

John's conversation with Karl moves to discussions about long-distance walks in general. He has walked three previous Caminos, and this is his second visit to the Via de la Plata, having walked as far as Salamanca on the first trip. He is confident he and Hermann will get to Santiago this time. Before we arrived at the albergue he ascertained there is a bar that also does food a short distance away and John agrees we will join him and Hermann there later.

There is no signal in the albergue, so it is impossible to text home to confirm where we are or that we are safe and well. Maybe we will get a signal from the bar later. A 14th peregrino arrives as John and I are resting on our beds and for a while, the rain eases before at around quarter-past four it gets heavier again. Pilgrims come and go from the albergue during the afternoon, presumably to venture to and from the bar.

The rest of the tortilla and a drink of water complete a late lunch before I turn my thoughts to what lies ahead. Contemplating our journey forward from here, it seems we may have different options on places to stay but we should be in Ourense in three days, where we plan to stay for two nights and have a rest day. The weather is supposed to be better tomorrow before getting wetter again for a further two days. Karl, however, reckons there will be rain every day now until after Sunday. Whatever will be, will be!

I didn't hear the first cuckoo today until we were in the albergue and I was in the shower. Thinking about it, there were no skylarks or any other birdsong at all heard between A Gudina and Campobecerros. It has been a while since any buzzards or other birds of prey have been seen, which is perhaps surprising. Less surprising is the fact we haven't seen any storks now since our unscheduled detour out of Puebla de Sanabria.

We had, at different times today, options of leaving the road. On other days a break from walking on tarmac would have been most welcome and I am sure on a dry and clear day we would have had no hesitation in enjoying such deviations. In any pilgrimage walk, however, it is the combination of weather, terrain and distances that create the challenge. Today the weather trumped all. I am writing up my notes warm and dry in my sleeping bag but can both see and hear the rain hammering down. I know outside rivulets of water are rushing down the street outside the albergue. For now, no-one else is contemplating venturing out.

The smell of damp clothing pervades the confined area of the single room we are all in and I ruminate there is not much chance any of the clothes hanging or draped around the place will be dry by morning. Even my pilgrim passport is wet, and I have pinned it, completely unfurled to a notice board in the vain hope doing this may dry it out. It has increasingly become a key aspect of the walk, the evidence that demonstrates the paths I have followed and the places I have stayed. From tomorrow it will be encased in plastic and kept in an inner pocket of the rucksack, where even torrential downpours cannot penetrate.

Today has been reminiscent of the wettest days on my 2012 Pennine Way walk and just like at the end of those days, my boots are stuffed with paper and are strategically placed under a radiator to catch any heat that may emerge.

It is by now quarter-past five and we have been dozing and writing notes, apart from our short lunch break for over two hours. Finally, the rain eases sufficiently for us to tog up and set off to go to the bar. Despite on several occasions being promised the prospect of an early dinner, we finally dine at quarter-past nine and leave at ten. Sergio is staying in a room at the bar and we are reunited with Martin and Marian, their B&B, far from being two kilometres beyond Campobecerros, is at the only bar in the middle of the village. We share a laugh at the vagaries of our communication skills. I am impressed at her ability to make a phone call and arrange accommodation and then to find where it is, recalling our earlier attempts to contact and find the private albergue that was supposed to be near to Caparra.

Whilst John is in conversation with Karl, I get chance to talk to Sergio. He has walked the whole Camino and set off from Sevilla two days before Maureen and I left there. Although he is a Spaniard he lives in Portugal. He seems to want to say more but we get interrupted by Hermann at this juncture and the moment passes. Sergio seems very troubled in some way, but he doesn't elucidate on what is bothering him, despite spending further time with us all during the evening.

It is Karl who initially believes we are promised to be able to eat at six before this gets amended to first seven, then eight and finally nine o'clock. One of the consequences of this is we get to drink several beers before we eat, and this affects the mood of all present. Karl certainly gets quite merry, Sergio seems to become increasingly sullen, whilst Marian just seems to radiate warmth, which Martin seems to fully appreciate.

Karl decides to tell us his favourite joke. "Two hillbillies were enjoying a meal together in a restaurant when at a nearby table a younger woman suddenly starts to choke on something she is eating. One hillbilly jumps and goes to her aid. He helps her to her feet, lifts her dress and pulls her pants down to expose her bare bottom. He then bends down and briefly runs his tongue along her left buttock. She is so shocked by this she coughs, and the piece of food is released. Whilst she is recovering her composure, the hillbilly returns to his table. He turns to his friend and says, I've heard great things about the hind lick manoeuvre, but I didn't know it was that effective!"

I am sure Hermann has probably heard it before, but he seems to laugh more than anyone. The joke elicits a smirk from Martin, who in turn gets a disapproving smile from Marian. It goes over the head of the Moon family and Sergio is unmoved. Like several of the pilgrims we have met who set out alone, (Bernhard, Millie and Inieste) he seems to prefer his own company and to be a troubled spirit.

For such pilgrims, the Camino has an element of self-punishment and the motivation to continue is about the search for redemption. Others, like Erico, Giovanni, Marie and Andreas set out alone but linked up with others. They are happy to share their daily experience of the Camino, and whilst each has their reasons for walking its path, none are soul searching to the same degree.

Perhaps it is as well the waitress finally arrives to attend to our needs, and we experience the start of 15 minutes of an almost theatrical performance from our hostess. She starts by bringing and carefully arranging glasses for us all and then five minutes later returns with cutlery which she puts in place settings and then decides to tamper with these until she appears satisfied. A further short delay follows whilst she goes in search of serviettes which are at first, placed in the middle of the place settings and then, picked up again and moved to sit alongside the knives. During this process she studiously avoids eye contact and twice ignores our attempts to have menus brought to the table.

Only when she is completely happy with the foodless tableau, does she go away and return with menus and then hovers, imploring us to decide on what to eat. Marion takes charge in terms of managing this on our collective behalf as the waitress is clearly not used to having to take meal orders from so many foreigners at the same time. The 11 of us, the Moon family, Karl, Hermann, Marian, Martin, Sergio and ourselves dine together and there are no further additions to our party in the albergue when we return, although 14 of us sleeping in the spaces we have is sufficient, I think! Teeth are cleaned, and I am in bed by half-past ten.

Campobecerros to Laza

(14 km or 8.5 m) a short and mainly downhill stretch
Total descent 501 metres

Tuesday 26th April

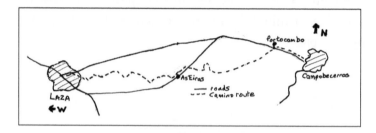

I don't sleep well adjusting to the noise of snoring from most of our company at some stage or other. It is difficult to discern who has the loudest or least musical snore and to be clear from where each noise emanates, although Karl is the most persistent culprit. It is also disconcerting to open my eyes at one point and be peering directly at John's face, less than six inches away. Later he reveals he too had a similarly uncomfortable nocturnal experience. Passing the night within the confined space of this albergue is certainly a one-off. I do drop off to sleep from time to time and am woken either by the snoring, or on the final occasion, by a whispered conversation in German between Karl and Hermann as they get up, dressed and ready themselves to leave; no doubt to be the first arrivals at the next accommodation stop, where they can seek the best bottom bunks.

It is still dark outside and isn't long after six o'clock when I first become aware of their whispering. They are trying so hard to not wake others, but the noise of their rustling bags and continued whispering soon wakes everyone else. Despite it becoming clear most in the room are now awake, their conversation continues in whispers. At half-past six I get up to use the bathroom, but clamber back into my bunk determined not to get up just yet. Whilst it is still dark outside, a glance through the window towards the street lights shows the rain has abated, not surprising given the amount of water thrown down yesterday.

With the group of us in the albergue and four more peregrinos using the accommodation at the bar, there were 18 pilgrims in Campobecerros last night; a real boost for the local economy. Judging by the way providing dinner for us all last night was handled, I imagine it is unusual to have so many pilgrims stay at the village on the same night. No doubt the weather played a part. Most of the group would have continued to Laza had it been kinder.

The Germans continue their whispering and packing, oblivious to everyone else. They are away by seven and silence returns to the albergue. The urge to metaphorically "bag a bottom bunk" first at the next stopping place must be a strong one. If we are away by nine o'clock, we will be in Laza by lunch time, which is where most people are planning to stay this evening, including Karl and Hermann.

It is a good hour later when we are ready to depart by which time we are on first name terms with the South Korean Moon family! They started from Sevilla a day after I did but managed to overtake us because of our unscheduled stay in Salamanca. They have a plane home on the 14th of May. Getting up and dressed into dampish clothes is not a great start and my boots are still wet. Hopefully, they will dry during the day's walk if the rain holds off. We say farewell to the albergue, (home for the last 19 hours) and head to the bar for breakfast where we discover there is nothing to eat and we must make do with a coffee!

Our walk starts pleasantly, without the rain of yesterday as we go uphill along a small road. There aren't any vehicles. Indeed, we don't encounter a single car between Campobecceros and Laza. At the top of a little rise in the path there is a cross and it is here we catch up with the Moon family again. They are all wearing brightly coloured ponchos each a different colour: green, pink, blue and yellow. The mist hangs above the valleys and high on the hills too, but we do have bright yellow gorse for company as we now start to drop down into the small hamlet of As Eiras.

After the breakfast disappointment, we are pleasantly surprised to discover, a little 'unofficial' café with homemade biscuits, cakes and jams. Casa Ultreia is a splendid find.

It serves toast and coffee too. Martin and Marian are already enjoying steaming mugs when we arrive and before we depart the New Zealander who was with us last night joins us, as does Francuesca. As we are getting ready to depart the Moon family appear at the door, look inside before disappearing again without stopping—they don't know what they are missing. The younger German couple arrives as we are bidding our farewells, feeling blessed that because we only had coffee at Campoberrecos, we were able to enjoy the homemade goodies on offer here.

The next stretch is a stunning downhill walk to Laza, with views down the valley to our right and far away to the Sierra de Queira. I reflect on a dry day with no low cloud and mist, yesterday's walk would have been equally memorable. The scenery of the morning has been reminiscent of Scotland: pine trees, gorse, quiet roads, valleys surrounded by hills. The only missing ingredient being the lochs.

For the last three kilometres we are joined by a black and tan dog. At times he is following and at others leading; he certainly seems to know where he is going. It is as if he just wants to share his journey with us rather than walk alone. I vaguely remember the same dog being outside our stopping place in As Eiras, which is a good six kilometres back! We arrive at the railway and cross a bridge before turning right to reach the outskirts of the town.

As we arrive in Laza under greying skies, it is carnival time. There is music and a small parade with villagers dressed in garb similar to Morris men wearing mainly white tunics and pantaloons with red, yellow and blue ribbons and tassels tied around their waists and ankles. Blouses on the women and shirts on the men are adorned with blue brocade. There is a large flag pole, with a long tapering log lashed to its end and a small flag tied high at the top.

As we wander round the small town, we can hear the explosive bangs of fireworks. Aside from the carnival gathering, the rest of the town seems at first soulless, as we start to become reunited with our 'pilgrim family', starting with Martin and Miriam. There are cooking facilities within a small kitchen in the albergue we are informed, as we link up with our Danish amigos and find the local supermarket to buy some provisions. We return with them to get our first experience of the albergue, a very pleasant surprise after last night. It is purpose-built and is all on one level, with wide corridors with several bedrooms along one corridor, each with four bunk beds. There are also ample showers and toilets and a large dining room and sitting area in addition to the small kitchen. The whole building is designed within a quadrant, the inner walls of which are primarily glass so you can see across to the different areas. There is an outside sitting area, too.

We leave our rucksacks and go back into Laza to find the Ayuntamiento, where we can register, pay for our stay, get a key for the albergue and get our pilgrim passport stamped. Back at our accommodation, there is time to get damp clothes on radiators to dry, shower and change, sort out rucksacks, before heading to the kitchen. A lunch of chicken noodle soup, bread and cheese and a glass of water will sustain us until later. More peregrinos arrive as the day wears on, the Moon family and the German couple, Francuesca and Sergio (who tells us he is from Merida), but is currently living in Porto in Portugal. No trace of Karl and Hermann, though. There are five other pilgrims I haven't come across before and by the end of the afternoon there are 23 of us in total, but as the albergue holds 32 there is plenty of space for us all, if not for all our clothes that desperately need drying.

By half-past two in the afternoon every inch of radiator space has some item of apparel draped over it, the South Koreans have even rigged up a zig-zag of wires above a radiator from which to hang their items, not all as brightly coloured as their ponchos. It is a shame the excellent facilities in the building don't run to a proper indoor drying area. There is no Wifi connection, either. Outside, the rain continues to beat down; most pilgrims are either resting on chosen bunks or sitting in the lounge/dining area reading or writing notes, like me. As the afternoon wears on, Sergio bravely togs up to face the elements.

"I think there is a bar serving food not far from here," he throws out, as if to justify his departure.

I use the inertia of this down time to conjecture on how far we have still to walk to Santiago de Compostela—155km, I reckon. It certainly seems a long time ago since I linked up with John in Zafra and even longer since I set off with Maureen on the Via de la Plata. For a long time, Santiago seemed an impossibly long way ahead, but now it seems almost within touching distance.

Outside the rain eases somewhat and we seize the opportunity to venture out into the town. Despite the rain, the carnival is in full swing. There is music to listen to, the bars are overflowing (as are the glasses in the hands of the animated village folk). There is dancing in the streets and it seems the whole population are out in their finery. Laza warms to me the longer we stay here. We are acknowledged and smiled at by many of the locals as they enjoy a special day on their town's calendar.

We find Sergio in a bar not far from the albergue and he negotiates some racciones for us to eat. He certainly seems to be another troubled spirit, in the space of an hour, I have almost all his life story.

"I smoke, I have a sedentary life-style, I have given up working and am living off my investments," he begins. "I am not wealthy, but I do okay". He goes on to tell us he has an Argentinian wife and a four-year-old son. "I am a Spaniard living in Portugal. I much prefer the passion and vividness of the Spanish way of life to the calmer considered, almost Britishness," he says and casts a smile in my direction, "of the Portuguese."

I am a little taken aback by what comes next.

"I didn't plan or intend to walk the Camino. I left the house one day and just decided to do it!" Indeed, he left home without kissing his wife or son goodbye! He fully intended to be home later.

Perhaps not surprisingly (referring to his wife) he says, "She was shocked when I rang her to tell her I would be away for a few weeks." He had decided on the spur of the moment to undertake his pilgrimage walk. Faith in God has got him thus far he states. "I have lost faith in politicians and politics, Spanish politics in particular." We then enter a deep discussion about the Spanish Civil War and how the older generations in Spain can't forget and don't want to change their positions. "They talk in adversarial terms about who they know and who was on the 'other' side." Younger Spaniards in general however seek to work towards reconciliation, so the whole country can move on. "I fear we may have to wait until more of the 'oldies' are no longer with us," he concludes.

His wife wants to return to Argentina, but he isn't at all sure that is what he wants. "At the moment though I am not living in Spain, I am only two hours away from my spiritual home. I have few friends but those I have are all Spaniards living here in Spain."

What lies next in his life is finishing the Camino, beyond that he doesn't want to contemplate. A look of tortured sorrow fleetingly crosses his face as if he knows at some point he will have to choose between his beloved Spain and his Argentinian wife and child. He has walked most of the way to Santiago and he still hasn't found the answer, the guidance, or the resolution he desperately hoped he would.

Leaving the bar, we head back into the centre of the town to experience more of the carnival atmosphere. We watch entranced as a young girl is serenaded and danced with by several of the young men of Laza, each one seeming to want to outdo their predecessors in whirling her around the little square. On the other side there is a stage and later a group play a mixture of pop and rock, whilst a statuesque young female singer on lead vocals commands the stage and the attention of most of her audience. We bump into Sergio in another bar just across from the square and share a drink. He is happier—he is on the Camino, he is going to get to Santiago, all is okay in his world. We both know it is the drink talking and he has suppressed his demons for another day.

We are back at the albergue by half-past nine after our enjoyable evening. The heating is on, which has certainly aided the drying process and there are now lots of empty places on radiators where dry garments have been removed. Now the atmosphere is stuffy, and it is necessary to open the window in the dormitory to let some fresh air in. Martin and Marian are preparing to go to bed, a young Japanese guy is already in his sleeping bag, there are two spare bunks and the remaining one awaits Sergio's return. It is about ten-past ten when he arrives back and by half-past, we are all tucked up in bed and the lights are out.

Outside the daylight is fast fading and the rain is falling heavier again.

Our Japanese pilgrim informed John, "It won't be raining from eight in the morning, though it still will be at seven!"

I think he is living more in hope than certain knowledge. Depending on the weather, our day tomorrow will either be 23 or 34km. Our fitness levels, feet and who knows what else may have a bearing on the matter, too. John has used the last of the cheese and bread to make bocadillos for tomorrow, which will serve as our lunch, if we can get breakfast at a bar in the morning, or as breakfast if we can't—such things are never a given on the Camino.

I reflect again on Sergio and the time we shared this evening. I felt for the past few days he wanted to share more with me. I don't, however, recognise his description of the Portuguese in Erico and ponder how many days ahead of us he may be and whether he has got to Orense yet and met up with his wife-to-be?

Sergio explained the tradition of a village girl, chosen the day before, to dance with the men of the town and Laza was famed throughout Spain for its 'fiesta'. I felt particularly fortunate to have been able to share in that experience today. The second bar we met him in was certainly the fullest Spanish bar I have ever been in. The brass band was still playing as we left the centre to return to the albergue and no-one seemed to have let the rain dampen their spirits in any way.

As Sergio said, "The Camino makes things happen in your head," which is true, but the one thing it can't do is resolve an issue of the allegiance between two powerful forces of love, your country or your wife. I am still thinking about Sergio as I drift off to sleep.

Laza to Xunquiera de Ambia

(34 km or 20.5 m) an undulating walk taking in several small villages
Total ascent 94 metres

Wednesday 27th April

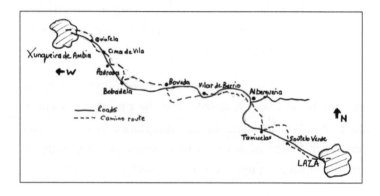

Another fitful night's sleep is endured before most people start getting up at around half-past six. Several times people leave the room in the night to use the facilities, with Sergio being the main culprit. Unusually for me, my first visit coincided with this hubbub of risings. It is still dark outside, so I can't tell whether it is raining or not. At least the rain is not hammering on the roof though.

A breakfast of fruit tea, apricots, bananas and a Madelaine are enjoyed before we set off. Everybody seems to be up and organised this morning, whilst it takes us until around ten-past eight to get out of the door. Ironically enough, only Sergio remains, still trying to get his stuff (and I suspect his head), together before departure. The keys are dropped off at the ayuntamiento as requested and we head out of the little town of Laza, which has, during our brief dalliance here, given us some very fond memories. The carnival was a real bonus and the warmth of its people, despite the inclement weather, will be well remembered, too.

Just as we are leaving Laza behind, we see a figure ahead of us and work out it is Francuesca, walking alone as usual. We are on a tree-lined road and there is rain in the air and at times light rain does fall. This means we keep waterproofs and rucksack covers in place. The first cuckoo is heard and not long after this, a cuckoo is spotted high on a tree to our left, giving vent to her oh so familiar refrain.

We are soon at the village of Soutelo Verde, where Alison informs us there is a place for swimming—what a shame we have forgotten our trunks! Just after, a hare dashes across our path—he doesn't appear to have his trunks with him either! He comes into view again in a field further ahead and to our left. He is a magnificent specimen and a spectacular sight as he eats up the ground in huge effortless bounds. This short but enjoyable distraction means we have, for the first time in the space of the last hour lost visual contact with Francuesca. More eucalyptus trees appear at about the moment I am trying to locate a road route to Tamicelas, which would, Alison informs us, avoid a steep 500-metre climb, stretching over six kilometres to Albergueria.

No such detour option is discovered, meaning we are committed to the climb, which even has a name— The Monte Requeixal. It provides some splendid views as we get higher and higher. It is steep, but enjoyable, although we do require three stops before we get to the top. Before the first of these, we can see Francuesca ahead. She walks quickly but we are gaining on her, before our first stop. For the rest of the climb it is as if she is on a long piece of elastic, the distance between us gets longer during our stops and then gradually shortens again when we are on the move. This pattern continues to the summit and on the drop into Abergueria, when she suddenly disappears between two houses on our left.

Looking left when we arrive, we find a little hidden bar, that offers a drink and food to take away, too. It is literally full of shells—every wall, ceiling, nook and cranny is covered with them. Most are encrypted with the names and nationalities of pilgrims and the dates they passed through. The bar offers shells for all visiting pilgrims to write on. We are assured all will find pride of place somewhere within the building. Francuesca, Martin, Marian, the Moon family and three other pilgrims are enjoying the hospitality and warmth provided and we join them around a group of small tables. It is just after half-past 11 and we have covered around 12km from Laza to get here, despite our stops on the way up the climb.

It starts to rain again as we arrive, and the bar provides a perfect haven to relax for a while. A rather tasty looking pie is added to our provisions and we enjoy a hot drink and a piece of cake. A blazing fire in the open grate and a country version of 'Ring of Fire' greet our arrival. One of the other three pilgrims is Dutch. Her name is Elsa who, it transpires, has also stayed in some of the same places as us over the last few days. She was in the albergue at Laza last night. Along with Elsa, we share experiences with Francuesca, Martin and Marian about the wonderful carnival atmosphere yesterday. Rather surprisingly, we discover none of the Moon family saw or experienced anything as they spent the whole of their time whilst in Laza at the albergue. That's the second time in as many days they have missed out on wonderful experiences shared by most of our Camino 'family'.

The soporific warmth of the fire in the bar is enticing us to dally and the sound system is now treating us to Dylan singing 'Coming Home'. Home seems a long way away and whilst returning there to Sandra and my family will be extremely welcome, I am going to miss my Camino family, too—several of whom I have grown very fond of during my journey of discovery.

We have a beautiful walk again with the lush, broad valley below us as we drop from the mountains that have been our companions for a week or so. A watery sun keeps us company during our morning descent into Vilar de Bario. Coffee is enjoyed outside a little bar on the corner of a square, which also contains a green, at the centre of which a fountain is at work. A leak in a spot where its footings meet the ground means there is a soggy semi-circle of grass to one side. After the coffee, we sit on a bench by the fountain and for the first time in what seems like ages, are blessed with a warming sun. Elsa arrives and waves to us. She is staying here tonight, so our paths may not cross again for a while.

Setting off again, the sunshine gradually overpowers the clouds and we have her warmth for the rest of the day. We start encountering strange structures which look like giant's coffins built on pillars at either end, usually with steps up the side of one of these pillars.

They reach up as high as nearby houses with their steep pantiled roofs and some have a small cross attached to them. I think they may be family places of prayer and contemplation.

Upon my return home I learn from Maureen they are horreos (grain stores), although, despite their much humbler purpose, the construction and ownership of them are seen as giving the family status.

A hoopoe is spotted after we pass through the village of Boreda and from here we have a long but effortless walk on an earth track between fields and on occasions these are also edged with streams. We experience a succession of crossroads at the sixth of which a memorial stone is evident, whilst at the seventh, we make a right turn to reach a road, which we soon leave again to take a track behind some properties and have woodland on our right. The word ANIMAITE is written in pebbles in the path as we walk a short stretch between two villages.

At one point a grisly gnarled tree ahead takes on almost human form and seems to be showing us our onward route.

From here we drop to tarmac again and soon arrive at the albergue—on the right before we get to the main centre of Xunquiera. It is full but has room for two more and there are familiar faces as well as some new ones, too!

Another cold shower experience, which whilst not pleasant leaves me feeling refreshed, especially after I am dry and dressed in my evening clothes. I try to write up notes and at the same time engage in conversation with fellow pilgrims. Initially I have a lengthy conversation with a fellow 'Brit' called David, a young man with shoulder-length hair and a wiry build. He is cycling the Camino and is the first person from the UK we have met since Keith and Susan. He picked up the cycle in Sevilla 15 days ago and has averaged between 50 and 60km each day. He pedalled a total of 100km one day. He will be in Santiago de Compostela in two days. It will take us six days more, which includes our planned rest day in Ourense. John, in particular, is looking forward to that.

David tells us he simply could not find the time to walk the Camino and as it was a journey he wanted to undertake, cycling was the next best thing. David, John and I are joined by two New Zealanders (one of whom was part of our party in Campobecerros) and an Aussie. We continue our English-speaking conversations about the Camino and our various experiences.

After we arrive, the sun is again usurped and the sky greys, the heavens open and it pours for a good hour.

Apparently, the person responsible for the albergue will arrive at seven o'clock to take any further fees and to stamp pilgrim passports. There are several bars in the town, so finding somewhere to eat tonight should not be a problem. After our dues are paid and pilgrim passports are stamped, we head towards the town. The road is still wet from the heavy downpour and the afternoon air has a fresh, cooler feel. We find the bar where the Aussie, two New Zealanders and David are dining. The remainder of our group is made up of the young Japanese guy, who was in our dormitory at Laza and a French pilgrim we haven't met before. A pilgrim menu is available for nine euros and I enjoy an excellent lentil soup, followed by chicken and potatoes with some wine and water. It is such a refreshing change to have boiled potatoes instead of chips!

Most people are in bed when we get back to the albergue. It is just turned nine o'clock. By ten everyone is in bed and I am soon asleep. Between half-past 12 and half-past one in the morning, however, I and most of the building are awake. It seems everyone needs to go to the toilet and the doors from the dormitories open out onto a corridor to access these, where the lights are on. One of the drawbacks of an albergue is in the challenge of resting and sleeping sufficiently. Everyone has a different time for when they sleep and rise. Most pilgrims, like ourselves, need to make some nights on the pilgrimage stopovers at small hostals or hotels where a good night's sleep may be had, enough to keep going. Staying every single night in a refugio or albergue would be a challenge.

As I am reflecting on these thoughts my watch tells me it is now half-past two. It is probably after three when I finally get to sleep, only to be woken again around six to endure another hour of German whispering and bag rustling as Karl and Hermann start their routine. By seven they have no reason to return to the dorm and are gone. The building has two dormitory rooms, each with ten beds and there are nine of us in each. In ours as well as Karl and Hermann, are the younger German couple, the Japanese guy, (whose name I believe to be Haru), the Aussie guy and another German man, who was also up before seven!

At least for the next two nights we should be able to find a hotel and have a room to ourselves and a chance to catch up on some laundry and sleep.

Xunquieria de Ambia to Ourense

(25 km or 15 m) another undulating day before dropping down into the city
Total descent 366 metres

Thursday 28th April

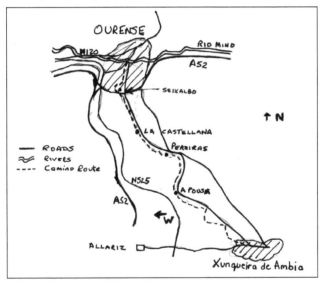

The German couple are the last to leave, about 15 minutes before us. We stop for breakfast in the bar we ate in last night—very good toast, jam and coffee. The arrows now take us on a fiddly route out of town, sending us down several short, grassy and wet paths only to re-join the main road again. Finally, after two kilometres the route sticks to the road. The sun comes out to warm us for about half an hour and we make steady progress, the kilometre markers along the roadside periodically ticking off how far we've walked from our overnight resting place.

Some very small villages and hamlets are passed through and we pause in one to take off the waterproofs. The sun is now hot enough to counteract the chill they have been protecting us from this morning. Soon afterwards I am blessed with another glimpse of an impressive golden oriole; her iridescent green plumage caught by shafts of sunlight, her flight across our paths being heralded by the first cuckoo of the morning. Ahead and to the right, it looks like it is raining over the mountains and at times there is moisture in the air, but so far we are dodging any showers.

We stop at a café and I enjoy the refreshing change of a cup of English tea and John and I share a pain-au-chocolat as good as the ones we had for breakfast at Padornelo. A further 100m beyond the bar is a bus shelter where we can sit and attend to our aching feet. Whilst we are sitting barefoot a local senor with a hoe approaches and engages us in a conversation about the weather, walking the Camino and his self-appointed role as a weed-finder along this stretch of footpath. The rain starts again and we re-emerge from the shelter in waterproofs once more. Our next stop will be in Orense itself.

The next eight kilometres require good concentration as we are walking through the industrial outskirts of the city and must negotiate at times busy road junctions. All around us factories, offices, shops, supermarkets and houses clamour for space, as we make our way towards the centre of the city. We spot a factory with a tall crooked chimney and a stork's nest on top, referred to in Alison's guide, so we know we are on the right road.

A short but pleasant interlude just before the city centre follows, as our route leaves the main road and down cobbled streets into what originally would have been a separate village on the outskirts of the then much smaller city—reminiscent of Saltaire, England. We rest in the small courtyard of an old chapel before finding larger roads to take us deeper into the heart of the city itself. The courtyard is also a perfect place for lunch and the pie we got in Albergueira is thoroughly enjoyed along with a banana and a refreshing drink. We meet the younger German couple again, who are very much in love and tend to keep themselves to themselves during the evening stopovers. They, too, are much taken by the cobbled streets, pretty houses and small tourist shops that are all around us. In conversation, we discover they are called Gunter and

Gertrude. They are walking from Salamanca to Santiago. Gunter walked from Sevilla to Salamanca a couple of years ago before he met Gertrude and they have been planning this walk together for the past six months.

It seems to take an age from leaving the sanctuary of the pretty village to negotiate the remaining suburbs until we get into the heart of Ourense itself. Typically, Tourist Information is not open when we finally get there and won't be until four o'clock in an hour and a quarter. We find a bench to rest on in a little park, behind the Tourist Information Office and take off our rucksacks. John explores whilst I stay guard. We are not far from the cathedral or from the Praza Maior and John discovers a hotel with a vacancy just up from our little park. We go back up together and view the room, it is a little small, but we take it. They may have a larger one tomorrow facing onto the street, whereas tonight's room is on the inside and looks upon an internal and rather utilitarian courtyard, where a mason is at work cutting stones as part of a refurbishment. Thankfully, he will stop work at six o'clock (we are informed by our hostess), our faces clearly portray concern at the level of noise he is generating.

The shower is small, but the water is hot, unlike the albergue from yesterday. Once we are clean several items of clothing are washed to give them maximum opportunity to dry before we depart in two days. There are some hangers in a small wardrobe to put things on. We open the window to the courtyard to let in air and allow us to hang items of laundry over the curtain pole. There is also a small radiator under the window, so we have a plan B if we need it. I certainly feel the need of a day's rest; the last six have been the toughest on the Camino so far. We have had the steepest and longest climbs, we have experienced some horrendous downpours, been up in the mountains, lost sleep, and we have been playing catch up ever since our unscheduled eight kilometres detour the morning after our last rest day in Puebla de Sanabria.

We go out to explore more of the city, which in the fading light and damp air is not as impressive as others we have seen. Some larger churches as well as the cathedral—one or two well laid out squares and the odd bar or two. Whilst we are out and about, we meet Gunter and Gertrude again and learn they are also staying two nights here and they are in a hotel just around the corner. A visit to Tourist Information is useful. Our plan for tomorrow is to eat at lunch time and just have a snack in the evening so we can get an early start on Wednesday morning. We return to the Hotel Irixo, which is certainly well placed to visit all the old city sights. The stone mason has finished his work for the day and though none of our washing is yet dry it is at least drier than when we left it.

Plate 25
Foot-stop in Requejo de Sanabria - Day 31

Plate 26
Blue flag irises in Lubian – Day 32

Plate 27
Welcome to Galicia sign bearing my initials at Alto da
Canda – Day 32

Plate 28
I almost step on a snake just before A Canda – Day 32

Plate 29
Casa Ultreia, the unofficial café in As Eiras – Day 34

Plate 30
Horreos (grain stores) start to appear in the villages – Day 35

Plate 31
The grisly gnarled tree presents an almost human form – Day 35

Plate 32
The crooked chimney, complete with stork's nest – Day 35

Chapter Nine

A day of rest in Ourense

Friday 29th April

A good night's sleep, only waking once, and it is after seven before I am fully awake and not until three-quarters of an hour later before I am up, washed and dressed. A check on the weather outside reveals it is dry, but rain is forecast from midday onwards and into the evening. Any outdoor sightseeing is therefore planned for this morning. The better news on the weather front is it is forecast to be warm and sunny on Wednesday and Thursday; the two days we will spend in Santiago at the end of our epic adventure. We plan to take four days from here to walk there. I am suddenly hit by how close we now are to our destination and a tinge of sadness briefly enters my head, as I contemplate no longer having a day walking on the Camino to look forward to!

However, last night I noticed a gash starting to open, on the inner side of my right walking shoe. Although four more days on the Camino might not be enough for me, they will certainly be enough for my footwear. They may just last to Santiago, but I already know there will be little point taking them home. They have served me well for two and a half years and over

900km along the Via de la Plata. I owe them nothing but gratitude. They have protected my feet well and there will be a tinge of sadness in leaving them behind.

"Breakfast then," John brings me out of my introspective footwear musings. "And a day of gentle exploration and sufficient rest before our final push," he adds.

As we go down to reception, we learn the larger room option will not be ready to view until later and we make three left turns to find our breakfast destination, sourced yesterday evening. Apart from John and I there is a solitary young woman, with blonde hair at a nearby table, dreamily finishing her coffee. The café is a splendid choice and we have a more leisurely than usual breakfast of juice, croissants and coffee, before strolling down to find the As Burgas hot springs and I remove my socks and shoes to dip my feet in the thermals. I cup the warm water in my hands and immerse my face in it. Several people are already taking to the thermal waters in swimwear to reap the reputed benefit of the spa.

Whether it is the effect of the waters or the benefit of a good night's sleep (or both), I suddenly start to feel more impressed with the architecture, buildings and the aura of Ourense, as we wander around its streets and squares. On our way back to Hotel Irixo, we meet

Gunter and Gertrude and advise them of the little café around the corner that provides butter croissants, freshly made juice and great coffee. They thank us and head off for breakfast, hand-in-hand. Back at the hotel, we are informed it will be at least another hour before our larger room will be ready and so we head back out. Across from the springs is an old market area and it is great fun to wander through, looking at the stalls. All the produce is expertly displayed to best effect. Two nectarines are purchased, and our wanderings bring us to the Parque de San Lazaro, where we enjoy a drink, the nectarines and a little people-watching time.

Wandering back towards our hotel we pass our breakfast café and on impulse, go back in for cake and coffee. Gunter and Gertrude are just finishing coffees and thank us for the recommendation. She reaches up and moves a stray hair from his forehead as they rise in unison and bid us farewell. A copy of the local paper is on the table and I am drawn to a picture on the front page which shows visitors to the cathedral. Centre stage is a picture of our Japanese peregrino, Haru, who we first met in Laza and was precise about what time it would rain in the morning. The picture was taken yesterday, and I manage to take a photograph of it to give to him, should we meet him again over the next few days.

It was by pure chance we went back there and found the paper and on our return to the hotel another missed opportunity reveals itself. The young woman we saw in the café earlier is in reception, checking out and waiting for a taxi to appear. I overhear her conversing in what I guess is an 'Aussie' accent and ask if she enjoyed her breakfast and whether she has been in the city long. It turns out her name is Sarah Mackenzie, she and her jazz quartet played at a club just around the corner last night. Today they are off to Belgium to play there, before flying south again. We bemoan the fact we were not aware of her gig last night, promise to look her up and wish her well for the rest of the tour. Later we listen to some of her music online and are impressed. So, whilst chance allowed us the opportunity to spot the picture of our Japanese fellow pilgrim (he will later be thrilled to receive it), it deprived us of the opportunity of hearing Sarah live. Next week the jazz club has the Benny Green Trio and in three weeks, Lucky Peterson will be headlining.

The room we have been waiting for, we surmise, must be the room Sarah had. It is certainly a step up from last night and is at the front of the small hotel, overlooking the street and square. It also has a balcony reminiscent of our room at Hostal Sara in Salamanca. It is well worth the additional five euros per night supplement. We gratefully move our things to the new room. It is once we have done this and settled in we listen to Sarah and her quartet on YouTube.

Back out in the city we visit the cathedral of Saint Martin that yesterday made front page news in the local paper. We then head southwards towards the river to find the bridge where we will cross as we leave tomorrow. The modern and sweeping curves of the cantilever structures on the new bridge to the left provide a perfect contrast to the solid stone Romanesque medieval Ponta Vella bridge on which we stand. They reflect the playful nature of the city of Ourense.

Some wonderful street sculptures similarly provide an interesting twist to its pull as a tourist destination. Whilst the rain holds off, the sun doesn't make a mark, though the city itself is warming. Whilst it might not quite captivate as Salamanca did, it has a lot to offer. It takes its name from the Roman Aquae Urientes, based on the discovery of the hot springs which are still used today. It has a population of just over 100,000 and is the largest place between Zamora and Santiago. It was renamed Sedes Auriensis in the fourth century and was a residence for the kings of the province in the sixth and seventh centuries. It has several renaissance and baroque churches and chapels as well as many Romanesque buildings. The Praza Maior is a splendid square, albeit not as large in scale as its equivalents in the other major cities we have navigated.

We return to the hotel to change before going out to an Italian restaurant we identified on our wanderings. La Tagliatella turns out to be an inspired choice. We sit down to eat at three o'clock and order a pasta dish each and a salad to share. The pasta comes in a huge bowl and there is plenty of parmesan to adorn it. Italian food is our favourite go-to choice and for me, this is as good as any Italian food I have ever tasted. The rain has held off, we have enjoyed our meanderings through the city and been treated to a splendid meal, and I am only four days away from Santiago. I am feeling particularly blessed.

Back at the hotel, we settle the bill, so we can leave early in the morning, before going up to our splendid room for a well-earned siesta. It is after seven when I wake and John has had a good sleep, too. We venture out for the last time to wander around the city and go in search of a beer. We have one in an Irish bar—with no football, but bump into Sergio who arrived this afternoon and like us is planning to stay for two nights. He should arrive in Santiago the day after we do if our respective onward journey goes according to plan. He still has not resolved his big dilemma, although he confides he is missing both his wife and son and is now looking forward to being reunited with them in less than a week.

After leaving the Irish pub, we find the jazz club and have a drink there, unfortunately without live music. A huge grand piano sits at one side of the stage area and pictures of the many artists who have graced the premises over the years adorn the walls. I close my eyes to recall the YouTube clip and can imagine what it would have been like here yesterday evening. Ah, well! Despite that, Ourense has provided an enjoyable rest day and given us all the energy we need for the final push to Santiago. Back at the hotel, we are in bed by ten o'clock. We plan an early start as the weather is forecast to be dry for the first half of the morning. We have a long day tomorrow, maybe 36km. We have probably clocked up five in our wanderings today.

Plate 33
I bathe my feet in the
spa waters at Ourense –
Day 37

Plate 34
Jazz Club in Ourense with
gig dates – Day 37

Chapter Ten

Ourense to Santiago de Compostella

***

**Ourense to Dozon (39 km or 23 m) uphill to start
with and then gently rolling
Gradient ascended 612 metres**

Saturday 30th April

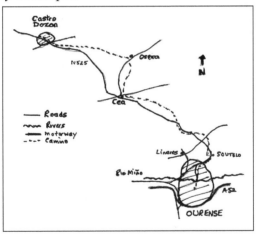

We have a long six kilometre climb out of Ourense
but first we retrace yesterday's steps to find the bridge
across the River Minho. Breakfast is enjoyed at a little
bar about two kilometres beyond our hotel and re-
joining our route, we manage to get lost for a while

before finally arriving at the Ponte Vella. This time, we cross fully over its many arches passing two older pilgrims we haven't seen before as we do so. There are two routes once on the other side, which come together in due course.

We decide to follow the route to the right as we start the long climb. On this stretch we meet two pilgrims who are new to us; Seamus, an Irish pensioner, who has just started, the final stage of his pilgrimage to Santiago today, and Gunter, another German pilgrim. He is a slow walker and we soon leave him behind, but Seamus matches our pace. The steepness of the climb means we have several stops, which each time, provides more conversation with him. He is quite a character and has walked a lot in both Spain and Italy as well as back in his native Ireland.

As we start to leave the city behind and climb along paved meandering roads, the views get more and more expansive each time there is a stop and a chance to look back to Ourense and beyond. We can see as far as the Sierra de Eixe mountains we came over several days ago, reaching up to well over 2,000m above sea level. A gleaming chestnut colt canters in a field to our left and some interesting and rather splendid houses are passed as well as a beautiful garden with palm trees and roses. We catch and then pass Gertrude and her beloved Gunter as they saunter along engrossed in each other's company. Warm smiles and waves are exchanged as our climb reaches another steeper section. We continue until the route finally flattens as we arrive in the village of Viastellae.

Here, we follow the directions to a bar (a detour well worth it), as we discover five other pilgrims there including Martin and Marian. This leads to hugs and greetings all round. Soon afterwards, we are joined by Seamus and Gertrude and Gunter and are a happy crew enjoying Fanta and cake together in the unexpected warm sun. We have covered around 11 and a half kilometres to get here and it is half-past 11. Most of the day's climbing is now over. Everyone gathered at the little bar is either stopping at Cea or going as far as Oseira. They will probably stay at Dozon tomorrow. We say our farewells around midday and head off again.

"What time do you think we will get to Dozon?" asks John.

"Around half-past five," is my confident yet considered reply.

Following Alison's directions, we are on our own again until we get to Cea, apart from our final crossing of paths with Seamus, as we are consulting our guide book at a junction. The three of us agree which is the correct route and we bid our final farewells to Seamus with his mop of white hair, green chequered shirt and faded blue shorts. He plans to take six days to cover the 105km from Ourense to Santiago, whereas we plan to be there on Tuesday. Cea is famous for its bread and as we negotiate our way through, we spot the albergue, which already has a group of pilgrims outside, including Francuesca.

Getting out of Cea proves a challenge and we waste 20 minutes trying to walk out before we get back on track. Again, the guide describes two options to get from here to Dozon, albeit the distances along each are supposed to be the same. It is very pleasant walking though, with rolling countryside, more fields with cows than we have seen for some time and some very pleasant diversions through dappled woodland, albeit some of the paths are a bit squelchy.

On the outskirts of Oseira we encounter two groups of comic life-sized model figures each framed and with a little roof to protect them from the worst of the elements. They are all fully dressed and cut quite a spectacle as they welcome pilgrims to the village.

According to Alison, it is a further four kilometres to Dozon from here and therefore we should be there around five o'clock, in another hour. Unfortunately, the route we take, which (follows the arrows we spot) takes us over two hours and we cover at least a further nine kilometres. It is still pleasant walking, although we are away from farmland for the most part and walking through woods and alongside hedges. A rain shower just before the end of the stretch means we must stop to put on our cagoules and rain covers for our rucksacks, which adds a little more time to what is certainly the longest day since we left Puebla de Sanabria. The greenery is certainly as verdant as any I have seen at any point along the Camino and the beauty of Galicia is evident.

Arriving in the village the albergue is at the other side, hence my calculations about the distance we have covered today. Karl and Hermann are just checking in as we arrive, (they have taken about three hours out of their day by stopping to eat before coming on here). Haru is also here and I show him the picture I took of the front page of the paper in Ourense. He is made up and asks whether he can download the picture onto his phone.

"Of course."

He tells us, "Haru means peaceful clear weather in Japanese."

"Of course, it does," I respond, casting an eye out of the window at the rain lashing down.

The Moon family are here too and are busy making an evening meal in the kitchen. There are two communal showers on the lower floor, one for the men and one for the women. I have it to myself, but as the water is either too hot or freezing it is a case of having to keep ducking in and out of the flow of water until I am fully showered. Afterwards there is time for me to catch up on some notes.

Outside, it is still pouring down; the bar is at least 400m back in the village, so it might be a wet walk for supper tonight. The dormitory has ten sets of bunks. Naturally, all the bottom bunks are taken and there are only four top ones left for John and me to choose from. We end up sleeping above Karl and Hermann again. Ah well, we will be awake by six then!

Apart from being the longest walk for some time, today has been very enjoyable, although tiring. We have also been able to catch up with quite a few of our 'family'. Whilst we had a rest day in Ourense yesterday, most of our fellow peregrinos took two days to walk from there. Three more days and we will probably all be in Santiago. I snuggle down in my sleeping bag to drown out the sound of Karl snoring, but the exertions of the day mean I am soon asleep.

Dozon to Silleda

(28.5 km or 17 m) rolling hills with one short but steep descent
Gradient descended 301 metres

Sunday 1st May

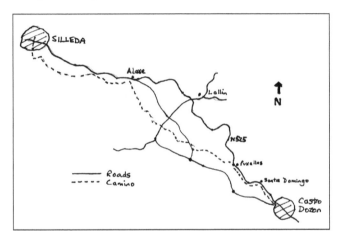

Despite my early descent into slumber, I have a poor night's sleep, at one point lying awake for around two hours. Two women have commandeered a little fan heater to keep warm during the night and instead of switching it off they have left it on and the noise is irritatingly disturbing. After over five weeks on the Camino I have grown to find ways of ignoring snoring, particularly German. But this 'new' distraction is a real pain. At one point I get up to use the facilities and as I creep back into the dorm I am tempted to go across and switch it off. As I tiptoe towards it, one of the two women (who are sleeping together in the bottom bunk, toe to tail) opens her eyes and I smile, swivel and tiptoe back to my bunk, cursing under my breath.

As I clamber wearily into the bunk, I gather up a blanket from the end of the bed, fold it and put it over my exposed ear to deaden the sound of the wretched heater. At least this gives me another couple of hours of sleep before the usual early morning risings. I think Karl and Hermann must have had their slumbers affected, too, as there is no attempt to speak in whispers.

There is also a lot of agitation amongst the Moon family as the husband of the sister has injured his leg. This eventually results in a taxi being summoned to transport him to Silleda, whilst his wife, her brother and partner will continue to walk and link up with him later. Technical problems with most of the mobiles carried by other peregrinos, means my phone summons the taxi and Haru makes the call. This is a typical example of Camino family teamwork in action. Despite all the mayhem the two women in the same bunk are still either asleep or feigning it, much to the chagrin of most of the other pilgrims. Normally, other pilgrims still asleep would be accorded the courtesy of an air of quietness as people went about their early morning ablutions and packing for the day ahead. However, the noise levels this morning are unusually loud as if an unspoken collective protest is being mounted.

It is still raining as we leave the albergue and head down to the bar for breakfast, before backtracking to head towards and then across the N525. It is a lot cooler today and we have some further confusion with Alison's distances. She indicates it is one kilometre to Santa Domingo and then a further five to Puxallos, whereas we walk three to the former and a further two to get to Puxallos. We are still walking in light rain along interesting little lanes as we pass through these two small hamlets. In each a cat is watching our every move from her position on the wall to the garden of a house. I might have thought I was seeing double had one not been a ginger cat and the other grey.

In the next hamlet of Pontenoufe, there is a house with a well-appointed garden with a statue of the 'apostel de Santiago' in pride of place. As we leave Xestas and go along a narrow path between a wall and a hedge I can reach up and pluck a lemon off a tree. I can, but I don't! This stretch is also noteworthy for some of the strange yellow arrow placements we discover, including one pointing skywards.

We stop in Botos de Abaixo for a hot drink in a bar and a blazing fire there offers additional warmth. It is May 1st, we are walking in Spain, but back home in the UK they are experiencing a heat-wave. Yet here we are huddled in front of a fire.

"Doesn't make sense, does it?" says John, as if reading my thoughts.

After the trials and tribulations of the first day walking with John from Zafra and the premature arrival in Salamanca, to provide respite to blistered and aching feet, his commitment to the pilgrimage and his camaraderie along the way have been second to none. As we get ready to depart and hit the trail again, I reach and pick up our two trusty walking poles. It is one of the unwritten rules we have. I am responsible for ensuring John has his pole after every stop we make. Not for the first time I'm met with a sheepish grin and an, "Oh Yes!" Next comes the adjustment to the straps on his rucksack to ensure it is as high as possible. A little unspoken routine that is a feature of our time together on the Camino.

Back on the road, we spot Karl and Hermann and two other pilgrims too; they had all stopped at another bar for warmth and a break. It is now around three hours since we left our breakfast bar in Dozon. As we leave tarmac again and continue along an earthen track, the two other pilgrims are lost from sight. It isn't long before we are well ahead of Karl and Hermann again. In a further six kilometres we stop at another bar, which is equally welcoming and obtain a pilgrim stamp and enjoy queso and jambón bocadillos.

Five other pilgrims are dining here as we arrive and before we leave the three remaining colourful members of the Moon family join us, too. It is only the blue poncho that is missing! As we leave our comfortable surroundings and fellow pilgrims, we discard the rain gear for the first time today and after a further half an hour, unzip our trouser bottoms and apply sun cream. For the first time since early yesterday afternoon, we are walking in warmth again. I spot a hoopoe and we have the usual range of dogs for company and a lot of cats, which seem to be far more numerous in Galicia.

We also hear cuckoos, swifts and swallows and have a comical encounter with a lady and a big black cow. She and the cow are languidly ambling along towards us and I start to get ready to take a picture, which I am 'bigging' up to John beforehand. Suddenly and without warning, she and the cow take a sharp right and she is shepherding the lumbering monster to her new grazing ground. I am left with no picture and egg on my face.

"Bit like fishing," quips John, "that'll be the one that got away!"

Plunging back into the woodland for the umpteenth time, we arrive at an old pack horse bridge across a stream and I instantly recognise the scene. I can recall a picture of Maureen on her 2010 pilgrimage pausing here and having a fellow pilgrim take a picture of her crossing the bridge. The opportunity is not to be missed!

"Do you mind?" I ask John, passing him my camera and taking a position at the apex of the bridge.

"I'm sure this one will be great fun to share with Maureen when we get back."

"Poser," he snaps.

The tenth century Ponta Taboada over the river Deza is in very good condition, with its medieval paved surface dating from 912 AD, Our next stop is at a picnic spot around two and a half kilometres before Silleda, according to both Gerald and Alison. The three Moons catch us up again, but no sign of Karl and Hermann. It is three o'clock and we should be at tonight's resting place in half an hour. I ponder however, just how many times our expected ETA did not match our actual experience.

"I won't put money on it," is John's retort, as if to emphasise the point.

We catch up the South Koreans again along a pleasant wooded stretch with eucalyptus trees. The effect of the warm sun after the morning rain means there is also a strong scent of eucalyptus in the air. We have a false end to the walk as we arrive at a small touristica albergue, but it is a further one and a half kilometres before Silleda is reached. The next challenge is to find our albergue, but between ourselves, the Moon family and eventually Karl and Hermann, we do.

We check in and have a small room overlooking farmland, in which two horses are maternally tending to two new-born foals. An adjacent room has two bijou showers and a toilet. We are on the second floor of three and at the end of a short corridor, past the shower/toilet room there is access to a veranda with tables, chairs and washing lines. Washing is duly done and hung out to dry. A sudden rain shower means this is quickly retrieved and brought back to our rather small room to be draped over every usable surface. Whilst it was only a shower, looking out of the window the sky is considerably darker. We meet Concetta, who was one of the women who stayed at Dozon last night —not one of the bed-sharing pair. Whilst Concetta is originally from Spain, she now lives and works in the USA. She is in Spain until the middle of June and she will link up with her husband and family later in Madrid as they have a family wedding to attend.

We can eat tonight in the bar on the ground floor and arrange to do so between half-past seven and eight, before going out to do some shopping. I purchase a new pen as my one remaining pen gave up the ghost soon after leaving Ourense. This allows me to do some much-needed catching up with my notes. John and I test each other's knowledge of naming the best BWFC ever and then try to come up with the best English 11. We also have some time for reminiscing about walks we have done together before and where this journey of discovery fits in the scheme of things. I know I am certainly going to miss the Camino once we arrive in Santiago.

I plan to speak to my brother, who has lived in France for around 12 years, about the idea of him joining me at a future date and for us to walk from Santiago the 75 or so kilometres to Finisterre on the northwest coast of Spain. Thinking of this, I wonder where Erico and his wife-to-be are, and whether our paths may yet cross before they head on to the coast to declare their undying love. I muse whether this would be an option Gunter and Gertrude would consider and whether Bernhard has found his Viennese señorita yet!

John breaks my musings with an intriguing and very pertinent question.

"What do we do when we get to Santiago—how do we get our pilgrim passport validated and stamped?"

I know Maureen indicated we must get our credentials certified, but like John, I was a bit hazy on how exactly we would do this. Seems daft I had walked all this way with a goal and destination in mind but wasn't quite sure of the 'end game', like dribbling a football from one end of the pitch to the other, then not realising I had to put the ball in the net!

"I'm sure if we go to the cathedral there will be somebody to ask, or maybe one of our fellow pilgrims will know," I offer.

"How about texting Maureen and asking her the question?" responds John.

"Great plan, John, far better to share our slight embarrassment with another mutual friend than the wider world."

Food in the bar is good with a warming soup, beef stifado, the obligatory flan and a couple of beers to wash it down with. Back in the hostal, we contemplate the reality it is unlikely any of the items we washed earlier are going to be dry by morning, particularly as there is no heat in the room. It is another night of dressing up to go to bed and I slither into the sheet-sleeping bag under the covers for extra warmth. We are in bed soon after half-past nine. Surprisingly, it doesn't take long to get warm and I drift off to sleep musing over all the pilgrims I have met throughout my journey and how many I might bump into in Santiago.

Silleda to Outiera

(25 km or 15 m) gently undulating with one steep descent and ascent into the Rio Ulla valley Gradient descended 12 metres

Monday 2nd May

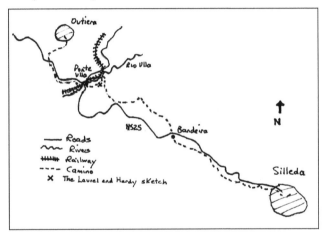

I sleep well, waking up once in the night to use the facilities, at which point I discard the sleeping bag as I am warm enough. It is around six o'clock when I am woken again by the sounds of people using the bathroom and getting up in other rooms on the 2nd floor. We are up and dressed after seven and by the time we have both used the bathroom and packed our rucksacks, the place is empty—a familiar scenario. We are also the only two peregrinos in the bar for breakfast, which is fine by us and then leave the albergue and head into town to pick up the Camino route. In larger places, it is often best to head for the church and start from there and this tactic works this morning. The clock strikes nine as we pass it.

We lazy English, heh?

At first, we are constantly leaving and re-joining the N525 as the route tries its best to keep us off the main road. Finally, we leave the main road behind and have more pleasant if damp rural routes to make our way through. After about an hour and a half walking, we arrive in Banderia and make a great call to stop at a little roadside café, where we enjoy coffee and cake; three euros for both of us and we also get a small complimentary piece of cake and a glass of orange free gratis.

Soon afterwards, we are walking through a woodland stretch again along damp paths, with occasional bursts of spring flowering colour and the scent of damp and decaying wood, mixed in with pine and eucalyptus. A shrine has been created in the belly of a decaying tree, a sure sign we are on the right path.

We are now walking along country lanes that could well be anywhere in middle England, if the buildings we encountered along this stretch weren't built in the Spanish style. We catch and pass three peregrinos we haven't seen before. I spot what I believe to be a nightingale. This is before another hamlet with a bar and we surmise the three pilgrims we passed went in there, as despite further stops by ourselves, they never catch up. Alison's guide promises us a picnic spot just ahead, which we look forward to utilising as a lunch stop. The place is off the Camino to the right, up a steep hill to a shelter on a summit. We decline the opportunity to visit and instead head down a steep and curving tarmac road into Ponte Ulla.

I stop to take a picture of the (unvisited) picnic site high on the hill and John continues down. Suddenly John's feet go from under him and he hits the deck and slides on his back for a short distance, his trusty walking pole flying up into the air. An audible shriek of pain emanates from the prostrate figure.

"Don't worry, John I'm on my way."

I run down towards my fallen comrade and as I get to the spot where he fell, my feet go from under me and because I am running the momentum takes me on my back, sliding past John.

"Fine lot of use you are," is John's remark.

As I am running towards him, I am hoping this is not another broken wrist scenario. Last year John, another friend Simon and I had been undertaking an alternative coast to coast walk and were coming down The Band on Bowfell, when John slipped. We had to cut short our trip and it subsequently emerged he had fractured a wrist. As it was me who arranged the itinerary and route of this trip, I was not popular with Caroline, John's wife. I was dreading having to make a phone call to the UK to share such news!

Luckily, the damage this time is more about cuts and grazes to his hands and the first aid kit has to be wrested from the rucksack to use an antiseptic wipe to clean the wound and apply plasters. He does also suffer a clean break, the bottom five centimetres of his walking pole has completely shorn off with the impact. In the immediate aftermath of our crazy recreation of a Laurel and Hardy sketch, it is good humour that takes over.

We both laugh at our ridiculous situation, lying like beached turtles on our backs in the middle of the road. Thankfully it is a minor road and no cars are on it at the time or immediately afterwards. Regaining our feet, we go back up to the place we both came a cropper and spot a fuel spillage on the road, which creates a surface as slippery as black ice. Of course, the rest of our descent is at a somewhat gingerly pace. Even Karl and Hermann would leave us in their wake.

Once Ponte Ulla is reached, we find a bench, under cover, as it has started to rain again, on which John can sit, whilst I do a better job of patching up the wound and John, still visibly shaken, recovers his composure. Luckily for both of us, the gradient of the hill meant we fell onto our backs and the rucksacks, therefore, took most of the force. As we are sitting there the rain starts to get heavier. Across the street is a little bar and we retreat into it and have a Fanta and a cheese and tomato bocadillo. We have covered 19km today, which would suggest we are only around 20km from Santiago.

We planned to do a further five today and to get to Santiago around lunch time tomorrow. There is also an option to stay here in Ponte Ulla, which given John's tumble may be a good plan. He is adamant however, he is okay and keen to carry on to Outiera, where we are promised there is a newish albergue and the possibility of food being available. Well, that's what both Haru and the Moon family have said.

"I'd rather reduce tomorrow's walk so we can spend more time in Santiago," is John's rationale.

Whilst we are enjoying our lunch and recovering our composure, we read texts to and from Maureen in response to yesterday's enquiry. We are now fully briefed around the protocol and place to go tomorrow. It is a long slog mainly on the roadside, which doesn't seem to accord with any description from either guide. We pass the threesome we saw earlier in the day again and are starting to regret our decision not to stay put in Ponte Ulla. Out of the blue, a sign appears for an albergue one kilometre away to our right. Soon after this, a sign to Outiera is seen; strange there was no such sign at the road junction itself. According to the map Outiera should be off the N252 to the left, anyway.

We keep the faith and carry on walking and our trust is rewarded as we arrive at a very modern looking and expansive albergue, where we are reunited with Haru and all four of the Moon family and several others who were in our accommodation at Silleda last night. Top bunks only of course, but who cares? A hot shower and a change of clothes are next, plus an opportunity to peg yesterday's damp washing on an indoor line. A coffee machine in the reception area provides both a hot drink and a small madeleine. I have time to sit, take stock and write up some notes on another eventful day.

It occurs to me we haven't seen any storks since Puebla de Sanabria and only one nest; on top of the crooked chimney on the outskirts of Ourense. Strangely, given the hills we walked up and over. I've seen no birds of prey since Mombuey. Leaving Ourense aside, the last five days walking has also seen rain commence soon after we have arrived at our overnight accommodation. The stretch from Puebla de Sanabria has given us both more time and opportunity to meet and stay as a 'family' with other pilgrims. I wonder whether we will see Martin and Marion or Inieste again.

It has stopped raining outside and there is no doubt the albergue is in a lovely setting. Mist is still hugging the valleys. We go and sit somewhere where we can take in the view and verbalise our thoughts as realisation sinks in as to just how much we have achieved and how much we have enjoyed this epic pilgrimage walk through rural Spain. Despite the setting, it is very cold sitting for more than a moment and it is still difficult to imagine we are in Spain in May, particularly as we are reminded from texts home that the UK is still enjoying its heat-wave.

Whilst I will miss the Camino, I am really looking forward to seeing Sandra—those blue-green eyes I fell in love with all those years ago—the woman who has been a part of my life for so long and whose support of me and my adventures, has been steadfast and sure. We have deliberately not covered the subject of 'moving or staying put' in the brief conversations and texts we have shared over the past five weeks. I am certain moving to a new home together will be the best option for us both and I am convinced she will have reached the same conclusion.

The hospitalerie arrives and we go and pay our six euros and get our pilgrim stamp and our mattress and pillow covers, these seem to have been a feature of the albergues in Galicia. There will not be any meal provided and it is about a mile to the nearest place which serves food. We have some bread and cheese and a couple of pears and can get more hot drinks from the vending machine, so we should be okay.

There are about five or six Italians in the group tonight, which turn my thoughts to both Giovanni and the 'master and his apprentice'. I also wonder where Seamus has got to, some fellow pilgrims, like him, made a mark on our journey in just one day. We discover there is no heat on in the building, despite requests to the hospitalierie to put it on. Wandering back to where our clothes are hanging over and next to a heat source that isn't switched on is frustrating. At least we will have three nights in a comfortable hotel room in Santiago from tomorrow. For today, we are pilgrims and must suffer.

The coffee machine has ceased to function but at least I manage to make a hot drink for us both with my one remaining liquorice teabag. As I am bringing the drinks back to John, I spot a hoopoe sitting on a fence post watching intently before taking off again. Whoopee for the hoopoe for brightening up what is turning into a grey and cold evening. More attempts are made to persuade the thickset cold-hearted woman who is the hospitalierie, to switch the heating on, this time by the two female Moons. Again, she refuses and soon after is gone. Our fate for the remainder of the evening is set. At least the long-range forecast promises us two warm days in Santiago before we fly home on Friday.

"A good meal out tomorrow night, then."

"Deal," I respond, "with a bottle of wine to wash it down."

There are one or two radiators dotted around the building and I check every single one, but none are on. It will certainly be a case of dressing for bed tonight. I will probably have to wear most of what I have, given a quarter of my items are still damply clinging to a line with no hope of getting any drier. According to the usually reliable "Gerald", the Hospitalierie here may provide food and 'other' refreshments and is reported to be good. There must have been a change or transformation of personnel. Our hostess behaves more like a prison wardress and is most put out to have to give up part of her Monday night to attend to the needs of some stupid peregrinos. I muse on what 'other' refreshments she may offer: cold showers, ice baths, body piercings?

The Moon family are walking around like mini Michelin people with every item of clothing about their bodies. Moon Deuk Yung managed to join the other three on the walk today, having rested up yesterday— not the reward he was expecting at the end of the day. Outside the rain is pouring again. The evening is turning into a real horror show, with pilgrims wandering around shivering with coats on to try and keep warm. Before she left, our 'prison wardress' did a bit of mopping. I'll wager the floors she mopped will still be wet in the morning. I risked her wrath by moving some chairs into the dormitory so I can drape damp clothes on them. There may be more heat from sleeping pilgrims if we close the door to the dorm than from anywhere else.

Other pilgrims quickly follow suit, and soon every chair is in the dormitory and each one has clothing draped over it. There is absolutely no point trying to stay up any longer and an almost unspoken collective decision is made to go to bed. As I don two pairs of socks, a base layer, fleece and slide my sleeping sack inside my sleeping bag and look around, others are clambering into bed in various states of full dress. I pull the sleeping bag tight around my neck and wait for my body heat to eventually start to warm me up. It takes a while (too long), and now I have a cacophony of snoring from those who have managed to get to sleep before me to contend with. I concentrate to distract me from this and eventually drop off to sleep.

Outiera to Santiago de Compostella

(17.5 km or 10 m) gradual descent
Gradient descended 37 metres

Tuesday 3rd May

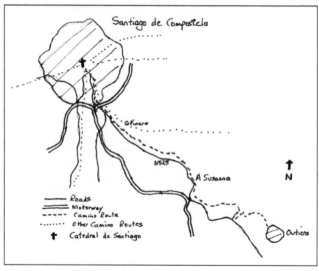

It is a difficult night and I get no more than three hours sleep. I am woken by the noises of people emerging from their cocoons, although nobody is in good enough humour to lay claim to having shed their pupae status. Everybody is in a rush to leave this morning and by quarter-past six, apart from John and I, the dormitory and the whole building is deserted. It is, however, still pitch-black outside.

"Is it something I said or did?" John resists the temptation to rise at first. "I think I'll stay another night; well we might as well get our money's worth!"

We fiddle more in hope than expectation with the coffee machine and it suddenly spews out one drink, but after that refuses to cooperate despite eating several one euro coins. We share the drink between us and as we do so are plunged into semi-darkness as the lights go off around us. They must be on a timer and the hospitalierie doesn't anticipate anyone lingering beyond seven o'clock. Let us take the hint and get out of this place! The last of our supplies provides breakfast, one pear, some dried apricots and a single mini pepperoni stick. We take a final look around to make sure we haven't left anything and then leave, shutting the door on the worst nocturnal experience of the whole Camino.

We now have a walk, as dawn breaks on another grey and drizzly day, along narrow roads and through a forest on a soft leafy track before we spot a bar on the main road away to our left. It is off the Camino but worth the detour to be sitting in some warmth and having a hot cup of coffee each to help us on our way. Another 11km and we will be in Santiago. The route from here once we have re-joined the Camino seems to want to take us on a meandering tour, in which we have lots of changes of direction.

"It just wants us to avoid the main road," ventures John, which is undoubtedly true.

The Camino now throws us one last steep climb before we start to drop down and can see the city ahead of us. I am wrapped up in thoughts of home as well as a real sense of anticipation. Although, I am not sure what exactly I am anticipating. I have walked from Sevilla, which seems a million miles away now and am on the threshold of entering Santiago de Compostella. Maureen was pivotal in my undertaking this journey and sharing the start of it with me, but I owe a huge debt of gratitude to John who has shared the bulk, despite at times being in considerable discomfort.

We catch up with the colourful Moon family by an overpass along which pilgrims have tied or left items from their journeys of discovery. The array of pilgrim memorabilia is too good not to both add to and take a picture.

As we enter the outskirts of the city, we can't yet see the cathedral spire. Following our noses, we continue walking towards the centre and eventually it reveals itself, albeit most of the main tower is shrouded in scaffolding. As we are standing there, I am sure somewhat bedraggled and a little bewildered, a cry of "Peter, John", is heard and as I turn my head in its direction, I am amazed to see Erico striding towards us with a woman by his side.

"You made it!" he says, "I was wondering whether I would see you guys before we left for Finisterre. This is Pauletta, by the way."

"Wow," is all I can muster at first, adding, "when did you get here, is Giovanni here too? Pleased to meet you," in a jumble of unconnected stumbling words.

We find a seat nearby and catch up. Pauletta is every bit the way Erico described her, and it is abundantly clear the two of them are very much in love. A wonderful 15 minutes is spent catching up on events since we were last together in Puebla de Sanabria. It appears we have effectively been a day behind Erico ever since. He and Pauletta stayed two nights together in Ourense. Amazingly they went to see the Sarah Mackenzie Quartet at the jazz club there! They stayed at Ponte Ulla, so missed out on the Outiera experience. Giovanni was with him until Xunqueira de Ambia. He thinks he didn't want to be the party pooper once he met up with Pauletta.

"Ever the gentleman," he sighs. "He is a great guy, I still miss him."

They saw Bernhard at Castro Dozon, but as he is probably staying at his mother's holiday house here in the city, we may not see him. He hadn't met any Viennese señoritas as far as he knew. All too soon we are saying our farewells as the pair of them have a 15 kilometre walk to Ponte Maceira this afternoon on their continuing journey. They plan to catch the sunset over the Atlantic Ocean on Friday evening and pledge their future lives to each other.

We start to follow the directions provided by Maureen to find the location of the pilgrim office where we will have our credentials checked and bump into Steve, the Aussie pilgrim we last saw in Xunqueira. He suggests we will have about an hour and a half to wait once we join the queue, which turns out to be a pretty accurate estimation. That's probably why everybody disappeared by quarter-past six this morning, to reduce their waiting time.

The queue bends around the courtyard and into and around the corridors of the building itself, like a huge pilgrim snake. This means at times you come face-to-face with people ahead of you in the queue and at other times with people behind you. There is an excited and almost hysterical sense of anticipation. Many pilgrim routes end here. The Via de la Plata is not as popular as other pilgrimage routes, like the French Camino, so most of the people around us are not only not familiar but have followed a different journey to get here. The queue is a mixture of people who have arrived today and others who arrived yesterday but may have been too late to get their credentials checked, like Steve.

Soon the Moon family are spotted, and mutual congratulations and hugs are exchanged. This strange mix of satisfied, yet weary pilgrims gradually unravels into a straight line as we near the entrance to where the 'officials' who will check our pilgrim passports and question us about our journeys sit. There is a large semi-circular desk with about a dozen cubicles partitioned off to give each official and each entering pilgrim the opportunity to converse without distraction. A form is provided for each peregrino, within which each must specify whether their journey has been undertaken for spiritual, personal or other reasons. John is stressing about the choice he should make.

"Shall I put personal or other?"

"I'm going to put personal, if that helps John?" I offer.

In the end he opts for other. I approach the counter and offer up my pilgrim passport and we discuss the journey I have undertaken. My credentials are stamped, and I am given a scroll which certifies the distance I have covered. This indicates I have walked 1006km from leaving Sevilla. Incredibly, this is only half a kilometre off from my calculations. John's conversation takes much longer but he joins me with a very satisfied, if somewhat relieved, look on his face.

We find our hotel after about a ten minute walk and bump into Francuesca, who is just checking out. She arrived yesterday too. Congratulatory exchanges are made, and we wish her well on her journey back home to Lille. At the hotel there is a laundry, so we can both wash and dry our clothes. There isn't much of my clobber that doesn't need washing and there are still several items damp from being washed two days ago, that could probably benefit from being rewashed. I ring home to confirm we have arrived and write up some notes. Our hotel is pleasant, recommended by Maureen. The hot shower is brilliant. I stand there luxuriating in the hot water almost as if the dirt of the last 42 days needs to be eradicated from my body. More likely, it's the need to warm up after last night's experience!

My mind wanders back to the Camino. I will miss it, as one misses an old friend. I will miss the journey, the peregrinos, the albergues, the holm oaks, the yellow arrows, the buzzards, storks, cuckoos and wild-flowers.

It is a strange feeling after so much of my energy and sense of purpose has been poured into getting here, to be now feeling at somewhat of a loss. What have I learned about myself? Maybe that I do have the inner resources to call upon when needed, I am determined enough to see things through. Whilst I originally planned to walk alone, having first Maureen and then John for company was, on reflection, a far more rewarding option. I had been impressed by the life stories and sheer willpower of many of my fellow pilgrims and of the care and comradeship, many offered along the way. My health and sense of well-being are sky-high.

On a more mundane level it is strangely satisfying to have a full set of freshly laundered clothes to choose from. We manage to print off our boarding passes for the flight home on Friday. We can now relax and set off back into the centre of Santiago, minus backpacks and with no more days of walking to contemplate. We cut a pretty picture as a pair of weather-beaten ageing buck sticks, sporting slightly sickly grins as we find somewhere to have something to eat and a beer. We are also keeping our eyes peeled to see if we can spot any other members of the 'family' who have been a huge part of our journey for many days. It is still quite cold, but at least it is not raining.

Exploring Santiago is an interesting experience. It is the third most popular Christian pilgrimage destination after Rome and Jerusalem. It is also a city that knows what it is and there are many shops selling pilgrimage mementoes. There are also lots of pilgrims around to buy them. I reckon at least one in four of the many people, we pass are pilgrims. They compete with locals, tourists and business folk as they hustle or saunter along the narrow streets or through the myriad of little squares that seem to be a feature of the old part of the city.

A group of Galician musicians are entertaining the crowds in one square. There are bagpipes, drums and tambourines as well as children in costume dancing to the music. As we are making our way back to the hotel, we turn a corner and almost collide with Marie, who is waiting for a taxi to take her to the airport. She, Andreas and the 'Gruppenführer' arrived here three days ago and they both set off for home yesterday. She is so pleased to see us, and it is great to know they all made it. The last time we saw them was on the final day of our recuperation in Salamanca before we returned to the Camino. It is a shame we haven't got more time to catch up. What we do find out is after his dereliction of duty in Galisteo, Jesus insisted he stay with them for the rest of the journey. She has never yet beaten him in a chess game. What we also discover is she and Andreas grew so fond of each other over the time they spent together they are going to make time to see each other regularly.

"We will see," she says, "he is 15 years younger than me and once he gets back home, I may be completely forgotten."

As she says this a tear comes to her eye and I feel the urge to hug her and wish the two of them all the very best. Her taxi arrives and we help her get the rucksack she has carted across Spain into the boot. She gets in the back of the taxi.

"Remember us to Andreas," John shouts after her as the car heads off.

"Fancy that." My head is spinning to take in what we have just heard, but more with a sense of joy, we have found a key missing piece of the jigsaw of our pilgrimage family tree.

"Who do you think we might bump into next?" enquires John, as we arrive back at our hotel and head to our room.

Who indeed? I think.

The Bayern Munich versus Atletico Madrid Champions League match is on the TV and I am half watching it and half contemplating John's question, when tiredness finally sets in and the TV is switched off. I don't need long to lapse into a welcome long night's repose.

Plate 35
Tableaux of figures on display in garden in Oseira – Day 39

Plate 36
Posing on the Ponta Taboada – Day 39

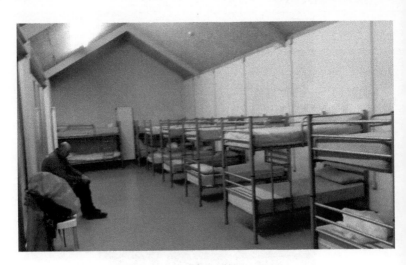

Plate 37
The dormitory at Outiera (our worst nocturnal experience) –
Day 41

Plate 38
Array of pilgrim memorabilia on the outskirts of Santiago –
Day 41

Chapter Eleven

Final Reflections

Wednesday 4th May

After my good night's sleep, I feel incredibly refreshed and we are up, showered and dressed and go out into bright sunshine for breakfast. This turns out to be at a bar in the little square where yesterday, the crowds were entertained with Galician folk music and dancing. We sit and enjoy croissants and coffee and are entertained by a guy playing blues on a guitar. He has the look of a young Robert Powell, (whom I had the pleasure of meeting when he was a young up-and-coming actor and part of the company at the Octagon Theatre in Bolton in the late 1960's). We return to the hotel to collect our pilgrim passports and head back to the cathedral.

The mass is full of pilgrims and we crane our necks to see if we recognise anyone we know. At the beginning of the mass, a list is read out, including the number of pilgrims who have registered at the office within the last 24 hours, their nationalities and from where they started. The spectacle of the swinging incense burner is an incredible sight to behold. It is tethered on a stout rope to a pillar and at the appointed time, two priests free the burner and steer it to the centre of the cathedral in front of the main altar and the seated statue of Saint James, the apostle. The bishop conducting the service then approaches, blesses and lights what is reputed to be the biggest 'censer' in the world.

The famous Botafumerio is made of silver and weighs nearly 80 kilograms. In total, it takes a team of eight men and a system of pulleys to swing the burner first one way and then the other. It gets higher and higher until it almost touches the ceiling above our heads at one end of the transept before dropping down and away to the ceiling of the transept at the other end of the cathedral. The trail of smoke and the aroma of the incense permeate the cathedral. It is a truly magnificent and awe-inspiring experience to be part of, not least of which that for every one of us standing there, it represents the end of our journeys of self-discovery along whichever pilgrim route we have travelled.

I think back to the excruciating chest pains that led to my emergency hospital admission and inwardly give thanks for being able to stand here now, shoulder to shoulder, with hundreds of fellow peregrinos. I feel connected to every one of them and my faith in the human spirit of endeavour and fellowship has never been stronger.

Back in the sunshine again and having stood for an hour, we now have a further hour aboard a little tourist train, which gives us a guided tour of some of the key places of interest within and around the city and an opportunity to determine which places we may want to visit on foot during our stay here. John is still taking in the impression the pilgrim mass has made on him, something he didn't really expect.

"They use so much incense to camouflage the smell of pilgrims you know." I am not sure whether he is saying this partly in jest or as a statement of fact.

"Well I smell sweeter than I've done for over a month," I quip.

After our ride around the city, we return to the Plaza del Obradoiro and wander through the narrow streets in search of a panaderia where we purchase two pasties, a small pizza and some water, and walk to the park behind and above the cathedral. We find a pleasant spot to sit under a huge tree and eat our lunch. There are perfect views of the whole cathedral facade and the tower of the impressive Portico de la Gloria can be seen, despite its lower part being hidden by scaffolding.

A stroll around the park reveals the one remaining arch of the old entrance to the city walls. There were originally many arches, and each served a specific purpose. This one remaining arch was the passage through which wine was brought into the fortress city. We also find a fairground with a huge Ferris wheel, with lots of different stalls and rides. A man approaches with some titbits for us to try and I think I am putting a piece of churros in my mouth. I soon discover it is a chewy piece of octopus and rush to find a bin in which to surreptitiously divest myself of the ghastly 'morsel'.

"How about a beer to take the taste away?" proffers John and we set off in search of a bar.

Whilst on this mission I spot an ice cream parlour and we stop for two delicious ice creams as a prelude to the beer. Sitting outside a little bar in one of the many little thoroughfares we share our reflections of our pilgrimage walk. Neither of us is religious but we both agree the journey has been a spiritual one for us both. Remembering the highs and lows of the last five weeks together is something we haven't allowed ourselves the luxury of doing until now. For me, those fellow pilgrims who have shared large chunks of our journey have had the most impact, but then there is so much else to treasure. The flock of bee-eaters, the fly pasts of the storks, the fragrance of the jara, the birdsong from the cuckoos and the larks. The comedy moments, the food, the language misunderstandings, the history of the many places we have passed through —and the beauty and majesty of cities like Salamanca.

By the time we get back to our hotel it is around half-past six. We decide to head out again around eight to find somewhere to eat. As it turns out, a siesta (probably influenced by drinking beer in the warm sun), means we don't wake up till after then and it is around half-past eight when we go in search of food. John has left the guidebook he bought and some postcards at the bar we were at earlier, so we retrace our steps.

"Isn't that Karl and Hermann?"

I point across the street to two men emerging from a bar. It sure is! Then it's man hugs all round and beaming smiles as we catch up with the latter stages of each other's journeys. They got here yesterday too and were in the pilgrim mass at lunch time.

"Sleep well last night?" asks Karl.

"Sure did," I respond, "because I didn't have your loud snoring to keep me awake."

Guffaws all around.

"No and we didn't have the early morning whispering chorus either," adds John, to more laughter.

427

Karl and Hermann are continuing to walk to Finisterre before they return to Germany. I feel like shouting out after them, "if you hurry you might catch up with Erico." But Karl and Hermann never hurry anywhere!

As the four of us are reminiscing, Inieste arrives on the scene and there is further hugging, slapping of backs and shaking of hands and catching up to be done. Inieste stayed at Outiera last night and shared her experiences of the place.

"She is a witch," says Inieste referring to the hospitalierie.

Apparently, two Spanish peregrinos had written negative words in the comments book and she had torn them out in a rage and ranted at them both. She had forbidden people to put the cooker on in the kitchen unless they were preparing food. She had told them all the mattresses in the dormitory had to be replaced recently because of bed bugs. When it was pointed out to her the bed bugs were probably caused by the place not being cleaned properly, she had another rant. The vending machine was still broken, and some pilgrims lost euros trying to get a drink from it.

When this was raised with her, she shrieked, "It should be unplugged, which one of you plugged it back in again?"

No suggestion of an apology or getting money back.

"I am definitely going to complain about that wicked witch."

From the way she voiced this, you knew she would. The slightly reclusive and reserved Inieste Maureen and I encountered on my first night on the Camino would not have dared to suggest such a thing. As to whether Inieste has conquered her inner demons in terms of not seeking out her Basque father whilst he was alive or not, I wasn't sure. I was sure, though, the Camino had given her greater self-confidence and a sense of self-assurance clearly reflected in the way she now carried herself and sought out fellow pilgrims.

Now the light is fading, but for once there is still some warmth in the air as we stroll around the city and neon lights start to appear to give it a different hue. I hear the strains of one of my favourite Santana numbers and turning a corner, our young Robert Powell is serenading in a different spot. We return to the cathedral square and opposite it, a crowd are gathered in the expansive and colonnaded entrance to the Romanesque library. We are royally entertained by some Galician folk minstrels and most of the audience are fellow pilgrims like ourselves. It is a fitting end to a splendid day. As we walk back to our hotel, I am pondering what tomorrow may bring.

"I hope we see Marian and Martin tomorrow," I verbalise.

"And maybe at least find out what happened to Sergio," adds John.

It is 11 when we get back and at least another half an hour before lights are switched off and sleep takes over. Only one more day here and so many pieces of our pilgrim jigsaw to put in place, I think as I drift off to sleep.

Thursday 5th May

I sleep through until six o'clock, but by the time we are up, showered and dressed and on our way out for breakfast it is quarter-past eight. According to the forecast, today will be the hottest since we left Puebla de Sanabria. We return after an uninspiring breakfast to clean our teeth, before going out again. This turns out to be fortuitous for, within five minutes, we meet Martin and Marian, who arrived yesterday. Whilst they may have originally considered going on to Finisterre, Martin has really struggled over the past two weeks and they will go no further. They too stayed with the 'witch' at Outiera and had familiar tales of woe to recall.

They are a wonderful couple and I know how much Marian has striven to nurse her husband across the finish line. He looks out on his feet but has a beaming smile when he sees us. They have shared so much of my journey and are a major piece of our pilgrim family jigsaw. I must admit, there is a tear in my eye as we exchange hugs and say our goodbyes.

"Well that's the first wish for the day fulfilled," I exclaim to John.

A walk around the parks and the outskirts of the city follows, taking in some of the routes our little train had shown us the other day. An exhibition inside the Anthropological Museum has some interesting data about Spain in general and Galicia in particular. Spain has the third oldest population in the world, after China and Japan. The Ourense district is the least populated part of Galicia and is continuing to shrink. In 2014 alone, it lost 1.2% of its population. Our experience of walking through the almost deserted small villages and hamlets from Laza to Ourense would affirm this trend, with only the older population seeming to want to remain.

Emerging from the exhibition we bump into Karl and Hermann again and inform them we have seen Martin and Marian.

"We have, too," says Hermann, as if it should have been obvious this would be the case.

A sunny spot is found to sit down in for lunch and a beer and a pleasant game of people watching.

"If we could only meet one more of our fellow pilgrims, who would you choose it to be?" asks John.

I think for a while and then announce, "Sergio, and you?"

"Suppose it's got to be Sergio, although it would be nice to confirm Giovanni got here."

This sets us off on a merry-go-round of reflections about all those fellow peregrinos who have left their indelible marks on our journey together. A further meander in the warming sun, another ice cream and a look inside the cathedral without the crowds are enjoyed before we head back to the hotel. Another dose of blues from our Robert Powell look alike, back in his original spot now, is taken in on the way.

We go out like condemned men for our last meal in Santiago and on our epic walk. Tomorrow we will be home with Sandra and Caroline, with the stories from our journey filling our brains. It will be so, so good to be reunited with Sandra and the rest of my family, particularly my granddaughter, Bella. Six weeks is such a long time when you are five! I am very clear moving to another house will be the best future option for Sandra and me and wonder whether she has reached a similar conclusion. Letting go of a chapter in life is important before planning the next one. I am still not quite ready and as we arrive at the cathedral, we sneak back inside to experience the evening mass.

It is clear there will be no incense swinging tonight and the mass is clearly for devout believers only, so we quietly slip away. The sun has been very hot today, but there is a cooler feel to the evening. We pass a little bar and see Martin and Marian dining at a table in the window and exchange waves and smiles. The city is much quieter this evening and not all the bars and restaurants are open. Our final meal is enjoyed indoors and we toast each other with a glass of wine at the end, before heading back to our hotel.

We are deliberately taking our time and certainly not taking the most direct route as we return to the library opposite the cathedral to see whether there is any music playing. As we walk back up the other side of the cathedral to re-join the narrow street that will take us back to our hotel, I can hear again the haunting sounds of a blues guitar.

He is back in his second home again and I turn to John. "We can linger for at least one number, can't we?"

Propped up against a wall across from 'Robert Powell', I am suddenly aware of a familiar figure leaning in a hunched manner against a streetlight about ten metres away.

"Sergio," I call.

He looks up with tears in his eyes and throws a half-smile in our direction as we approach.

"Powerful stuff, heh?" I say pointing to young Robert.

"She's gone," he blurts out. "I haven't been able to get hold of her for the past few days and so I rang a friend tonight and it turns out she's gone back to Argentina with our son."

He leans into my shoulder and sobs. John is rubbing his back and trying to comfort him, but he is inconsolable. I can feel my shirt getting wet with his tears. I wanted us to find Sergio, but not like this!

Friday 6th May

I wake on my last morning in Santiago with thoughts of Sergio still reeling in my head. Packing for our homeward journey helps to distract me and I know there is one more task I must complete before our taxi arrives in two hours.

In the square where we breakfasted yesterday is a plinth, on which sits the bronze casts of a pair of feet. I have my walking shoes in my hand as we leave our hotel room for the last time and we return to the square. I photograph my shoes between the large bronze feet, before discarding them in a nearby bin—a sad but necessary sacrifice. I now just have my sandals to return home in.

The bin is on the corner at the back of the cathedral right next to the entrance we took when we attended the pilgrim mass. The door is slightly ajar.

"Just one more peek inside," says John.

The cathedral is eerily silent, with shafts of light from the stained-glass windows creating pools of colour and darkness within its cavernous interior.

John sighs! "I wouldn't have missed this for the world."

He is remembering again the pilgrim mass and not our impromptu current visit.

I am thinking of the words of a colleague at work, after I had lost a lot of weight and taken up running after my almost heart attack. He stopped me in a corridor and, in an apologetic and almost whispered voice enquired, "You're not dying, are you?"

"Far from it," I replied, "I am very much alive."

I looked around the cathedral one last time and inwardly thanked my almost heart attack for jolting me out of complacency and giving me new-found purposes and ambitions, for leading me on a journey across most of the length of Spain, and for the opportunity to share most of it with a special and currently humbled friend.

"I wouldn't have missed this for the world," his voice echoes.

"Neither would I, John, neither would I!"

Plate 39
Cathedral at Santiago de Compostela from behind the big
tree – Day 42

Plate 40
Last image of my walking shoes before they hit the bin – Day

Postscript

When I got home, Sandra had not only reached the same conclusion as myself that we should move to a new house, but had seen a bungalow with an incredible garden that ticked all her boxes and had arranged for us both to see it two days later. I fell in love with the garden too and knew we could extend the house to make it ideal. 11 weeks later, we moved into our new home together.

Later in the year, my grandson Sammy was born, and Bella had the baby brother she had been so excited to tell me about when I was in Morille.

Despite giving my email address to Keith, I never did hear from him or Susan.

Maureen and I later met with Alison and discussed with her the sections of the route that seemed to have been changed since her guide was written. She planned to re-walk the Camino before the end of 2019 so her guidebook can be updated.

John and I returned to Spain in 2017 and walked from Cadiz to Sevilla, along the Via Augusta. Navigating was, at times, a challenge and it wasn't anywhere near as scenic as the Via de la Plata, but it was a promise fulfilled and well worth it. Only the stretch from Santiago de Compostela to Finisterre now remains in my quest to have walked from the south west Atlantic coast of Spain to the most westerly part, in the north.

Acknowledgements

I must first start by acknowledging the vital role of Maureen in defining my ambition to undertake this walk. Maureen undertook the Via de la Plata in 2010 and her tales and pictures of the route inspired me to want to take up the challenge. Maureen taught Spanish at night school and she also helped John and I to gain enough of an understanding of the language to feel confident about negotiating our way through rural Spain. Maureen was happy and prepared to return to Spain at the start of my journey and her presence during the first week of my pilgrimage helped to cement that confidence on what was to become a real journey of discovery. Finally, she was more than happy to check all the Spanish language references in the book, too!

I secondly want to state my appreciation of the contribution and companionship provided by John on my pilgrimage from Zafra onwards. Being together made it easier to work through translations and have conversations in Spanish as the need dictated. It also means I now have someone else who has and can continue to recall the many (and at times unusual) experiences we shared.

I would also wish to recognise the part played by all those fellow pilgrims whose own journeys coincided with mine. Their stories are at times intrinsically interwoven. My fellow travellers came from all parts of the world, including: Germany, France, Belgium, Holland, Poland, Denmark, Australia, Portugal, Switzerland, England, Canada, Spain, New Zealand, Brazil, USA, South Korea, Japan and Italy. But, they all shared a common purpose. All followed in the footsteps of others on a journey that served many elements of this unforeseen self-discovery.

A big thank you to all the people who helped and advised me in relation to the narrative, pictures, maps and lay-out of the book: Jenny, Maureen, John, Kevin and Sandra, to Debz for her initial proof-reading and finally to my editor E. Rachael Hardcastle of Curious Cat Books, for her help and support in getting the book published. Thank you also to my peers within 'The Invisible Writers' group; Matt, Liz, Jane, David, Stephen, Tanya and Charlotte. Their comments and suggestions made this a far better book than otherwise would have been the case.

I should also like to thank Steve and Celeste for their hospitality in Caceres and for their continued interest in the journey. Celeste also helped to identify in advance some of the many highlights of Salamanca —her home city—that only served to assist in my subsequent love affair with its beauty, architecture and history. Steve provided information about where we should dine in Puebla de Sanabria, a quite memorable culinary experience.

Finally, I would like to thank Julie and Simon for the loan of their cottage in Newbiggin-by-the-Sea for a few days to facilitate the last push to finish the writing and self-editing.

I should point out to the reader the names of those fellow pilgrims who have not been able to directly give their consent to appearing in this book, have been changed. The part they played in my journey is as accurate as my memory of it allows.

Bibliography

'VIA DE LA PLATA THE WAY OF ST. JAMES: SEVILLE TO SANTIAGO A CICERONE GUIDE' by Alison Raju, published in 2001

'WALKING GUIDE TO THE VIA DE LA PLATA AND THE CAMINO SANABRES FROM SEVILLE TO SANTIAGO AND ASTORGA'

'CAMINOGUIDE.NET' printed by Amazon.co.uk by Gerald Kelly, published in 2014

Appendix One

STAGES OF CAMINO FROM SEVILLA TO SANTIAGO DE COMPOSTELA:

For the benefit of the reader, I have broken the Camino down into four distinct stages, spanning a period of six weeks.

STAGE ONE:

The first stage was undertaken with a friend, Maureen, who first enthused and encouraged me to undertake the walk. Maureen walked with me for a period of seven days and this 'stage' took me from Sevilla to Zafra (covering 157km).

STAGE TWO:

Stage two involved John and me taking nine days to walk from Zafra to Aldeneuva del Camino, walking 273km. A combination of tiredness, sun, blisters and a hefty dose of realism meant on the tenth day we travelled 95km to Salamanca by bus and spent three days recuperating there, before backtracking to continue our pilgrimage.

STAGE THREE:

Stage three, therefore, describes our journey back to and then onwards from Aldeneuva del Camino to Puebla de Sanabria, spanning 321km and which covered a period of 11 days. We had a rest day there before recommencing our journey.

STAGE FOUR:

The final stage saw us walking from Puebla de Sanabria to Santiago de Compestela over ten days, during which we completed the remaining 258km. Nine days were spent walking and we enjoyed a rest day in Ourense.

STAGE ONE

SEVILLA TO ZAFRA

Date	From	To	Distance
23/03/16	Sevilla	Guillena	23k
24/03/16	Guillena	Castiblanco de los Arroyos	20k
25/03/16	Castiblanco de los Arroyos	Almaden de la Plata	29k
26/03/16	Almaden de la Plata	El Real de la Jara	16k
27/03/16	El Real de la Jara	Monasterio	22k
28/03/16	Monasterio	Fuente de Cantos	22k
29/03/16	Fuenta de Cantos	Zafra	25k
		Total Distance	*157k*

STAGE TWO

ZAFRA TO ALDEANUEVA DEL CAMINO

30/03/16	Zafra	Villafranca de los Barros	20k
31/03/16	Villafranca de los Barros	Torremejia	25k
1/04/16	Torremejia	Aljucen	30k
2/04/16	Aljucen	Aldea del Cano	35k
3/04/16	Aldea del Cano	Caceres	22k
4/04/16	Caceres	Embalse de Alcantara	33k
5/04/16	Embalse de Alcantara	Galisteo	42k
6/04/16	Galisteo	Olivia de Plasencia	33k
7/04/16	Olivia de Plasencia	Aldeanueva del Camino	33k
8/04/16	Aldeanueva del Camino	Salamanca	By bus!
		Total Distance	*273k*
		Overall Distance walked	*430k*

STAGE THREE

ALDEANUEVA DEL CAMINO TO PUEBLA DE SANABRIA

Date	From	To	Distance
11/04/16	Salamanca	Aldeanueva del Camino	By bus!
11/04/16	Aldenueva del Camino	Banos de Montemayor	10k
12/04/16	Banos de Montemayor	Fuenterroble de Salvatierra	30k
13/04/16	Fuenterroble de Salvatierra	Morille	30k
14/04/16	Morille	Salamanca	18k
15/04/16	Salamanca	El Cubo del Vino	34k
16/04/16	El Cubo del Vino	Zamora	29k
17/04/16	Zamora	Riego del Camino	34k
18/04/16	Riego del Camino	Tabara	32.5k
19/04/16	Tabara	Santa Croya de Tera	22.5k

20/04/16	Santa Croya de Tera	Mombuey	40.5k
21/04/16	Mombuey	Puebla de Sanabria	40.5k(38k)
		Total Distance	*321k (318.5k)*
		Overall Distance walked	*751k (748.5k)*

STAGE FOUR

PUEBLA DE SANABRIA TO SANTIAGO DE COMPOSTELLA

Date	From	To	Distance
23/04/16	Puebla de Sanabria	Padornelo	31k (23k)
24/04/16	Padornelo	A Gudina	32k
25/04/16	A Gudina	Campobecerros	20k
26/04/16	Campobecerros	Laza	14k
27/04/16	Laza	Xunquiera de Ambia	34k
28/04/16	Xunquiera de Ambia	Orense	25k
30/04/16	Orense	Dozon	39k

01/05/16	Dozon	Silleda	28.5k
2/05/16	Silleda	Outiera	25k
3/05/16	Outiera	Santiago de Compostella	17.5k
		Total Distance	*266k(258k)*
		Overall Distance walked	*1017k (1006.5k)*

NB. The distances identified are based on the actual kilometres covered and include on two days 'unscheduled' diversions. According to the certificate of completion presented to me at the end of my pilgrimage the overall distance from Sevilla to Santiago de Compostella is 1006km, which leaving aside the major diversions is only half a kilometre different to my own calculations.

Appendix Two

Spanish Glossary

- *refugio* - small hostel or bunkhouse, seen more in the earlier part of the walk

- *albergue* - larger hostel, like a youth hostel, with bunk-beds and dormitories

- *hostal* - a small hotel, where you would have your own room

- *ermita* - a small church or chapel often dedicated to a Saint or religious icon

- *peregrino* - a fellow pilgrim who is walking the Camino to Santiago

- *embalse* - a man-made reservoir often serving a nearby city

- *jara* - the incense plant which is often described as a Spanish rose

- *holm* - the native Spanish oak tree, much smaller in stature

- *bocadillo* - Spanish sandwich with different fillings served within a baguette

- *aseos*- toilet and washroom facilities within cafés or hotels

- *jambón ibérico*- Spanish dry cured ham

- *desayuno*- breakfast

- *rationes*- a larger portion of a dish, unlike a 'tapas', a smaller taster dish

- *queso*- the name for cheese

- *queso manchego*- a typical Spanish cheese

- *beunos nocha*- the Spanish greeting for good night

- *formaccia*- chemist

- *plátanos falsas*- plane trees

- *fincas*- Spanish farmsteads

- *castillo*- castle

- *gazpacho*- cold soup

- *hospitalierie*- warden at an albergue

- *churro*- cylindrical tubes of doughnut sprinkled with sugar

- *pandería*- bread and pastries shop

- *tosta*- toast, the most popular option available for breakfast

- *tiera*- an earth or green pathway or track

- *segundo*- the second course on a menu, often the 'main' course

- *postre*- this is the sweet course served at the end of your meal

- *vino tinto*- red wine

- *botafumerio*- incense burner

- *señoritas*- young women, often used to denote unmarried females

- *touíristica albergue*- hostel for tourists generally and not just for pilgrims

- *ayuntamiento*- town hall

- *buenos días*- good morning

- *milarios*- Roman distance marker stones

- *cocida*- stew

- *verredas*- walled lane between two dry stone walls

- *buenas nochas*- good night

- *romeríos*- church services

Lightning Source UK Ltd.
Milton Keynes UK
UKHW020303231222
414318UK00007BA/68

9 780957 490529